Jorrocks' Jaunts and Jollities

by

Robert Smith Surtees

The Echo Library 2006

Published by

The Echo Library

Echo Library
131 High St.
Teddington
Middlesex TW11 8HH

www.echo-library.com

Please report serious faults in the text to complaints@echo-library.com

ISBN 1-40683-142-5

CONTENTS

I
THE SWELL AND THE SURREY

WHAT true-bred city sportsman has not in his day put off the most urgent business—perhaps his marriage, or even the interment of his rib—that he might "brave the morn" with that renowned pack, the Surrey subscription foxhounds? Lives there, we would ask, a thoroughbred, prime, bang-up, slap-dash, break-neck, out-and-out artist, within three miles of the Monument, who has not occasionally "gone a good 'un" with this celebrated pack? And shall we, the bard of Eastcheap, born all deeds of daring to record, shall we, who so oft have witnessed—nay, shared—the hardy exploits of our fellow-cits, shall we sit still, and never cease the eternal twirl of our dexter around our sinister thumb, while other scribes hand down to future ages the paltry feats of beardless Meltonians, and try to shame old Father Thames himself with muddy Whissendine's foul stream? Away! thou vampire, Indolence, that suckest the marrow of imagination, and fattenest on the cream of idea ere yet it float on the milk of reflection. Hence! slug-begotten hag, thy power is gone—the murky veil thou'st drawn o'er memory's sweetest page is rent!

Harp of Eastcheap, awake!

Our thoughts hark back to the cover-side, and our heart o'erflows with recollections of the past, when life rode the pace through our veins, and the bark of the veriest mongrel, or the bray of the sorriest costermonger's sorriest "Jerusalem," were far more musical sounds than Paganini's pizzicatos or Catalani's clamorous caterwaulings.

And, thou, Goddess of the Silver Bow—chaste Diana—deign to become the leading star of our lucubrations; come perch upon our grey goose quill; shout in our ear the maddening Tally-ho! and ever and anon give a salutary "refresher" to our memory with thy heaven-wrought spurs—those spurs old Vulcan forged when in his maddest mood—whilst we relate such feats of town-born youths and city squires, as shall "harrow up the souls" of milk-sop Melton's choicest sons, and "fright their grass-galloping garrons from their propriety." But gently, Pegasus!—Here again, boys, and "let's to business," as they say on 'Change.

'Twere almost needless to inform our readers, that such portion of a county as is hunted by any one pack of hounds is technically denominated their country; and of all countries under the sun, that of the Surrey subscription foxhounds undoubtedly bears the bell. This superiority arises from the peculiar nature of the soil—wretched starvation stuff most profusely studded with huge sharp flints—the abundance of large woods, particularly on the Kent side, and the range of mountainous hills that run directly through the centre, which afford accommodation to the timid, and are unknown in most counties and unequalled in any.

One of the most striking features in the aspect of this chosen region of fox-hunting, is the quiet easy manner in which the sportsmen take the thing. On they go—now trotting gently over the flints—now softly ambling along the grassy ridge of some stupendous hill—now quietly following each other in long-drawn files, like geese, through some close and deep ravine, or interminable wood, which re-echoes to their never-ceasing holloas—every man shouting in proportion to the amount of his subscription, until day is made horrible with their yelling. There is no pushing, jostling, rushing, cramming, or riding over one another; no jealousy, discord, or daring; no ridiculous foolhardy feats; but each man cranes and rides, and rides and cranes in a style that would gladden the eye of a director of an insurance office.

The members of the Surrey are the people that combine business with pleasure, and even in the severest run can find time for sweet discourse, and talk about the price of stocks or stockings. "Yooi wind him there, good dog, yooi wind him."—"Cottons is fell."—"Hark to Cottager! Hark!"—"Take your bill at three months, or give you three and a half discount for cash." "Eu in there, eu in, Cheapside, good dog."—"Don't be in a hurry, sir, pray. He may be in the empty casks behind the cooper's. Yooi, try for him, good bitch. Yooi, push him out."—"You're not going down that bank, surely sir? Why, it's almost perpendicular! For God's sake, sir, take care—remember you are not insured. Ah! you had better get off—here, let me hold your nag, and when you're down you can catch mine;—that's your sort but mind he doesn't break the bridle. He won't run away, for he knows I've got some sliced carrots in my pocket to reward him if he does well.—Thank you, sir, and now for a leg up—there we are—that's your sort—I'll wait till you are up also, and we'll be off together."

It is this union of the elegant courtesies and business of life with the energetic sports of the field, that constitutes the charm of Surrey hunting; and who can wonder that smoke-dried cits, pent up all the week, should gladly fly from their shops to enjoy a day's sport on a Saturday? We must not, however, omit to express a hope that young men, who have their way to make in the world, may not be led astray by its allurements. It is all very well for old-established shopkeepers "to do a bit of pleasure" occasionally, but the apprentice or journeyman, who understands his duties and the tricks of his trade, will never be found capering in the hunting field. He will feel that his proper place is behind the counter; and while his master is away enjoying the pleasures of the chase, he can prig as much "pewter" from the till as will take both himself and his lass to Sadler's Wells theatre, or any other place she may choose to appoint.

But to return to the Surrey. The town of Croydon, nine miles from the standard in Cornhill, is the general rendezvous of the gallant sportsmen. It is the principal market town in the eastern division of the county of Surrey; and the chaw-bacons who carry the produce of their acres to it, instead of to the neighbouring village of London, retain much of their pristine barbarity. The town furnishes an interesting scene on a hunting morning, particularly on a Saturday. At an early hour, groups of grinning cits may be seen pouring in from the London side, some on the top of Cloud's coaches,[1] some in taxed carts, but the greater number mounted on good serviceable-looking nags, of the invaluable species, calculated for sport or business, "warranted free from vice, and quiet both to ride and in harness"; some few there are, who, with that kindness and considerate attention which peculiarly mark this class of sportsmen, have tacked a buggy to their hunter, and given a seat to a friend, who leaning over the back of the gig, his jocund phiz turned towards his fidus Achates, leads his own horse behind, listening to the discourse of "his ancient," or regaling him "with sweet converse"; and thus they onward jog, until the sign of the "Greyhound," stretching quite across the main street, greets their expectant optics, and seems to forbid their passing the open portal below. In they wend then, and having seen their horses "sorted," and the collar marks (as much as may be) carefully effaced by the shrewd application of a due quantity of grease and lamp-black, speed in to "mine host" and order a sound repast of the good things of this world; the which to discuss, they presently apply themselves with a vigour that indicates as much a determination to recruit fatigue endured, as to lay in stock against the effects of future exertion. Meanwhile the bustle increases; sportsmen arrive by the score, fresh tables are laid out, covered with "no end" of vivers; and towards the hour of nine, may be heard to perfection, that pleasing assemblage of sounds issuing from the masticatory organs of a number of men steadfastly and studiously employed in the delightful occupation of preparing their mouthfuls for deglutition. "O noctes coenæque Deûm," said friend Flaccus. Oh, hunting breakfasts! say we. Where are now the jocund laugh, the repartee, the oft-repeated tale, the last debate? As our sporting contemporary, the *Quarterly*, said, when describing the noiseless pursuit of old reynard by the Quorn: "Reader, there is no crash now, and not much music." It is the tinker that makes a great noise over a little work, but, at the pace these men are eating, there is no time for babbling. So, gentle lector, there is now no leisure for bandying compliments, 'tis your small eater alone who chatters o'er his meals; your true-born sportsman is ever a silent and, consequently, an assiduous grubber. True it is that occasionally space is found between mouthfuls to vociferate "WAITER!" in a tone that requires not repetition; and most sonorously do the throats of the assembled eaters re-echo the sound; but this is all—no useless exuberance of speech—no, the knife or fork is directed towards what is wanted, nor needs there any more expressive intimation of the applicant's wants.

At length the hour of ten approaches; bills are paid, pocket-pistols filled, sandwiches stowed away, horses accoutred, and our bevy straddle forth into the town, to the infinite gratification of troops of dirty-nosed urchins, who, for the last hour, have been peeping in at the windows, impatiently watching for the *exeunt* of our worthies.—They mount, and away—trot, trot—bump, bump— trot, trot—bump, bump—over Addington Heath, through the village, and up the hill to Hayes Common, which having gained, spurs are applied, and any

---

[1] The date of this description, it must be remembered, is put many years back.

slight degree of pursiness that the good steeds may have acquired by standing at livery in Cripplegate, or elsewhere, is speedily pumped out of them by a smart brush over the turf, to the "Fox," at Keston, where a numerous assemblage of true sportsmen patiently await the usual hour for throwing off. At length time being called, say twenty minutes to eleven, and Mr. Jorrocks, Nodding Homer, and the principal subscribers having cast up, the hounds approach the cover. "Yooi in there!" shouts Tom Hills, who has long hunted this crack pack; and crack! crack! crack! go the whips of some scores of sportsmen. "Yelp, yelp, yelp," howl the hounds; and in about a quarter of an hour Tom has not above four or five couple at his heels. This number being a trifle, Tom runs his prad at a gap in the fence by the wood-side; the old nag goes well at it, but stops short at the critical moment, and, instead of taking the ditch, bolts and wheels round. Tom, however, who is "large in the boiling pieces," as they say at Whitechapel, is prevented by his weight from being shaken out of his saddle; and, being resolved to take no denial, he lays the crop of his hunting-whip about the head of his beast, and runs him at the same spot a second time, with an *obligato* accompaniment of his spur-rowels, backed by a "curm along then!" issued in such a tone as plainly informs his quadruped he is in no joking humour. These incentives succeed in landing Tom and his nag in the wished-for spot, when, immediately, the wood begins to resound with shouts of "Yoicks True-bo-y, yoicks True-bo-y, yoicks push him up, yoicks wind him!" and the whole pack begin to work like good 'uns. Occasionally may be heard the howl of some unfortunate hound that has been caught in a fox trap, or taken in a hare snare; and not unfrequently the discordant growls of some three or four more, vociferously quarrelling over the venerable remains of some defunct rabbit. "Oh, you rogues!" cries Mr. Jorrocks, a cit rapturously fond of the sport. After the lapse of half an hour the noise in the wood for a time increases audibly. 'Tis Tom chastising the gourmands. Another quarter of an hour, and a hound that has finished his coney bone slips out of the wood, and takes a roll upon the greensward, opining, no doubt, that such pastime is preferable to scratching his hide among brambles in the covers. "Hounds have no right to opine," opines the head whipper-in; so clapping spurs into his prad, he begins to pursue the delinquent round the common, with "Markis, Markis! what are you at, Markis? get into cover, Markis!" But "it's no go"; Marquis creeps through a hedge, and "grins horribly a ghastly smile" at his ruthless tormentor, who wends back, well pleased at having had an excuse for taking "a bit gallop"! Half an hour more slips away, and some of the least hasty of our cits begin to wax impatient, in spite of the oft-repeated admonition, "don't be in a hurry!" At length a yokel pops out of the cover, and as soon as he has recovered breath, informs the field that he has been "a-hollorin' to 'em for half an hour," and that the fox had "gone away for Tatsfield, 'most as soon as ever the 'oounds went into 'ood."

All is now hurry-scurry—girths are tightened—reins gathered up—half-munched sandwiches thrust into the mouth—pocket-pistols applied to—coats comfortably buttoned up to the throat; and, these preparations made, away goes the whole field, "coolly and fairly," along the road to Leaves Green and Crown

Ash Hill—from which latter spot, the operations of the pack in the bottom may be comfortably and securely viewed—leaving the whips to flog as many hounds out of cover as they can, and Tom to entice as many more as are willing to follow the "twang, twang, twang" of his horn.

And now, a sufficient number of hounds having been seduced from the wood, forth sallies "Tummas," and making straight for the spot where our yokel's "mate" stands leaning on his plough-stilts, obtains from him the exact latitude and longitude of the spot where reynard broke through the hedge. To this identical place is the pack forthwith led; and, no sooner have they reached it, than the wagging of their sterns clearly shows how genuine is their breed. Old Strumpet, at length, first looking up in Tom's face for applause, ventures to send forth a long-drawn howl, which, coupled with Tom's screech, setting the rest agog, away they all go, like beans; and the wind, fortunately setting towards Westerham, bears the melodious sound to the delighted ears of our "roadsters," who, forthwith catching the infection, respond with deafening shouts and joyous yells, set to every key, and disdaining the laws of harmony. Thus, what with Tom's horn, the holloaing of the whips, and the shouts of the riders, a very pretty notion may be formed of what Virgil calls:

"Clamorque virûm, clangorque tubarum."

A terrible noise is the result!

At the end of nine minutes or so, the hounds come to fault in the bottom, below the blacksmith's, at Crown Ash Hill, and the fox has a capital chance; in fact, they have changed for the blacksmith's tom cat, which rushed out before them, and finding their mistake, return at their leisure. This gives the most daring of the field, on the eminence, an opportunity of descending to view the sport more closely; and being assembled in the bottom, each congratulates his neighbour on the excellent condition and stanchness of the hounds, and the admirable view that has been afforded them of their peculiar style of hunting. At this interesting period, a "regular swell" from Melton Mowbray, unknown to everyone except his tailor, to whom he owes a long tick, makes his appearance and affords abundance of merriment for our sportsmen. He is just turned out of the hands of his valet, and presents the very beau-ideal of his caste—"quite the lady," in fact. His hat is stuck on one side, displaying a profusion of well-waxed ringlets; a corresponding infinity of whisker, terminating at the chin, there joins an enormous pair of moustaches, which give him the appearance of having caught the fox himself and stuck its brush below his nose. His neck is very stiff; and the exact Jackson-like fit of his coat, which almost nips him in two at the waist, and his superlatively well-cleaned leather Andersons,[2] together with the perfume and the general puppyism of his appearance, proclaim that he is a "swell" of the very first water, and one that a Surrey sportsman would like to buy at his own price and sell at the other's. In addition to this, his boots, which

---

[2] Anderson, of South Audley Street, is, or was, a famous breeches-maker.

his "fellow" has just denuded from a pair of wash-leather covers, are of the finest, brightest, blackest patent leather imaginable; the left one being the identical boot by which Warren's monkey shaved himself, while the right is the one at which the game-cock pecked, mistaking its own shadow for an opponent, the mark of its bill being still visible above the instep; and the tops—whose pampered appetites have been fed on champagne—are of the most delicate cream-colour, the whole devoid of mud or speck. The animal he bestrides is no less calculated than himself to excite the risible faculties of the field, being a sort of mouse colour, with dun mane and tail, got by Nicolo, out of a flibbertigibbet mare, and he stands seventeen hands and an inch. His head is small and blood-like, his girth a mere trifle, and his legs, very long and spidery, of course without any hair at the pasterns to protect them from the flints; his whole appearance bespeaking him fitter to run for half-mile hunters' stakes at Croxton Park or Leicester, than contend for foxes' brushes in such a splendid country as the Surrey. There he stands, with his tail stuck tight between his legs, shivering and shaking for all the world as if troubled with a fit of ague. And well he may, poor beast, for—oh, men of Surrey, London, Kent, and Middlesex, hearken to my word—on closer inspection he proves to have been shaved!!![3]

After a considerable time spent in casting to the right, the left, and the rear, "True-bouy" chances to take a fling in advance, and hitting upon the scent, proclaims it with his wonted energy, which drawing all his brethren to the spot, they pick it slowly over some brick-fields and flint-beds, to an old lady's flower-garden, through which they carry it with a surprising head into the fields beyond, when they begin to fall into line, and the sportsmen doing the same—"one at a time and it will last the longer"—"Tummas" tootles his horn, the hunt is up, and away they all rattle at "Parliament pace," as the hackney-coachmen say.

Our swell, who flatters himself he can "ride a few," according to the fashion of his country, takes up a line of his own, abreast of the leading hounds, notwithstanding the oft vociferated cry of "Hold hard, sir!" "Pray, hold hard, sir!" "For God's sake, hold hard, sir!" "G—d d—n you, hold hard, sir!" "Where the h—ll are you going to, sir?" and other familiar inquiries and benedictions, with which a stranger is sometimes greeted, who ventures to take a look at a strange pack of hounds.

In the meantime the fox, who has often had a game at romps with his pursuers, being resolved this time to give them a tickler, bears straight away for Westerham, to the infinite satisfaction of the "hill folks," who thus have an excellent opportunity of seeing the run without putting their horses to the trouble of "rejoicing in their strength, or pawing in the valley." But who is so fortunate as to be near the scene of action in this second scurry, almost as fast as the first? Our fancy supplies us, and there not being many, we will just initialise them all, and let he whom the cap fits put it on.

If we look to the left, nearly abreast of the three couple of hounds that are

---

[3] Shaving was in great vogue at Melton some seasons back. It was succeeded by clipping, and clipping by singeing.

leading by some half mile or so, we shall see "Swell"—like a monkey on a giraffe—striding away in the true Leicestershire style; the animal contracting its stride after every exertion in pulling its long legs out of the deep and clayey soil, until the Bromley barber, who has been quilting his mule along at a fearful rate, and in high dudgeon at anyone presuming to exercise his profession upon a dumb brute, overtakes him, and in the endeavour to pass, lays it into his mule in a style that would insure him rotatory occupation at Brixton for his spindles, should any member of the Society for the Prevention of Cruelty to Animals witness his proceedings; while his friend and neighbour old B——, the tinker, plies his little mare with the Brummagems, to be ready to ride over "Swell" the instant the barber gets him down. On the right of the leading hounds are three crack members of the Surrey, Messrs. B—e, S—bs, and B—l, all lads who can go; while a long way in the rear of the body of the pack are some dozen, who, while they sat on the hills, thought they could also, but who now find out their mistake. Down Windy Lane, a glimpse of a few red coats may be caught passing the gaps and weak parts of the fence, among whom we distinctly recognise the worthy master of the pack, followed by Jorrocks, with his long coat-laps floating in the breeze, who thinking that "catching-time" must be near at hand, and being dearly fond of blood, has descended from his high station to witness the close of the scene. "Vot a pace! and vot a country!" cries the grocer, standing high in his stirrups, and bending over the neck of his chestnut as though he were meditating a plunge over his head; "how they stick to him! vot a pack! by Jove they are at fault again. Yooi, Pilgrim! Yooi, Warbler, ma load! (lad). Tom, try down the hedge-row." "Hold your jaw, Mr. J——," cries Tom, "you are always throwing that red rag of yours. I wish you would keep your potato-trap shut. See! you've made every hound throw up, and it's ten to one that ne'er a one among 'em will stoop again." "Yonder he goes," cries a cock of the old school, who used to hunt with Colonel Jolliffe's hounds, and still sports the long blue surtout lined with orange, yellow-ochre unmentionables, and mahogany-coloured knee-caps, with mother-of-pearl buttons. "Yonder he goes among the ship (sheep), for a thousand! see how the skulking waggabone makes them scamper." At this particular moment a shrill scream is heard at the far end of a long shaw, and every man pushes on to the best of his endeavour. "Holloo o-o-u, h'loo o-o-u, h'loo—o-o-u, gone away! gone away! forward! forrard! hark back! hark forrard! hark forrard! hark back!" resounds from every mouth. "He's making for the 'oods beyond Addington, and we shall have a rare teaser up these hills," cries Jorrocks, throwing his arms round his horse's neck as he reaches the foot of them.—"D—n your hills," cries "Swell," as he suddenly finds himself sitting on the hindquarters of his horse, his saddle having slipped back for want of a breastplate,—"I wish the hills had been piled on your back, and the flints thrust down your confounded throat, before I came into such a cursed provincial." "Haw, haw, haw!" roars a Croydon butcher. "What don't 'e like it, sir, eh? too sharp to be pleasant, eh?—Your nag should have put on his boots before he showed among us."

"He's making straight for Fuller's farm," exclaims a thirsty veteran on reaching the top, "and I'll pull up and have a nip of ale, please God." "Hang your ale," cries a certain sporting cheesemonger, "you had better come out with a barrel of it tacked to your horse's tail."—"Or 'unt on a steam-engine," adds his friend the omnibus proprietor, "and then you can brew as you go." "We shall have the Croydon Canal," cries Mr. H———n, of Tottenham, who knows every flint in the country, "and how will you like that, my hearties?" "Curse the Croydon Canal," bawls the little Bromley barber, "my mule can swim like a soap-bladder, and my toggery can't spoil, thank God!"

The prophecy turns up. Having skirted Fuller's farm, the villain finds no place to hide; and in two minutes, or less, the canal appears in view. It is full of craft, and the locks are open, but there is a bridge about half a mile to the right. "If my horse can do nothing else he can jump this," cries "Swell," as he gathers him together, and prepares for the effort. He hardens his heart and goes at it full tilt, and the leggy animal lands him three yards on the other side. "Curse this fellow," cries Jorrocks, grinning with rage as he sees "Swell" skimming through the air like a swallow on a summer's eve, "he'll have a laugh at the Surrey, for ever and ever, Amen. Oh, dear! oh, dear! I wish I durst leap it. What shall I do? Here bargee," cries he to a bargeman, "lend us a help over and I'll give you ninepence." The bargeman takes him at his word, and getting the vessel close to the water's edge, Jorrocks has nothing to do but ride in, and, the opposite bank being accommodating, he lands without difficulty. Ramming his spurs into his nag, he now starts after "Swell," who is sailing away with a few couple of hounds that took the canal; the body of the pack and all the rest of the field— except the Bromley barber, who is now floundering in the water—having gone round to the bridge.

The country is open, the line being across commons and along roads, so that Jorrocks, who is not afraid of "the pace" so long as there is no leaping, has a pretty good chance with "Swell." The scene now shifts. On turning out of a lane, along which they have just rattled, a fence of this description appears: The bottom part is made of flints, and the upper part of mud, with gorse stuck along the top, and there is a gutter on each side. Jorrocks, seeing that a leap is likely, hangs astern, and "Swell," thinking to shake off his only opponent, and to have a rare laugh at the Surrey when he gets back to Melton, puts his nag at it most manfully, who, though somewhat blown, manages to get his long carcass over, but, unfortunately alighting on a bed of flints on the far side, cuts a back sinew, and "Swell" measures his length on the headland. Jorrocks then pulls up.

The tragedy of George Barnwell ends with a death, and we are happy in being able to gratify our readers with a similar entertainment. Already have the best-mounted men in the field attained the summit of one of the Mont Blancs of the country, when on looking down the other side of the "mountain's brow," they, to their infinite astonishment, espy at some distance our "Swell" dismounted and playing at "pull devil, pull baker" with the hounds, whose discordant bickerings rend the skies. "Whoo-hoop!" cries one; "whoo-hoop!" responds another; "whoo-hoop!" screams a third; and the contagion spreading, and each man dismounting, they descend the hill with due caution, whoohooping, hallooing, and congratulating each other on the splendour of the run, interspersed with divers surmises as to what mighty magic had aided the hounds in getting on such good terms with the warmint, and exclamations at the good fortune of the stranger, in being able (by nicking,[4] and the fox changing his line) to get in at the finish.

And now some dozens of sportsmen quietly ambling up to the scene of action, view with delight (alone equalled by their wonder at so unusual and unexpected an event) the quarrels of the hounds, as they dispute with each other the possession of their victim's remains, when suddenly a gentleman, clad in a bright green silk-velvet shooting-coat, with white leathers, and Hessian boots with large tassels, carrying his Joe Manton on his shoulder, issues from an adjoining coppice, and commences a loud complaint of the "unhandsome conduct of the gentlemen's 'ounds in devouring the 'are (hare) which he had taken so much pains to shoot." Scarcely are these words out of his mouth than the whole hunt, from Jorrocks downwards, let drive such a rich torrent of abuse at our unfortunate *chasseur*, that he is fain to betake himself to his heels, leaving them undisputed masters of the field.

The visages of our sportsmen become dismally lengthened on finding that their fox has been "gathered unto his fathers" by means of hot lead and that villainous saltpetre "digged out of the bowels of the harmless earth"; some few, indeed, there are who are bold enough to declare that the pack has actually made a meal of a hare, and that their fox is snugly earthed in the neighbouring cover. However, as there are no "reliquias Danaum," to prove or disprove this assertion, Tom Hills, having an eye to the cap-money, ventures to give it as his opinion, that pug has fairly yielded to his invincible pursuers, without having "dropped to shot." This appearing to give very general satisfaction, the first whip makes no scruple of swearing that he saw the hounds pull him down fairly; and Peckham, drawing his mouth up on one side, with his usual intellectual grin, takes a similar affidavit. The Bromley barber too, anxious to have it to say that he has for once been in at the death of a fox, vows by his beard that he saw the "varmint" lathered in style; and these protestations being received with clamorous applause, and everyone being pleased to have so unusual an event to record to his admiring spouse, agrees that a fox has not only been killed, but killed in a most sportsmanlike, workmanlike, businesslike manner; and long and loud are the congratulations, great is the increased importance of each man's physiognomy, and thereupon they all lug out their half-crowns for Tom Hills.

In the meantime our "Swell" lays hold of his nag—who is sorely damaged with the flints, and whose wind has been pretty well pumped out of him by the hills—and proceeds to lead him back to Croydon, inwardly promising himself for the future most studiously to avoid the renowned county of Surrey, its woods, its barbers, its mountains, and its flints, and to leave more daring spirits to overcome the difficulties it presents; most religiously resolving, at the same time, to return as speedily as possible to his dear Leicestershire, there to amble

---

[4] A stranger never rides straight if he beats the members of the hunt.

o'er the turf, and fancy himself an "angel on horseback." The story of the country mouse, who must needs see the town, occurs forcibly to his recollection, and he exclaims aloud:

> "me sylva, cavusque
> Tutus ab insidiis tenui solabitur ervo."

On overhearing which, Mr. Jorrocks hurries back to his brother subscribers, and informs them, very gravely, that the stranger is no less a personage than "Prince Matuchevitz, the Russian ambassador and minister plenipotentiary extraordinary," whereupon the whole field join in wishing him safe back in Russia—or anywhere else—and wonder at his incredible assurance in supposing that he could cope with THE SURREY HUNT.

II
THE YORKSHIREMAN AND THE SURREY

IT is an axiom among fox-hunters that the hounds they individually hunt with are the best—compared with them all others are "slow."

Of this species of pardonable egotism, Mr. Jorrocks—who in addition to the conspicuous place he holds in the Surrey Hunt, as shown in the preceding chapter, we should introduce to our readers as a substantial grocer in St. Botolph's Lane, with an elegant residence in Great Coram Street, Russell Square—has his full, if not rather more than his fair share. Vanity, however, is never satisfied without display, and Mr. Jorrocks longed for a customer before whom he could exhibit the prowess of his[5] pack.

Chance threw in his way a young Yorkshireman, who frequently appearing in subsequent pages, we may introduce as a loosish sort of hand, up to anything in the way of a lark, but rather deficient in cash—a character so common in London, as to render further description needless.

Now it is well known that a Yorkshireman, like a dragoon, is nothing without his horse, and if he does understand anything better than racing—it is hunting. Our readers will therefore readily conceive that a Yorkshireman is more likely to be astonished at the possibility of fox-hunting from London, than captivated by the country, or style of turn-out; and in truth, looking at it calmly and dispassionately, in our easy-chair drawn to a window which overlooks the cream of the grazing grounds in the Vale of White Horse, it does strike us with astonishment, that such a thing as a fox should be found within a day's ride of the suburbs. The very idea seems preposterous, for one cannot but associate the charms of a "find" with the horrors of "going to ground" in an omnibus, or the fox being headed by a great Dr. Eady placard, or some such monstrosity. Mr. Mayne,[6] to be sure, has brought racing home to every man's door, but fox-hunting is not quite so tractable a sport. But to our story.

It was on a nasty, cold, foggy, dark, drizzling morning in the month of February, that the Yorkshireman, having been offered a "mount" by Mr. Jorrocks, found himself shivering under the Piazza in Covent Garden about seven o'clock, surrounded by cabs, cabbages, carrots, ducks, dollys, and drabs of all sorts, waiting for his horse and the appearance of the friend who had seduced him into the extraordinary predicament of attiring himself in top-boots and breeches in London. After pacing up and down some minutes, the sound of a horse's hoofs were heard turning down from Long Acre, and reaching the lamp-post at the corner of James Street, his astonished eyes were struck with the sight of a man in a capacious, long, full-tailed, red frock coat reaching nearly to his spurs, with mother-of-pearl buttons, with sporting devices—which afterwards proved to be foxes, done in black—brown shag breeches, that would have been

---

[5] Subscribers, speaking to strangers, always talk of the hounds as their own.
[6] The promoter of the Hippodrome, near Bayswater—a speculation that soon came to grief.

spurned by the late worthy master of the Hurworth,[7] and boots, that looked for all the world as if they were made to tear up the very land and soil, tied round the knees with pieces of white tape, the flowing ends of which dangled over the mahogany-coloured tops. Mr. Jorrocks—whose dark collar, green to his coat, and *tout ensemble*, might have caused him to be mistaken for a mounted general postman—was on a most becoming steed—a great raking, raw-boned chestnut, with a twisted snaffle in his mouth, decorated with a faded yellow silk front, a nose-band, and an ivory ring under his jaws, for the double purpose of keeping the reins together and Jorrocks's teeth in his head—the nag having flattened the noses and otherwise damaged the countenances of his two previous owners, who had not the knack of preventing him tossing his head in their faces. The saddle—large and capacious—made on the principle of the impossibility of putting a round of beef upon a pudding plate—was "spick and span new," as was an enormous hunting-whip, whose iron-headed hammer he clenched in a way that would make the blood curdle in one's veins, to see such an instrument in the hands of a misguided man.

"Punctuality is the politeness of princes," said Mr. Jorrocks, raising a broad-brimmed, lowish-crowned hat, as high as a green hunting-cord which tackled it to his yellow waistcoat by a fox's tooth would allow, as he came upon the Yorkshireman at the corner. "My soul's on fire and eager for the chase! By heavens, I declare I've dreamt of nothing else all night, and the worst of it is, that in a par-ox-ism of delight, when I thought I saw the darlings running into the warmint, I brought Mrs. J—— such a dig in the side as knocked her out of bed, and she swears she'll go to Jenner, and the court for the protection of injured ribs! But come—jump up—where's your nag? Binjimin, you blackguard, where are you? The fog is blinding me, I declare! Binjimin, I say! Binjimin! you willain, where are you?"

"Here, sir! coming!" responded a voice from the bottom of one of the long mugs at a street breakfast stall, which the fog almost concealed from their view, and presently an urchin in a drab coat and blue collar came towing a wretched, ewe-necked, hungry-looking, roan rosinante along from where he had been regaling himself with a mug of undeniable bohea, sweetened with a composition of brown sugar and sand.

"Now be after getting up," said Jorrocks, "for time and the Surrey 'ounds wait for no man. That's not a werry elegant tit, but still it'll carry you to Croydon well enough, where I'll put you on a most undeniable bit of 'orse-flesh—a reg'lar clipper. That's a hack—what they calls three-and-sixpence a side, but I only pays half a crown. Now, Binjimin, cut away home, and tell Batsay to have dinner ready at half-past five to a minute, and to be most particular in doing the lamb to a turn."

The Yorkshireman having adjusted himself in the old flat-flapped hack saddle, and got his stirrups let out from "Binjimin's" length to his own, gathered

---

[7] The late Mr. Wilkinson, commonly called "Matty Wilkinson," master of the Hurworth foxhounds, was a rigid adherent of the "d——n-all-dandy" school of sportsmen.

up the stiff, weather-beaten reins, gave the animal a touch with his spurs, and fell into the rear of Mr. Jorrocks. The morning appeared to be getting worse. Instead of the grey day-dawn of the country, when the thin transparent mist gradually rises from the hills, revealing an unclouded landscape, a dense, thick, yellow fog came rolling in masses along the streets, obscuring the gas lights, and rendering every step one of peril. It could be both eat and felt, and the damp struck through their clothes in the most summary manner. "This is bad," said Mr. Jorrocks, coughing as he turned the corner by Drury Lane, making for Catherine Street, and upset an early breakfast and periwinkle stall, by catching one corner of the fragile fabric with his toe, having ridden too near to the pavement. "Where are you for now? and bad luck to ye, ye boiled lobster!" roared a stout Irish wench, emerging from a neighbouring gin-palace on seeing the dainty viands rolling in the street. "Cut away!" cried Jorrocks to his friend, running his horse between one of George Stapleton's dust-carts and a hackney-coach, "or the Philistines will be upon us." The fog and crowd concealed them, but "Holloa! mind where you're going, you great haw-buck!" from a buy-a-hearth-stone boy, whose stock-in-trade Jorrocks nearly demolished, as he crossed the corner of Catherine Street before him, again roused his vigilance. "The deuce be in the fog," said he, "I declare I can't see across the Strand. It's as dark as a wolf's mouth.—Now where are you going to with that meazly-looking cab of yours?—you've nearly run your shafts into my 'oss's ribs!" cried he to a cabman who nearly upset him. The Strand was kept alive by a few slip-shod housemaids, on their marrow-bones, washing the doorsteps, or ogling the neighbouring pot-boy on his morning errand for the pewters. Now and then a crazy jarvey passed slowly by, while a hurrying mail, with a drowsy driver and sleeping guard, rattled by to deliver their cargo at the post office. Here and there appeared one of those beings, who like the owl hide themselves by day, and are visible only in the dusk. Many of them appeared to belong to the other world. Poor, puny, ragged, sickly-looking creatures, that seemed as though they had been suckled and reared with gin. "How different," thought the Yorkshireman to himself, "to the fine, stout, active labourer one meets at an early hour on a hunting morning in the country!" His reverie was interrupted on arriving opposite the *Morning Chronicle* office, by the most discordant yells that ever issued from human beings, and on examining the quarter from whence they proceeded, a group of fifty or a hundred boys, or rather little old men, were seen with newspapers in their hands and under their arms, in all the activity of speculation and exchange. "A clean *Post* for Tuesday's *Times*!" bellowed one. "I want the *Hur!* (Herald) for the *Satirist*!" shouted another. "Bell's *Life* for the *Bull! The Spectator* for the *Sunday Times*!"

The approach of our sportsmen was the signal for a change of the chorus, and immediately Jorrocks was assailed with "A hunter! a hunter! crikey, a hunter! My eyes! there's a gamecock for you! Vot a beauty! Vere do you turn out to-day? Vere's the stag? Don't tumble off, old boy! 'Ave you got ever a rope in your pocket? Take Bell's *Life in London*, vot contains all the sporting news of the country! Vot a vip the gemman's got! Vot a precious basternadering he could give us—my eyes, vot a swell!—vot a shocking bad hat![8]—vot shocking bad breeches!"

The fog, which became denser at every step, by the time they reached St. Clement's Danes rendered their further progress almost impossible.—"Oh, dear! oh, dear! how unlucky," exclaimed Jorrocks, "I would have given twenty pounds of best Twankay for a fine day—and see what a thing we've got! Hold my 'oss," said he to the Yorkshireman, "while I run into the 'Angel,' and borrow an argand burner, or we shall be endorsed[9] to a dead certainty." Off he got, and ran to the inn. Presently he emerged from the yard—followed by horse-keepers, coach-washers, porters, cads, waiters and others, amid loud cries of "Flare up, flare up, old cock! talliho fox-hunter!"—with a bright mail-coach footboard lamp, strapped to his middle, which, lighting up the whole of his broad back now cased in scarlet, gave him the appearance of a gigantic red-and-gold insurance office badge, or an elderly cherub without wings.

The hackney-coach-and cab-men, along whose lines they passed, could not make him out at all. Some thought he was a mail-coach guard riding post with the bags; but as the light was pretty strong he trotted on regardless of observation. The fog, however, abated none of its denseness even on the "Surrey side," and before they reached the "Elephant and Castle," Jorrocks had run against two trucks, three watercress women, one pies-all-ot!-all-ot! man, dispersed a whole covey of Welsh milkmaids, and rode slap over one end of a buy 'at (hat) box! bonnet-box! man's pole, damaging a dozen paste-boards, and finally upsetting Balham Hill Joe's Barcelona "come crack 'em and try 'em" stall at the door of the inn, for all whose benedictions, the Yorkshireman, as this great fox-hunting knight-errant's "Esquire," came in.

Here the Yorkshireman would fain have persuaded Mr. Jorrocks to desist from his quixotic undertaking, but he turned a deaf ear to his entreaties. "We are getting fast into the country, and I hold it to be utterly impossible for this fog to extend beyond Kennington Common—'twill ewaporate, you'll see, as we approach the open. Indeed, if I mistake not, I begin to sniff the morning air already, and hark! there's a lark a-carrolling before us!" "Now, spooney! where are you for?" bellowed a carter, breaking off in the middle of his whistle, as Jorrocks rode slap against his leader, the concussion at once dispelling the pleasing pastoral delusion, and nearly knocking Jorrocks off his horse.

As they approached Brixton Hill, a large red ball of lurid light appeared in the firmament, and just at the moment up rode another member of the Surrey Hunt in uniform, whom Jorrocks hailed as Mr. Crane. "By Jove, 'ow beautiful the moon is," said the latter, after the usual salutations. "Moon!" said Mr. Jorrocks, "that's not never no moon—I reckon it's Mrs. Graham's balloon." "Come, that's a good 'un," said Crane, "perhaps you'll lay me an 'at about it". "Done!" said Mr. Jorrocks, "a guinea one—and we'll ax my friend here.—Now, what's that?" "Why, judging from its position and the hour, I should say it is the

---

[8] "Vot a shocking bad hat!"—a slang cockney phrase of 1831.
[9] City—for having a pole run into one's rear.

sun!" was the reply.

We have omitted to mention that this memorable day was a Saturday, one on which civic sportsmen exhibit. We may also premise, that the particular hunt we are about to describe, took place when there were very many packs of hounds within reach of the metropolis, all of which boasted their respective admiring subscribers. As our party proceeded they overtook a gentleman perusing a long bill of the meets for the next week, of at least half a dozen packs, the top of the list being decorated with a cut of a stag-hunt, and the bottom containing a notification that hunters were "carefully attended to by Charles Morton,[10] at the 'Derby Arms,' Croydon," a snug rural *auberge* near the barrack. On the hunting bill-of-fare, were Mr. Jolliffe's foxhounds, Mr. Meager's harriers, the Derby staghounds, the Sanderstead harriers, the Union foxhounds, the Surrey foxhounds, rabbit beagles on Epsom Downs, and dwarf foxhounds on Woolwich Common. What a list to bewilder a stranger! The Yorkshireman left it all to Mr. Jorrocks.

"You're for Jolliffe, I suppose," said the gentleman with the bill, to another with a blue coat and buff lining. "He's at Chipstead Church—only six miles from Croydon, a sure find and good country." "What are you for, Mr. Jorrocks?" inquired another in green, with black velvet breeches, Hessian boots, and a red waistcoat, who just rode up. "My own, to be sure," said Jorrocks, taking hold of the green collar of his coat, as much as to say, "How can you ask such a question?" "Oh, no," said the gentleman in green, "Come to the stag—much better sport—sure of a gallop—open country—get it over soon—back in town before the post goes out." Before Mr. Jorrocks had time to make a reply to this last interrogatory, they were overtaken by another horseman, who came hopping along at a sort of a butcher's shuffle, on a worn-out, three-legged, four-cornered hack, with one eye, a rat-tail, and a head as large as a fiddle-case.—"Who's for the blue mottles?" said he, casting a glance at their respective coats, and at length fixing it on the Yorkshireman. "Why, Dickens, you're not going thistle-whipping with that nice 'orse of yours," said the gentleman in the velvets; "come and see the stag turned out—sure of a gallop—no hedges—soft country—plenty of publics—far better sport, man, than pottering about looking for your foxes and hares, and wasting your time; take my advice, and come with me." "But," says Dickens, "my 'orse won't stand it; I had him in the shay till eleven last night, and he came forty-three mile with our traveller the day before, else he's a 'good 'un to go,' as you know. Do you remember the owdacious leap he took over the tinker's tent, at Epping 'Unt, last Easter? How he astonished the natives within!" "Yes; but then, you know, you fell head-foremost through the canvas, and no wonder your ugly mug frightened them," replied he of the velvets. "Ay; but that was in consequence of my riding by balance instead of gripping with my legs," replied Dickens; "you see, I had taken seven lessons in

[10] Where the carrion is, there will be the crow, and on the demise of the "Surrey staggers," Charley brushed off to the west, to valet the gentlemen's hunters that attend the Royal Stag Hunt.—*Vide* Sir F. Grant's picture of the meet of the Royal Staghounds.

riding at the school in Bidborough Street, Burton Crescent, and they always told me to balance myself equally on the saddle, and harden my heart, and ride at whatever came in the way; and the tinker's tent coming first, why, naturally enough, I went at it. But I have had some practice since then, and, of course, can stick on better. I have 'unted regularly ever since, and can 'do the trick' now." "What, summer and winter?" said Jorrocks. "No," replied he, "but I have 'unted regularly every fifth Saturday since the 'unting began."

After numerous discourses similar to the foregoing, they arrived at the end of the first stage on the road to the hunt, namely, the small town of Croydon, the rendezvous of London sportsmen. The whole place was alive with red coats, green coats, blue coats, black coats, brown coats, in short, coats of all the colours of the rainbow. Horsemen were mounting, horsemen were dismounting, one-horse "shays" and two-horse chaises were discharging their burdens, grooms were buckling on their masters' spurs, and others were pulling off their overalls. Eschewing the "Greyhound," they turn short to the right, and make for the "Derby Arms" hunting stables.

Charley Morton, a fine old boy of his age, was buckling on his armour for the fight, for his soul, too, was "on fire, and eager for the chase." He was for the "venison"; and having mounted his "deer-stalker," was speedily joined by divers perfect "swells," in beautiful leathers, beautiful coats, beautiful tops, beautiful everything, except horses, and off they rode to cut in for the first course—a stag-hunt on a Saturday being usually divided into three.

The ride down had somewhat sharpened Jorrocks's appetite; and feeling, as he said, quite ready for his dinner, he repaired to Mr. Morton's house—a kind of sporting snuggery, everything in apple-pie order, and very good—where he baited himself on sausages and salt herrings, a basin of new milk, with some "sticking powder" as he called it, *alias* rum, infused into it; and having deposited a half-quartern loaf in one pocket, as a sort of balance against a huge bunch of keys which rattled in the other, he pulled out his watch, and finding they had a quarter of an hour to spare, proposed to chaperon the Yorkshireman on a tour of the hunting stables. Jorrocks summoned the ostler, and with great dignity led the way. "Humph," said he, evidently disappointed at seeing half the stalls empty, "no great show this morning—pity—gentleman come from a distance—should like to have shown him some good nags.—What sort of a devil's this?" "Oh, sir, he's a good 'un, and nothing but a good 'un!—Leap! Lord love ye, he'll leap anything. A railway cut, a windmill with the sails going, a navigable river with ships—anything in short. This is the 'orse wot took the line of houses down at Beddington the day they had the tremendious run from Reigate Hill." "And wot's the grey in the far stall?" "Oh, that's Mr. Pepper's old nag—Pepper-Caster as we call him, since he threw the old gemman, the morning they met at the 'Leg-of-Mutton' at Ashtead. But he's good for nothing. Bless ye! his tail shakes for all the world like a pepper-box afore he's gone half a mile. Those be yours in the far stalls, and since they were turned round I've won a bob of a gemman who I bet I'd show him two 'osses with their heads vere their tails should be.[11] I always says," added he with a leer, "that you rides the best 'osses of any gemman vot comes to our governor's." This flattered Jorrocks, and sidling up, he slipped a shilling into his hand, saying, "Well—bring them out, and let's see how they look this morning." The stall reins are slipped, and out they step with their hoods on their quarters. One was a large, fat, full-sized chestnut, with a white ratch down the full extent of his face, a long square tail, bushy mane, with untrimmed heels. The other was a brown, about fifteen two, coarse-headed, with a rat-tail, and collar-marked. The tackle was the same as they came down with. "You'll do the trick on that, I reckon," said Jorrocks, throwing his leg over the chestnut, and looking askew at the Yorkshireman as he mounted. "Tatt., and old Tatt., and Tatt. sen. before him, all agree that they never knew a bad 'oss with a rat-tail."

"But, let me tell you, you must be werry lively, if you mean to live with our 'ounds. They go like the wind. But come! touch him with the spur, and let's do a trot." The Yorkshireman obeyed, and getting into the main street, onwards they jogged, right through Croydon, and struck into a line of villas of all sorts, shapes, and sizes, which extend for several miles along the road, exhibiting all sorts of architecture, Gothic, Corinthian, Doric, Ionic, Dutch, and Chinese. These gradually diminished in number, and at length they found themselves on an open heath, within a few miles of the meet of the "Surrey foxhounds". "Now", says Mr. Jorrocks, clawing up his smalls, "you will see the werry finest pack of hounds in all England; I don't care where the next best are; and you will see as good a turn-out as ever you saw in your life, and as nice a country to ride over as ever you were in".

They reach the meet—a wayside public-house on a common, before which the hounds with their attendants and some fifty or sixty horsemen, many of them in scarlet, were assembled. Jorrocks was received with the greatest cordiality, amid whoops and holloas, and cries of "now Twankay!—now Sugar!—now Figs!" Waving his hand in token of recognition, he passed on and made straight for Tom Hill, with a face full of importance, and nearly rode over a hound in his hurry. "Now, Tom," said he, with the greatest energy, "do, my good fellow, strain every nerve to show sport to-day.—A gentleman has come all the way from the north-east side of the town of Boroughbridge, in the county of York, to see our excellent 'ounds, and I would fain have him galvanised.—Do show us a run, and let it end with blood, so that he may have something to tell the natives when he gets back to his own parts. That's him, see, sitting under the yew-tree, in a bottle-green coat with basket buttons, just striking a light on the pommel of his saddle to indulge in a fumigation.—Keep your eye on him all day, and if you can lead him over an awkward place, and get him a purl, so much the better.—If he'll risk his neck I'll risk my 'oss's."

The Yorkshireman, having lighted his cigar and tightened his girths, rode leisurely among the horsemen, many of whom were in eager council, and a gentle breeze wafted divers scraps of conversation to his ear.

---

[11] A favourite joke among grooms when a horse is turned round in his stall.

What is that hound got by? No. How is that horse bred? No. What sport had you on Wednesday? No. Is it a likely find to-day? No, no, no; it was not where the hounds, but what the Consols, left off at; what the four per cents, and not the four horses, were up to; what the condition of the money, not the horse, market. "Anything doing in Danish bonds, sir?" said one. "You must do it by lease and release, and levy a fine," replied another. Scott *v.* Brown, crim. con. to be heard on or before Wednesday next.—Barley thirty-two to forty-two.—Fine upland meadow and rye grass hay, seventy to eighty.—The last pocket of hops I sold brought seven pounds fifteen shillings. Sussex bags six pounds ten shillings.—There were only twenty-eight and a quarter ships at market, "and coals are coals." "Glad to hear it, sir, for half the last you sent me were slates."—"Best qualities of beef four shillings and eightpence a stone—mutton three shillings and eightpence, to four shillings and sixpence.—He was exceedingly ill when I paid my last visit—I gave him nearly a stone of Epsom-salts, and bled him twice.—This horse would suit you to a T, sir, but my skip-jack is coming out on one at two o'clock that can carry a house.—See what a bosom this one's got.—Well, Gunter, old boy, have you iced your horse to-day?—Have you heard that Brown and Co. are in the *Gazette?* No, which Brown—not John Brown? No, William Brown. What, Brown of Goodman's Fields? No, Brown of—— Street—Brown*e* with an *e*; you know the man I mean.—Oh, Lord, ay, the man wot used to be called Nosey Browne." A general move ensued, and they left "the meet."

"Vere be you going to turn out pray, sir, may I inquire?" said a gentleman in green to the huntsman, as he turned into a field. "Turn out," said he, "why, ye don't suppose we be come calf-hunting, do ye? We throws off some two stones'-throw from here, if so be you mean what cover we are going to draw." "No," said green-coat, "I mean where do you turn out the stag?"—"D—n the stag, we know nothing about such matters," replied the huntsman. "Ware wheat! ware wheat! ware wheat!" was now the general cry, as a gentleman in nankeen pantaloons and Hessian boots with long brass spurs, commenced a navigation across a sprouting crop. "Ware wheat, ware wheat!" replied he, considering it part of the ceremony of hunting, and continued his forward course. "Come to my side," said Mr.——, to the whipper-in, "and meet that gentleman as he arrives at yonder gate; and keep by him while I scold you."—"Now, sir, most particularly d—n you, for riding slap-dash over the young wheat, you most confounded insensible ignorant tinker, isn't the headland wide enough both for you and your horse, even if your spurs were as long again as they are?" Shouts of "Yooi over, over, over hounds—try for him—yoicks—wind him! good dogs—yoicks! stir him up—have at him there!"—here interrupted the jawbation, and the whip rode off shaking his sides with laughter. "Your horse has got a stone in each forefoot, and a thorn in his near hock," observed a dentist to a wholesale haberdasher from Ludgate Hill, "allow me to extract them for you—no pain, I assure—over before you know it." "Come away, hounds! come away!" was heard, and presently the huntsman, with some of the pack at his horse's heels, issued from the wood playing *Rule, Britannia!* on a key-bugle, while the cracks of heavy-thonged whips warned the stragglers and loiterers to follow. "Music hath charms to soothe the savage beast," observed Jorrocks, as he tucked the laps of his frock over his thighs, "and I hope we shall find before long, else that quarter of house-lamb will be utterly ruined. Oh, dear, they are going below hill I do believe! why we shall never get home to-day, and I told Mrs. Jorrocks half-past five to a minute, and I invited old Fleecy, who is a most punctual man."

Jorrocks was right in his surmise. They arrived on the summit of a range of steep hills commanding an extensive view over the neighbouring country—almost, he said, as far as the sea-coast. The huntsman and hounds went down, but many of the field held a council of war on the top. "Well! who's going down?" said one. "I shall wait for the next turn," said Jorrocks, "for my horse does not like collar work." "I shall go this time," said another, "and the rest next." "And so will I," said a third, "for mayhap there will be no second turn." "Ay," added a fourth, "and he may go the other way, and then where-shall we all be?" "Poh!" said Jorrocks, "did you ever know a Surrey fox not take to the hills?—If he does not, I'll eat him without mint sauce," again harping on the quarter of lamb. Facilis descensus Averni—two-thirds of the field went down, leaving Jorrocks, two horse-dealers in scarlet, three chicken-butchers, half a dozen swells in leathers, a whip, and the Yorkshireman on the summit. "Why don't you go with the hounds?" inquired the latter of the whip. "Oh, I wait here, sir," said he, "to meet Tom Hills as he comes up, and to give him a fresh horse." "And who is Tom Hills?" inquired the Yorkshireman. "Oh, he's our huntsman," replied he; "you know Tom, don't you?" "Why, I can't say I do, exactly," said he; "but tell me, is he called Hills because he rides up and down these hills, or is that his real name?" "Hought! you know as well as I do," said he, quite indignantly, "that Tom Hills is his name."

The hounds, with the majority of the field, having effected the descent of the hills, were now trotting on in the valley below, sufficiently near, however, to allow our hill party full view of their proceedings. After drawing a couple of osier-beds blank, they assumed a line parallel to the hills, and moved on to a wood of about ten acres, the west end of which terminated in a natural gorse. "They'll find there to a certainty," said Mr. Jorrocks, pulling a telescope out of his breeches' pocket, and adjusting the sight. "Never saw it blank but once, and that was the werry day the commercial panic of twenty-five commenced.—I remember making an entry in my ledger when I got home to that effect. Humph!" continued he, looking through the glass, "they are through the wood, though, without a challenge.—Now, my booys, push him out of the gorse! Let's see vot you're made of.—There goes the first 'ound in.—It's Galloper, I believe.—I can almost see the bag of shot round his neck.—Now they all follow.—One—two—three—four—five—all together, my beauties! Oh, vot a sight! Peckham's cap's in the air, and it's a find, by heavens!" Mr. Jorrocks is right.—The southerly wind wafts up the fading notes of the "Huntsman's Chorus" in *Der Frieschutz* and confirms the fact.—Jorrocks is in ecstasies.— "Now," said he, clawing up his breeches (for he dispenses with the article of braces when out hunting), "that's what I calls fine. Oh, beautiful! beautiful!—

Now, follow me if you please, and if yon gentleman in drab does not shoot the fox, he will be on the hills before long." Away they scampered along the top of the ridge, with a complete view of the operations below. At length Jorrocks stopped, and pulling the telescope out, began making an observation. "There he is, at last," cried he, "just crossed the corner of yon green field—now he creeps through the hedge by the fir-tree, and is in the fallow one. Yet, stay—that's no fox—it's a hare: and yet Tom Hills makes straight for the spot—and did you hear that loud tally-ho? Oh! gentlemen, gentlemen, we shall be laughed to scorn—what can they be doing—see, they take up the scent, and the whole pack have joined in chorus. Great heavens, it's no more a fox than I am!—No more brush than a badger! Oh, dear! oh, dear! that I should live to see my old friends, the Surrey fox'ounds, 'unt hare, and that too in the presence of a stranger." The animal made direct for the hills—whatever it was, the hounds were on good terms with it, and got away in good form. The sight was splendid—all the field got well off, nor between the cover and the hills was there sufficient space for tailing. A little elderly gentleman, in a pepper-and-salt coat, led the way gallantly—then came the scarlets—then the darks—and then the fustian-clad countrymen. Jorrocks was in a shocking state, and rolled along the hill-tops, almost frantic. The field reached the bottom, and the foremost commenced the steep ascent.

"Oh, Tom Hills!—Tom Hills!—'what are you at? what are you after?"' demanded Jorrocks, as he landed on the top. "Here's a gentleman come all the way from the north-east side of the town of Boroughbridge, in the county of York, to see our excellent 'ounds, and here you are running a hare. Oh, Tom Hills! Tom Hills! ride forward, ride forward, and whip them off, ere we eternally disgrace ourselves." "Oh," says Tom, laughing, "he's a fox! but he's so tarnation frightened of our hounds, that his brush dropped off through very fear, as soon as ever he heard us go into the wood; if you go back, you'll find it somewhere, Mr. Jorrocks; haw, haw, haw! No fox indeed!" said he.—"Forrard, hounds, forrard!" And away he went—caught the old whipper-in, dismounted him in a twinkling, and was on a fresh horse with his hounds in full cry. The line of flight was still along the hill-tops, and all eagerly pressed on, making a goodly rattle over the beds of flints. A check ensued. "The guard on yonder nasty Brighton coach has frightened him with his horn," said Tom; "now we must make a cast up to yonder garden, and see if he's taken shelter among the geraniums in the green-house. As little damage as possible, gentlemen, if you please, in riding through the nursery grounds. Now, hold hard, sir—pray do—there's no occasion for you to break the kale pots; he can't be under them. Ah, yonder he goes, the tailless beggar; did you see him as he stole past the corner out of the early-cabbage bed? Now bring on the hounds, and let us press him towards London."

"See the conquering hero comes", sounded through the avenue of elms as Tom dashed forward with the merry, merry pack. "I shall stay on the hills", said one, "and be ready for him as he comes back; I took a good deal of the shine out of my horse in coming up this time". "I think I will do the same", said two or three more. "Let's be doing", said Jorrocks, ramming his spurs into his nag to seduce him into a gallop, who after sending his heels in the air a few times in token of his disapprobation of such treatment, at last put himself into a round-rolling sort of canter, which Jorrocks kept up by dint of spurring and dropping his great bastinaderer of a whip every now and then across his shoulders. Away they go pounding together!

The line lies over flint fallows occasionally diversified with a turnip-field or market-garden, and every now and then a "willa" appears, from which emerge footmen in jackets, and in yellow, red and green plush breeches, with no end of admiring housemaids, governesses, and nurses with children in their arms.

Great was the emulation when any of these were approached, and the rasping sportsmen rushed eagerly to the "fore." At last they approach "Miss Birchwell's finishing and polishing seminary for young ladies," whose great flaring blue-and-gold sign, reflecting the noonday rays of the sun, had frightened the fox and caused him to alter his line and take away to the west. A momentary check ensued, but all the amateur huntsmen being blown, Tom, who is well up with his hounds, makes a quick cast round the house, and hits off the scent like a workman. A private road and a line of gates through fields now greet the eyes of our M'Adamisers. A young gentleman on a hired hunter very nattily attired, here singles himself out and takes place next to Tom, throwing the pebbles and dirt back in the eyes of the field. Tom crams away, throwing the gates open as he goes, and our young gentleman very coolly passes through, without a touch, letting them bang-to behind him. The Yorkshireman, who had been gradually creeping up, until he has got the third place, having opened two or three, and seeing another likely to close for want of a push, cries out to our friend as he approaches, "Put out your hand, sir!" The gentleman obediently extends his limb like the arm of a telegraph, and rides over half the next field with his hand in the air! The gate, of course, falls to.

A stopper appears—a gate locked and spiked, with a downward hinge to prevent its being lifted. To the right is a rail, and a ha-ha beyond it—to the left a quick fence. Tom glances at both, but turns short, and backing his horse, rides at the rail. The Yorkshireman follows, but Jorrocks, who espies a weak place in the fence a few yards from the gate, turns short, and jumping off, prepares to lead over. It is an old gap, and the farmer has placed a sheep hurdle on the far side. Just as Jorrocks has pulled that out, his horse, who is a bit of a rusher, and has got his "monkey" completely up, pushes forward while his master is yet stooping—and hitting him in the rear, knocks him clean through the fence, head foremost into a squire-trap beyond!—"Non redolet sed olet!" exclaims the Yorkshireman, who dismounts in a twinkling, lending his friend a hand out of the unsavoury cesspool.—"That's what comes of hunting in a new[12] saddle, you see," added he, holding his nose. Jorrocks scrambles upon "terra firma" and exhibits such a spectacle as provokes the shouts of the field. He has lost his wig,

---

[12] There is a superstition among sportsmen that they are sure to get a fall the first day they appear in anything new.

his hat hangs to his back, and one side of his person and face is completely japanned with black odoriferous mixture. "My vig!" exclaims he, spitting and spluttering, "but that's the nastiest hole I ever was in—Fleet Ditch is lavender-water compared to it! Hooi yonder!" hailing a lad, "Catch my 'oss, boouy!" Tom Hills has him; and Jorrocks, pocketing his wig, remounts, rams his spurs into the nag, and again tackles with the pack, which had come to a momentary check on the Eden Bridge road. The fox has been headed by a party of gipsies, and, changing his point, bends southward and again reaches the hills, along which some score of horsemen have planted themselves in the likeliest places to head him. Reynard, however, is too deep for them, and has stolen down unperceived. Poor Jorrocks, what with the violent exertion of riding, his fall, and the souvenir of the cesspool that he still bears about him, pulls up fairly exhausted. "Oh, dear," says he, scraping the thick of the filth off his coat with his whip, "I'm reglarly blown, I earn't go down with the 'ounds this turn; but, my good fellow," turning to the Yorkshireman, who was helping to purify him, "don't let me stop you, go down by all means, but mind, bear in mind the quarter of house-lamb—at half-past five to a minute."

Many of the cits now gladly avail themselves of the excuse of assisting Mr. Jorrocks to clean himself for pulling up, but as soon as ever those that are going below hill are out of sight and they have given him two or three wipes, they advise him to let it "dry on," and immediately commence a different sort of amusement—each man dives into his pocket and produces the eatables.

Part of Jorrocks's half-quartern loaf was bartered with the captain of an East Indiaman for a slice of buffalo-beef. The dentist exchanged some veal sandwiches with a Jew for ham ones; a lawyer from the Borough offered two slices of toast for a hard-boiled egg; in fact there was a petty market "ouvert" held. "Now, Tomkins, where's the bottle?" demanded Jenkins. "Vy, I thought you would bring it out to-day," replied he; "I brought it last time, you know." "Take a little of mine, sir," said a gentleman, presenting a leather-covered flask—"real Thomson and Fearon, I assure you." "I wish someone would fetch an ocean of porter from the nearest public," said another. "Take a cigar, sir?" "No; I feel werry much obliged, but they always make me womit." "Is there any gentleman here going to Halifax, who would like to make a third in a new yellow barouche, with lavender-coloured wheels, and pink lining?" inquired Mr.——, the coach-maker. "Look at the hounds, gentlemen sportsmen, my noble sportsmen!" bellowed out an Epsom Dorling's correct—cardseller—and turning their eyes in the direction in which he was looking, our sportsmen saw them again making for the hills. Pepper-and-salt first, and oh, what a goodly tail was there!—three quarters of a mile in length, at the least. Now up they come—the "corps de reserve" again join, and again a party halt upon the hills. Again Tom Hills exchanges horses; and again the hounds go on in full cry. "I must be off," said a gentleman in balloon-like leathers to another tiger; "we have just time to get back to town, and ride round by the park before it is dark—much better than seeing the end of this brute. Let us go"; and away they went to canter through Hyde Park in their red coats. "I must go and all," said another gentleman; "my dinner will be ready at five, and it is now three." Jorrocks was game; and forgetting the quarter of house-lamb, again tackled with the pack. A smaller sweep sufficed this time, and the hills were once more descended, Jorrocks the first to lead the way. He well knew the fox was sinking, and was determined to be in at the death. Short running ensued—a check—the fox had lain down, and they had overrun the scent. Now they were on him, and Tom Hills's who-whoop confirmed the whole.

"Ah! Tom Hills, Tom Hills!" exclaimed Jorrocks, as the former took up the fox, "'ow splendid, 'ow truly brilliant—by Jove, you deserve to be Lord Hill— oh, had he but a brush that we might present it to this gentleman from the north-east side of the town of Boroughbridge, in the county of York, to show the gallant doings of the men of Surrey!" "Ay," said Tom, "but Squire——'s keeper has been before us for it."

"Now," said a gentleman in a cap, to another in a hat, "if you will ride up the hill and collect the money there, I will do so below—half-a-crown, if you please, sir—half-a-crown, if you please, sir.—Have I got your half-a-crown, sir?"—"Here's three shillings if you will give me sixpence." "Certainly, sir— certainly." "We have no time to spare," said Jorrocks, looking at his watch. "Good afternoon, gentlemen, good afternoon," muttering as he went, "a quarter of house-lamb at half-past five—Mrs. Jorrocks werry punctual—old Fleecy werry particular." They cut across country to Croydon, and as they approached the town, innumerable sportsmen came flocking in from all quarters. "What sport have you had?" inquired Jorrocks of a gentleman in scarlet; "have you been with Jolliffe?" "No, with the staghounds; three beautiful runs; took him once in a millpond, once in a barn, and once in a brickfield—altogether the finest day's sport I ever saw in my life." "What have you done, Mr. J——?" "Oh, we have had a most gallant thing; a brilliant run indeed—three hours and twenty minutes without a check—over the finest country imaginable." "And who got the brush?" inquired the stag-man. "Oh, it was a gallant run," said Jorrocks, "by far the finest I ever remember." "But did you kill?" demanded his friend. "Kill! to be sure we did. When don't the Surrey kill, I should like to know?" "And who got his brush, did you say?" "I can't tell," said he—"didn't hear the gentleman's name." "What sport has Mr. Meager had to-day?" inquired he of a gentleman in trousers, who issued from a side lane into the high road. "I have been with the Sanderstead, sir—a very capital day's sport—run five hares and killed three. We should have killed four—only—we didn't." "I don't think Mr. Meager has done anything to-day." "Yes, he has," said a gentleman, who just joined with a hare buckled on in front of his saddle, and his white cords all stained with blood; "we killed this chap after an hour and forty-five minutes' gallop; and accounted for another by losing her after running upwards of-three-quarters of an hour." "Well, then, we have all had sport," said Jorrocks, as he spurred his horse into a trot, and made for Morton's stables—"and if the quarter of house-lamb is but right, then indeed am I a happy man."

III
SURREY SHOOTING: MR. JORROCKS IN TROUBLE

OUR readers are now becoming pretty familiar with our principal hero, Mr. Jorrocks, and we hope he improves on acquaintance. Our fox-hunting friends, we are sure, will allow him to be an enthusiastic member of the brotherhood, and though we do not profess to put him in competition with Musters, Osbaldeston, or any of those sort of men, we yet mean to say that had his lot been cast in the country instead of behind a counter, his keenness would have rendered him as conspicuous—if not as scientific—as the best of them.

For a cockney sportsman, however, he is a very excellent fellow—frank, hearty, open, generous, and hospitable, and with the exception of riding up Fleet Street one Saturday afternoon, with a cock-pheasant's tail sticking out of his red coat pocket, no one ever saw him do a cock tail action in his life.

The circumstances attending that exhibition are rather curious.—He had gone out as usual on a Saturday to have a day with the Surrey, but on mounting his hunter at Croydon, he felt the nag rather queer under him, and thinking he might have been pricked in the shoeing, he pulled up at the smith's at Addington to have his feet examined. This lost him five minutes, and unfortunately when he got to the meet, he found that a "travelling[13] fox" had been tallied at the precise moment of throwing off, with which the hounds had gone away in their usual brilliant style, to the tune of "Blue bonnets are over the border." As may be supposed, he was in a deuce of a rage; and his first impulse prompted him to withdraw his subscription and be done with the hunt altogether, and he trotted forward "on the line," in the hopes of catching them up to tell them so. In this he was foiled, for after riding some distance, he overtook a string of Smithfield horses journeying "foreign for Evans," whose imprints he had been taking for the hoof-marks of the hunters. About noon he found himself dull, melancholy, and disconsolate, before the sign of the "Pig and Whistle," on the Westerham road, where, after wetting his own whistle with a pint of half-and-half, he again journeyed onward, ruminating on the uncertainty and mutability of all earthly affairs, the comparative merits of stag-, fox-, and hare-hunting, and the necessity of getting rid of the day somehow or other in the country.

Suddenly his reverie was interrupted by the discharge of a gun in the field adjoining the hedge along which he was passing, and the boisterous whirring of a great cock-pheasant over his head, which caused his horse to start and stop short, and to nearly pitch Jorrocks over his head. The bird was missed, but the sportsman's dog dashed after it, with all the eagerness of expectation, regardless of the cracks of the whip—the "comes to heel," and "downs to charge" of the master. Jorrocks pulled out his hunting telescope, and having marked the bird down with the precision of a billiard-table keeper, rode to the gate to acquaint the shooter with the fact, when to his infinite amazement he discovered his

---

[13] He might well be called a "travelling fox," for it was said he had just travelled down from Herring's, in the New Road, by the Bromley stage.

friend, Nosey Browne (late of "The Surrey"), who, since his affairs had taken the unfortunate turn mentioned in the last paper, had given up hunting and determined to confine himself to shooting only. Nosey, however, was no great performer, as may be inferred, when we state that he had been in pursuit of the above-mentioned cock-pheasant ever since daybreak, and after firing thirteen shots at him had not yet touched a feather.

His dog was of the right sort—for Nosey at least—and hope deferred had not made his heart sick; on the contrary, he dashed after his bird for the thirteenth time with all the eagerness he displayed on the first. "Let me have a crack at him," said Jorrocks to Nosey, after their mutual salutations were over. "I know where he is, and I think I can floor him." Browne handed the gun to Jorrocks, who, giving up his hunter in exchange, strode off, and having marked his bird accurately, he kicked him up out of a bit of furze, and knocked him down as "dead as a door-nail." By that pheasant's tail hangs the present one.

Now Nosey Browne and Jorrocks were old friends, and Nosey's affairs having gone crooked, why of course, like most men in a similar situation, he was all the better for it; and while his creditors were taking twopence-halfpenny in the pound, he was taking his diversion on his wife's property, which a sagacious old father-in-law had secured to the family in the event of such a contingency as a failure happening; so knowing Jorrock's propensity for sports, and being desirous of chatting over all his gallant doings with "The Surrey," shortly after the above-mentioned day he dispatched a "twopenny," offering him a day's shooting on his property in Surrey, adding, that he hoped he would dine with him after. Jorrocks being invited himself, with a freedom peculiar to fox-hunters, invited his friend the Yorkshireman, and visiting his armoury, selected him a regular shot-scatterer of a gun, capable of carrying ten yards on every side.

At the appointed hour on the appointed morning, the Yorkshireman appeared in Great Coram Street, where he found Mr. Jorrocks in the parlour in the act of settling himself into a new spruce green cut-away gambroon butler's pantry-jacket, with pockets equal to holding a powder-flask each, his lower man being attired in tight drab stocking-net pantaloons, and Hessian boots with large tassels—a striking contrast to the fustian pocket-and-all-pocket jackets marked with game-bag strap, and shot-belt, and the weather-beaten many-coloured breeches and gaiters, and hob-nail shoes, that compose the equipment of a shooter in Yorkshire. Mr. Jorrocks not keeping any "sporting dogs," as the tax-papers call them, had borrowed a fat house-dog—a cross between a setter and a Dalmatian—of his friend Mr. Evergreen the greengrocer, which he had seen make a most undeniable point one morning in the Copenhagen Fields at a flock of pigeons in a beetroot garden. This valuable animal was now attached by a trash-cord through a ring in his brass collar to a leg of the sideboard, while a clean licked dish at his side, showed that Jorrocks had been trying to attach him to himself, by feeding him before starting.

"We'll take a coach to the Castle", said Jorrocks, "and then get a go-cart or a cast somehow or other to Streatham, for we shall have walking enough when we get there. Browne is an excellent fellow, and will make us range every acre of his estate over half a dozen times before we give in". A coach was speedily summoned, into which Jorrocks, the dog Pompey, the Yorkshireman, and the guns were speedily placed, and away they drove to the "Elephant and Castle."

There were short stages about for every possible place except Streatham. Greenwich, Deptford, Blackheath, Eltham, Bromley, Footscray, Beckenham, Lewisham—all places but the right. However, there were abundance of "go-carts," a species of vehicle that ply in the outskirts of the metropolis, and which, like the watering-place "fly," take their name from the contrary—in fact, a sort of *lucus a non lucendo*. They are carts on springs, drawn by one horse (with curtains to protect the company from the weather), the drivers of which, partly by cheating, and partly by picking pockets, eke out a comfortable existence, and are the most lawless set of rascals under the sun. Their arrival at the "Elephant and Castle" was a signal for a general muster of the fraternity, who, seeing the guns, were convinced that their journey was only what they call "a few miles down the road," and they were speedily surrounded by twenty or thirty of them, all with "excellent 'osses, vot vould take their honours fourteen miles an hour." All men of business are aware of the advantages of competition, and no one more so than Jorrocks, who stood listening to their offers with the utmost sang-froid, until he closed with one to take them to Streatham Church for two shillings, and deliver them within the half-hour, which was a signal for all the rest to set-to and abuse them, their coachman, and his horse, which they swore had been carrying "stiff-uns" [14] all night, and "could not go not none at all". Nor were they far wrong; for the horse, after scrambling a hundred yards or two, gradually relaxed into something between a walk and a trot, while the driver kept soliciting every passer-by to "ride," much to our sportsmen's chagrin, who conceived they were to have the "go" all to themselves. Remonstrance was vain, and he crammed in a master chimney-sweep, Major Ballenger the licensed dealer in tea, coffee, tobacco, and snuff, of Streatham (a customer of Jorrocks), and a wet-nurse; and took up an Italian organ-grinder to ride beside himself on the front, before they had accomplished Brixton Hill. Jorrocks swore most lustily that he would fine him, and at every fresh assurance, the driver offered a passer-by a seat; but having enlisted Major Ballenger into their cause, they at length made a stand, which, unfortunately for them, was more than the horse could do, for just as he was showing off, as he thought, with a bit of a trot, down they all soused in the mud. Great was the scramble; guns, barrel-organ, Pompey, Jorrocks, driver, master chimney-sweep, Major Ballenger, were all down together, while the wet-nurse, who sat at the end nearest the door, was chucked clean over the hedge into a dry ditch. This was a signal to quit the vessel, and having extricated themselves the best way they could, they all set off on foot, and left the driver to right himself at his leisure.

Ballenger looked rather queer when he heard they were going to Nosey Browne's, for it so happened that Nosey had managed to walk into his books for groceries and kitchen-stuff to the tune of fourteen pounds, a large sum to a

---

[14] Doing a bit of resurrection work.

man in a small way of business; and to be entertaining friends so soon after his composition, seemed curious to Ballenger's uninitiated suburban mind.

Crossing Streatham Common, a short turn to the left by some yew-trees leads, by a near cut across the fields, to Browne's house; a fiery-red brick castellated cottage, standing on the slope of a gentle eminence, and combining almost every absurdity a cockney imagination can be capable of. Nosey, who was his own "Nash," set out with the intention of making it a castle and nothing but a castle, and accordingly the windows were made in the loophole fashion, and the door occupied a third of the whole frontage. The inconveniences of the arrangements were soon felt, for while the light was almost excluded from the rooms, "rude Boreas" had the complete run of the castle whenever the door was opened. To remedy this, Nosey increased the one and curtailed the other, and the Gothic oak-painted windows and door flew from their positions to make way for modern plate-glass in rich pea-green casements, and a door of similar hue. The battlements, however, remained, and two wooden guns guarded a brace of chimney-pots and commanded the wings of the castle, one whereof was formed into a green-, the other into a gig-house.

The peals of a bright brass-handled bell at a garden-gate, surmounted by a holly-bush with the top cut into the shape of a fox, announced their arrival to the inhabitants of "Rosalinda Castle," and on entering they discovered young Nosey in the act of bobbing for goldfish, in a pond about the size of a soup-basin; while Nosey senior, a fat, stupid-looking fellow, with a large corporation and a bottle nose, attired in a single-breasted green cloth coat, buff waistcoat, with drab shorts and continuations, was reposing, *sub tegmine fagi*, in a sort of tea-garden arbour, overlooking a dung-heap, waiting their arrival to commence an attack upon the sparrows which were regaling thereon. At one end of the garden was a sort of temple, composed of oyster-shells, containing a couple of carrier-pigeons, with which Nosey had intended making his fortune, by the early information to be acquired by them: but "there is many a slip," as Jorrocks would say.

Greetings being over, and Jorrocks having paid a visit to the larder, and made up a stock of provisions equal to a journey through the Wilderness, they adjourned to the yard to get the other dog, and the man to carry the game—or rather, the prog, for the former was but problematical. He was a character, a sort of chap of all work, one, in short, "who has no objection to make himself generally useful"; but if his genius had any decided bent, it was, perhaps, an inclination towards sporting.

Having to act the part of groom and gamekeeper during the morning, and butler and footman in the afternoon, he was attired in a sort of composition dress, savouring of the different characters performed. He had on an old white hat, a groom's fustian stable-coat cut down into a shooting-jacket, with a whistle at the button-hole, red plush smalls, and top-boots.

There is nothing a cockney delights in more than aping a country gentleman, and Browne fancied himself no bad hand at it; indeed, since his London occupation was gone, he looked upon himself as a country gentleman in fact.

"Vell, Joe," said he, striddling and sticking his thumbs into the arm-holes of his waistcoat, to this invaluable man of all work, "we must show the gemmem some sport to-day; vich do you think the best line to start upon—shall we go to the ten hacre field, or the plantation, or Thompson's stubble, or Timms's turnips, or my meadow, or vere?" "Vy, I doesn't know," said Joe; "there's that old hen-pheasant as we calls Drab Bess, vot has haunted the plantin' these two seasons, and none of us ever could 'it (hit), and I hears that Jack, and Tom, and Bob, are still left out of Thompson's covey; but, my eyes! they're 'special vild!" "Vot, only three left? where is old Tom, and the old ramping hen?" inquired Browne. "Oh, Mr. Smith, and a party of them 'ere Bankside chaps, com'd down last Saturday's gone a week, and rattled nine-and-twenty shots at the covey, and got the two old 'uns; at least it's supposed they were both killed, though the seven on 'em only bagged one bird; but I heard they got a goose or two as they vent home. They had a shot at old Tom, the hare, too, but he is still alive; at least I pricked him yesterday morn across the path into the turnip-field. Suppose we goes at him first?"

The estate, like the game, was rather deficient in quantity, but Browne was a wise man and made the most of what he had, and when he used to talk about his "manor" on 'Change, people thought he had at least a thousand acres—the extent a cockney generally advertises for, when he wants to take a shooting-place. The following is a sketch of what he had: The east, as far as the eye could reach, was bounded by Norwood, a name dear to cockneys, and the scene of many a furtive kiss; the hereditaments and premises belonging to Isaac Cheatum, Esq. ran parallel with it on the west, containing sixty-three acres, "be the same more or less," separated from which, by a small brook or runner of water, came the estate of Mr. Timms, consisting of sixty acres, three roods, and twenty-four perches, commonly called or known by the name of Fordham; next to it were two allotments in right of common, for all manner of cattle, except cows, upon Streatham Common, from whence up to Rosalinda Castle, on the west, lay the estate of Mr. Browne, consisting of fifty acres and two perches. Now it so happened that Browne had formerly the permission to sport all the way up to Norwood, a distance of a mile and a half, and consequently he might have been said to have the right of shooting in Norwood itself, for the keepers only direct their attention to the preservation of the timber and the morals of the visitors; but since his composition with his creditors, Mr. Cheatum, who had "gone to the wall" himself in former years, was so scandalised at Browne doing the same, that no sooner did his name appear in the *Gazette*, than Cheatum withdrew his permission, thereby cutting him off from Norwood and stopping him in pursuit of his game.

Joe's proposition being duly seconded, Mr. Jorrocks, in the most orthodox manner, flushed off his old flint and steel fire-engine, and proceeded to give it an uncommon good loading. The Yorkshireman, with a look of disgust, mingled with despair, and a glance at Joe's plush breeches and top-boots, did the same, while Nosey, in the most considerate sportsmanlike manner, merely shouldered a stick, in order that there might be no delicacy with his visitors, as to who should shoot first—a piece of etiquette that aids the escape of many a bird in the neighbourhood of London.

Old Tom—a most unfortunate old hare, that what with the harriers, the shooters, the snarers, and one thing and another, never knew a moment's peace, and who must have started in the world with as many lives as a cat—being doomed to receive the first crack on this occasion, our sportsmen stole gently down the fallow, at the bottom of which were the turnips, wherein he was said to repose; but scarcely had they reached the hurdles which divided the field, before he was seen legging it away clean out of shot. Jorrocks, who had brought his gun to bear upon him, could scarcely refrain from letting drive, but thinking to come upon him again by stealth, as he made his circuit for Norwood, he strode away across the allotments and Fordham estate, and took up a position behind a shed which stood on the confines of Mr. Timms's and Mr. Cheatum's properties. Here, having procured a rest for his gun, he waited until old Tom, who had tarried to nip a few blades of green grass that came in his way, made his appearance. Presently he came cantering along the outside of the wood, at a careless, easy sort of pace, betokening either perfect indifference for the world's mischief, or utter contempt of cockney sportsmen altogether.

He was a melancholy, woe-begone-looking animal, long and lean, with a slight inclination to grey on his dingy old coat, one that looked as though he had survived his kindred and had already lived beyond his day. Jorrocks, however, saw him differently, and his eyes glistened as he came within range of his gun. A well-timed shot ends poor Tom's miseries! He springs into the air, and with a melancholy scream rolls neck over heels. Knowing that Pompey would infallibly spoil him if he got up first, Jorrocks, without waiting to load, was in the act of starting off to pick him up, when, at the first step, he found himself in the grasp of a Herculean monster, something between a coal-heaver and a gamekeeper, who had been secreted behind the shed. Nosey Browne, who had been watching his movements, holloaed out to Jorrocks to "hold hard," who stood motionless, on the spot from whence he fired, and Browne was speedily alongside of him. "You are on Squire Cheatum's estate," said the man; "and I have authority to take up all poachers and persons found unlawfully trespassing; what's your name?" "He's not on Cheatum's estate," said Browne. "He is," said the man. "You're a liar," said Browne. "You're another," said the man. And so they went on; for when such gentlemen meet, compliments pass current. At length the keeper pulled out a foot-rule, and keeping Jorrocks in the same position he caught him, he set-to to measure the distance of his foot from the boundary, taking off in a line from the shed; when it certainly did appear that the length of a big toe was across the mark, and putting up his measure again, he insisted upon taking Jorrocks before a magistrate for the trespass. Of course, no objection could be made, and they all adjourned to Mr. Boreem's, when the whole case was laid before him. To cut a long matter short—after hearing the pros and cons, and referring to the Act of Parliament, his worship decided that a trespass had been committed; and though, he said, it went against the grain to do so, he fined Jorrocks in the mitigated penalty of one pound one.

This was a sad damper to our heroes, who returned to the castle with their prog untouched and no great appetite for dinner. Being only a family party, when Mrs. B—— retired, the subject naturally turned upon the morning's mishap, and at every glass of port Jorrocks waxed more valiant, until he swore he would appeal against the "conwiction"; and remaining in the same mind when he awoke the next morning, he took the Temple in his way to St. Botolph Lane and had six-and-eightpence worth with Mr. Capias the attorney, who very judiciously argued each side of the question without venturing an opinion, and proposed stating a case for counsel to advise upon.

As usual, he gave one that would cut either way, though if it had any tendency whatever it was to induce Jorrocks to go on; and he not wanting much persuasion, it will not surprise our readers to hear that Jorrocks, Capias, and the Yorkshireman were seen a few days after crossing Waterloo Bridge in a yellow post-chaise, on their way to Croydon sessions.

After a "guinea" consultation at the "Greyhound," they adjourned to the court, which was excessively crowded, Jorrocks being as popular with the farmers and people as Cheatum was the reverse. Party feeling, too, running rather high at the time, there had been a strong "whip" among the magistrates to get a full attendance to reverse Boreem's conviction, who had made himself rather obnoxious on the blue interest at the election. Of course they all came in new hats,[15] and sat on the bench looking as wise as gentlemen judges generally do.

One hundred and twenty-two affiliation cases (for this was in the old Poor Law time) having been disposed of, about one o'clock in the afternoon, the chairman, Mr. Tomkins of Tomkins, moved the order of the day. He was a perfect prototype of a county magistrate—with a bald powdered head covered by a low-crowned, broad-brimmed hat, hair terminating behind in a *queue*, resting on the ample collar of a snuff-brown coat, with a large bay-window of a corporation, with difficulty retained by the joint efforts of a buff waistcoat, and the waistband of a pair of yellow leather breeches. His countenance, which was solemn and grave in the extreme, might either be indicative of sense or what often serves in the place of wisdom—when parties can only hold their tongues—great natural stupidity. From the judge's seat, which he occupied in the centre of the bench, he observed, with immense dignity, "There is an appeal of Jorrocks against Cheatum, which we, the bench of magistrates of our lord the king, will take if the parties are ready," and immediately the court rang with "Jorrocks and Cheatum! Jorrocks and Cheatum! Mr. Capias, attorney-at-law! Mr. Capias answer to his name! Mr. Sharp attorney-at-law! Mr. Sharp's in the jury-room.—Then go fetch him directly," from the ushers and bailiffs of the court; for though Tomkins of Tomkins was slow himself, he insisted upon others being quick, and was a great hand at prating about saving the time of the suitors. At length the bustle of counsel crossing the table, parties coming in and others

---

[15] Magistrates always buy their hats about session times, as they have the privilege of keeping their hats on their blocks in court.

leaving court, bailiffs shouting, and ushers responding, gradually subsided into a whisper of, "That's Jorrocks! That's Cheatum!" as the belligerent parties took their places by their respective counsel. Silence having been called and procured, Mr. Smirk, a goodish-looking man for a lawyer, having deliberately unfolded his brief, which his clerk had scored plentifully in the margin, to make the attorney believe he had read it very attentively, rose to address the court—a signal for half the magistrates to pull their newspapers out of their pockets, and the other half to settle themselves down for a nap, all the sport being considered over when the affiliation cases closed.

"I have the honour to appear on behalf of Mr. Jorrocks," said Mr. Smirk, "a gentleman of the very highest consideration—a fox-hunter—a shooter—and a grocer. In ordinary cases it might be necessary to prove the party's claim to respectability, but, in this instance, I feel myself relieved from any such obligation, knowing, as I do, that there is no one in this court, no one in these realms—I might almost add, no one in this world—to whom the fame of my most respectable, my most distinguished, and much injured client is unknown. Not to know JORROCKS is indeed to argue oneself unknown."

"This is a case of no ordinary interest, and I approach it with a deep sense of its importance, conscious of my inability to do justice to the subject, and lamenting that it has not been entrusted to abler hands. It is a case involving the commercial and the sporting character of a gentleman against whom the breath of calumny has never yet been drawn—of a gentleman who in all the relations of life, whether as a husband, a fox-hunter, a shooter, or a grocer, has invariably preserved that character and reputation, so valuable in commercial life, so necessary in the sporting world, and so indispensable to a man moving in general society. Were I to look round London town in search of a bright specimen of a man combining the upright, sterling integrity of the honourable British merchant of former days with the ardour of the English fox-hunter of modern times, I would select my most respectable client, Mr. Jorrocks. He is a man for youth to imitate and revere! Conceive, then, the horror of a man of his delicate sensibility—of his nervous dread of depreciation—being compelled to appear here this day to vindicate his character, nay more, his honour, from one of the foulest attempts at conspiracy that was ever directed against any individual. I say that a grosser attack was never made upon the character of any grocer, and I look confidently to the reversion of this unjust, unprecedented conviction, and to the triumphant victory of my most respectable and public-spirited client. It is not for the sake of the few paltry shillings that he appeals to this court—it is not for the sake of calling in question the power of the constituted authorities of this county—but it is for the vindication and preservation of a character dear to all men, but doubly dear to a grocer, and which once lost can never be regained. Look, I say, upon my client as he sits below the witness-box, and say, if in that countenance there appears any indication of a lawless or rebellious spirit; look, I say, if the milk of human kindness is not strikingly portrayed in every feature, and truly may I exclaim in the words of the poet:"

   If to his share some trifling errors fall,
   Look in his face, and you'll forget them all.'

  "I regret to be compelled to trespass upon the valuable time of the court; but, sir, this appeal is based on a trespass, and one good trespass deserves another."

  The learned gentleman then proceeded to detail the proceedings of the day's shooting, and afterwards to analyse the enactments of the new Game Bill, which he denounced as arbitrary, oppressive, and ridiculous, and concluded a long and energetic speech, by calling upon the court to reverse the decision of the magistrate, and not support the preposterous position of fining a man for a trespass committed by his toe.

  After a few minutes had elapsed, Mr. Sergeant Bumptious, a stiff, bull-headed little man, desperately pitted with the smallpox, rose to reply, and looking round the court, thus commenced:

  "Five-and-thirty years have I passed in courts of justice, but never, during a long and extensive practice, have I witnessed so gross a perversion of that sublimest gift, called eloquence, as within the last hour"—here he banged his brief against the table, and looked at Mr. Smirk, who smiled.—"I lament, sir, that it has not been employed in a better cause—(bang again—and another look). My learned friend has, indeed, laboured to make the worse appear the better cause—to convert into a trifle one of the most outrageous acts that ever disgraced a human being or a civilised country. Well did he describe the importance of this case!—important as regards his client's character—important as regards this great and populous county—important as regards those social ties by which society is held together—important as regards a legislative enactment, and important as regards the well-being and prosperity of the whole nation—(bang, bang, bang). I admire the bombastic eloquence with which my learned friend introduced his most distinguished client—his most delicate minded—sensitive client!—Truly, to hear him speaking I should have thought he had been describing a lovely, blushing young lady, but when he comes to exhibit his paragon of perfection, and points out that great, red-faced, coarse, vulgar-looking, lubberly lump of humanity—(here Bumptious looked at Jorrocks as he would eat him)—sitting below the witness-box, and seeks to enlist the sympathies of your worships on the Bench—of you, gentlemen, the high-minded, shrewd, penetrating judges of this important cause—(and Bumptious smiled and bowed along the Bench upon all whose eyes he could catch)—on behalf of such a monster of iniquity, it does make one blush for the degradation of the British Bar—(bang—bang—bang—Jorrocks here looked unutterable things). Does my learned friend think by displaying his hero as a fox-hunter, and extolling his prowess in the field, to gain over the sporting magistrates on the Bench? He knows little of the upright integrity—the uncompromising honesty—the undeviating, inflexible impartiality that pervades the breast of every member of this tribunal, if he thinks for the sake of gain, fear, favour, hope, or reward, to influence the opinion, much less turn the judgment, of any one of them." (Here Bumptious bowed very low to them all and laid his hand upon his heart. Tomkins nodded approbation.) "Far, far be it from me to dwell with unbecoming asperity on the conduct of anyone—we are all mortals—and alike liable to err; but when I see a man who has been guilty of an act which has brought him all but within the verge of the prisoners' dock; I say, when I see a man who has been guilty of such an outrage on society as this ruffian Jorrocks, come forward with the daring effrontery that he has this day done, and claim redress where he himself is the offender, it does create a feeling in my mind divided between disgust and amazement"—(bang).

Here Jorrock's cauldron boiled over, and rising from his seat with an outstretched shoulder-of-mutton fist, he bawled out, "D—n you, sir, what do you mean?"

The court was thrown into amazement, and even Bumptious quailed before the fist of the mighty Jorrocks. "I claim the protection of the court," he exclaimed. Mr. Tomkins interposed, and said he should certainly order Mr. Jorrocks into custody if he repeated his conduct, adding that it was "most disrespectful to the justices of our lord the king."

Bumptious paused a little to gather breath and a fresh volume of venom wherewith to annihilate Jorrocks, and catching his eye, he transfixed him like a rattlesnake, and again resumed.

"How stands the case?" said he. "This cockney grocer—for after all he is nothing else—who I dare say scarcely knows a hawk from a hand-saw—leaves his figs and raisins, and sets out on a marauding excursion into the county of Surrey, and regardless of property—of boundaries—of laws—of liberties—of life itself—strides over every man's land, letting drive at whatever comes in his way! The hare he shot on this occasion was a pet hare!—For three successive summers had Miss Cheatum watched and fed it with all the interest and anxiety of a parent. I leave it to you, gentlemen, who have daughters of your own, with pets also, to picture to yourselves the agony of her mind in finding that her favourite had found its way down the throat of that great guzzling, gormandising, cockney cormorant; and then, forsooth, because he is fined for the outrageous trespass, he comes here as the injured party, and instructs his counsel to indulge in Billingsgate abuse that would disgrace the mouth of an Old Bailey practitioner! I regret that instead of the insignificant fine imposed upon him, the law did not empower the worthy magistrate to send him to the treadmill, there to recreate himself for six or eight months, as a warning to the whole fraternity of lawless vagabonds." Here he nodded his head at Jorrocks as much as to say, "I'll trounce you, my boy!" He then produced maps and plans of the different estates, and a model of the shed, to show how it had all happened, and after going through the case in such a strain as would induce one to believe it was a trial for murder or high treason, concluded as follows:

"The eyes of England are upon us—reverse this conviction, and you let loose a rebel band upon the country, ripe for treason, stratagem, or spoil—you overturn the finest order of society in the world; henceforth no man's property will be safe, the laws will be disregarded, and even the upright, talented, and independent magistracy of England brought into contempt. But I feel convinced that your decision will be far otherwise—that by it you will teach these hot-headed—rebellious—radical grocers that they cannot offend with impunity, and show them that there is a law which reaches even the lowest and meanest inhabitant of these realms, that amid these days of anarchy and innovation you will support the laws and aristocracy of this country, that you will preserve to our children, and our children's children, those rights and blessings which a great and enlightened administration have conferred upon ourselves, and raise for Tomkins of Tomkins and the magistracy of the proud county of Surrey, a name resplendent in modern times and venerated to all eternity."

Here Bumptious cast a parting frown at Jorrocks, and banging down his brief, tucked his gown under his arm, turned on his heel and left the court, to indulge in a glass of pale sherry and a sandwich, regardless which way the verdict went, so long as he had given him a good quilting. The silence that followed had the effect of rousing some of the dozing justices, who nudging those who had fallen asleep, they all began to stir themselves, and having laid their heads together, during which time they settled the dinner-hour for that day, and the meets of the staghounds for the next fortnight, they began to talk of the matter before the court.

"I vote for reversing," said Squire Jolthead; "Jorrocks is such a capital fellow." "I must support Boreem," said Squire Hicks: "he gave me a turn when I made the mistaken commitment of Gipsy Jack." "What do you say, Mr. Giles?" inquired Mr. Tomkins. "Oh, anything you like, Mr. Tomkins." "And you, Mr. Hopper?" who had been asleep all the time. "Oh! guilty, I should say—three months at the treadmill—privately whipped, if you like," was the reply. Mr. Petty always voted on whichever side Bumptious was counsel—the learned serjeant having married his sister—and four others always followed the chair.

Tomkins then turned round, the magistrates resumed their seats along the bench, and coming forward he stood before the judge's chair, and taking off his hat with solemn dignity and precision, laid it down exactly in the centre of the desk, amid cries from the bailiffs and ushers for "Silence, while the justices of the peace of our sovereign lord the king, deliver the judgment of the court."

"The appellant in this case," said Mr. Tomkins, very slowly, "seeks to set aside a conviction for trespass, on the ground, as I understand, of his not having committed one. The principal points of the case are admitted, as also the fact of Mr. Jorrocks's toe, or a part of his toe, having intruded upon the respondent's estate. Now, so far as that point is concerned, it seems clear to myself and to my brother magistrates, that it mattereth not how much or how little of the toe was upon the land, so long as any part thereof was there. 'De minimis non curat lex'—the English of which is 'the law taketh no cognisance of fractions'—is a maxim among the salaried judges of the inferior courts in Westminster Hall, which we the unpaid, the in-cor-rup-ti-ble magistrates of the proud county of Surrey, have adopted in the very deep and mature deliberation that preceded the formation of our most solemn judgment. In the present great and important case, we, the unpaid magistrates of our sovereign lord the king, do not consider it necessary that there should be 'a toe, a whole toe, and nothing but a toe,' to constitute a trespass, any more than it would be necessary in the case of an assault to prove that the kick was given by the foot, the whole foot, and nothing but the foot. If any part of the toe was there, the law considers that it was there *in toto*. Upon this doctrine, it is clear that Mr. Jorrocks was guilty of a trespass, and the conviction must be affirmed. Before I dismiss the case I must say a few words on the statute under which this decision takes place.

"This is the first conviction that has taken place since the passing of the Act, and will serve as a precedent throughout all England. I congratulate the country upon the efficacy of the tribunal to which it has been submitted. The court has listened with great and becoming attention to the arguments of the counsel on both sides: and though one gentleman with a flippant ignorance has denounced this new law as inferior to the pre-existing system, and a curse to the country, we, the magistrates of the proud county of Surrey, must enter our protest against such a doctrine being promulgated. Peradventure, you are all acquainted with my prowess as a shooter; I won two silver tankards at the Red House, Anno Domini 1815. I mention this to show that I am a practical sportsman, and as to the theory of the Game Laws, I derive my information from the same source that you may all derive yours—from the bright refulgent pages of the *New Sporting Magazine*!"

IV
MR. JORROCKS AND THE SURREY STAGHOUNDS

THE Surrey foxhounds had closed their season—a most brilliant one—but ere Mr. Jorrocks consigned his boots and breeches to their summer slumber, he bethought of having a look at the Surrey staghounds, a pack now numbered among the things that were.

Of course he required a companion, were it only to have some one to criticise the hounds with, so the evening before the appointed day, as the Yorkshireman was sitting in his old corner at the far end of the Piazza Coffee-room in Covent Garden, having just finished his second marrowbone and glass of white brandy, George—the only waiter in the room with a name—came smirking up with a card in his hand, saying, that the gentleman was waiting outside to speak with him. It was a printed one, but the large round hand in which the address had been filled up, encroaching upon the letters, had made the name somewhat difficult to decipher. At length he puzzled out "Mr. John Jorrocks—Coram Street"; the name of the city house or shop in the corner (No.—, St. Botolph's Lane) being struck through with a pen. "Oh, ask him to walk in directly," said the Yorkshireman to George, who trotted off, and presently the flapping of the doors in the passage announced his approach, and honest Jorrocks came rolling up the room—not like a fox-hunter, or any other sort of hunter, but like an honest wholesale grocer, fresh from the city.

"My dear fellow, I'm so glad to see you, you can't think," said he, advancing with both hands out, and hugging the Yorkshireman after the manner of a Polar bear. "I have not time to stay one moment; I have to meet Mr. Wiggins at the corner of Bloomsbury Square at a quarter to six, and it wants now only seven minutes to," casting his eye up at the clock over the sideboard.—"I have just called to say that as you are fond of hunting, and all that sort of thing, if you have a mind for a day with the staghounds to-morrow, I will mount you same as before, and all that sort of thing—you understand, eh?" "Thank you, my good friend," said the Yorkshireman; "I have nothing to do to-morrow, and am your man for a stag-hunt." "That's right, my good fellow," said Jorrocks, "then I'll tell you what do—come and breakfast with me in Great Coram Street, at half-past seven to a minute. I've got one of the first 'ams (hams) you ever clapt eyes on in the whole course of your memorable existence.—Saw the hog alive myself—sixteen score within a pound; must come—know you like a fork breakfast—dejeune à la fauchette, as we say in France, eh? Like my Lord Mayor's fool I guess, love what's good; well, all right too—so come without any ceremony—us fox-hunters hates ceremony—where there's ceremony there's no friendship.—Stay—I had almost forgotten," added he, checking himself as he was on the point of departure. "When you come, ring the area bell, and then Mrs. J—— won't hear; know you don't like Mrs. J—— no more than myself."

At the appointed hour the Yorkshireman reached Great Coram Street, just as Old Jorrocks had opened the door to look down the street for him. He was dressed in a fine flowing, olive-green frock (made like a dressing-gown), with a black velvet collar, having a gold embroidered stag on each side, gilt stag-buttons, with rich embossed edges; an acre of buff waistcoat, and a most antediluvian pair of bright yellow-ochre buckskins, made by White, of Tarporley, in the twenty-first year of the reign of George the Third; they were double-lashed, back-stiched, front-stiched, middle-stiched, and patched at both knees, with a slit up behind. The coat he had won in a bet, and the breeches in a raffle, the latter being then second or third hand. His boots were airing before the fire, consequently he displayed an amplitude of calf in grey worsted stockings, while his feet were thrust into green slippers. "So glad to see you"! said he; "here's a charming morning, indeed—regular southerly wind and a cloudy sky—rare scenting it will be—think I could almost run a stag myself. Come in—never mind your hat, hang it anywhere, but don't make a noise. I stole away and left Mrs. J—— snoring, so won't do to wake her, you know. By the way, you should see my hat;—Batsey, fatch my hat out of the back parlour. I've set up a new green silk cord, with a gold frog to fasten it to my button-hole—werry illigant, I think, and werry suitable to the dress—quite my own idea—have a notion all the Surrey chaps will get them; for, between you and me, I set the fashions, and what is more, I sometimes set them at a leap too. But now tell me, have you any objection to breakfasting in the kitchen?—more retired, you know, besides which you get everything hot and hot, which is what I call doing a bit of plisure." "Not at all," said the Yorkshireman, "so lead the way"; and down they walked to the lower regions.

It was a nice comfortable-looking place, with a blazing fire, half the floor covered with an old oil-cloth, and the rest exhibiting the cheerless aspect of the naked flags. About a yard and a half from the fire was placed the breakfast table; in the centre stood a magnificent uncut ham, with a great quartern loaf on one side and a huge Bologna sausage on the other; besides these there were nine eggs, two pyramids of muffins, a great deal of toast, a dozen ship-biscuits, and half a pork-pie, while a dozen kidneys were spluttering on a spit before the fire, and Betsy held a gridiron covered with mutton-chops on the top; altogether there was as much as would have served ten people. "Now, sit down," said Jorrocks, "and let us be doing, for I am as hungry as a hunter. Hope you are peckish too; what shall I give you? tea or coffee?—but take both—coffee first and tea after a bit. If I can't give you them good, don't know who can. You must pay your devours, as we say in France, to the 'am, for it is an especial fine one, and do take a few eggs with it; there, I've not given you above a pound of 'am, but you can come again, you know—waste not want not. Now take some muffins, do, pray. Batsey, bring some more cream, and set the kidneys on the table, the Yorkshireman is getting nothing to eat. Have a chop with your kidney, werry luxterous—I could eat an elephant stuffed with grenadiers, and wash them down with a ocean of tea; but pray lay in to the breakfast, or I shall think you don't like it. There, now take some tea and toast or one of those biscuits, or whatever you like; would a little more 'am be agreeable? Batsey, run into the larder and see if your Missis left any of that cold chine of pork last night—and hear, bring the cold goose, and any cold flesh you can lay hands on, there are really no wittles on the table. I am quite ashamed to set you down to such a scanty fork breakfast; but this is what comes of not being master of your own house. Hope your hat may long cover your family: rely upon it, it is cheaper to buy your bacon than to keep a pig". Just as Jorrocks uttered these last words the side door opened, and without either "with your leave or by your leave", in bounced Mrs. Jorrocks in an elegant dishabille (or "dish-of-veal", as Jorrocks pronounced it), with her hair tucked up in papers, and a pair of worsted slippers on her feet, worked with roses and blue lilies.

"Pray, Mister J——," said she, taking no more notice of the Yorkshireman than if he had been enveloped in Jack the Giant-killer's coat of darkness, "what is the meaning of this card? I found it in your best coat pocket, which you had on last night, and I do desire, sir, that you will tell me how it came there. Good morning, sir (spying the Yorkshireman at last), perhaps you know where Mr. Jorrocks was last night, and perhaps you can tell me who this person is whose card I have found in the corner of Mr. Jorrocks's best coat pocket?" "Indeed, madam", replied the Yorkshireman, "Mr. Jorrocks's movements of yesterday evening are quite a secret to me. It is the night that he usually spends at the Magpie and Stump, but whether he was there or not I cannot pretend to say, not being a member of the free and easy club. As for the card, madam..." "There, then, take it and read it," interrupted Mrs. J——; and he took the card accordingly—a delicate pale pink, with blue borders and gilt edge—and read— we would fain put it all in dashes and asterisks—"Miss Juliana Granville, John Street, Waterloo Road."

This digression giving Mr. Jorrocks a moment or two to recollect himself, he pretended to get into a thundering passion, and seizing the card out of the Yorkshireman's hand, he thrust it into the fire, swearing it was an application for admission into the Deaf and Dumb Institution, where he wished he had Mrs. J——. The Yorkshireman, seeing the probability of a breeze, pretended to have forgotten something at the Piazza, and stole away, begging Jorrocks to pick him up as he passed. Peace had soon been restored; for the Yorkshireman had not taken above three or four turns up and down the coffee-room, ere George the waiter came to say that a gentleman waited outside. Putting on his hat and taking a coat over his arm, he turned out; when just before the door he saw a man muffled up in a great military cloak, and a glazed hat, endeavouring to back a nondescript double-bodied carriage (with lofty mail box-seats and red wheels), close to the pavement. "Who-ay, who-ay," said he, "who-ay, who-ay, horse!" at the same time jerking at his mouth. As the Yorkshireman made his exit, a pair eyes of gleamed through the small aperture between the high cloak collar and the flipe of the glazed hat, which he instantly recognised to belong to Jorrocks. "Why, what the deuce is this you are in?" said he, looking at the vehicle. "Jump up," said Jorrocks, "and I'll tell you all about it," which having done, and the machine being set in motion he proceeded to relate the manner in which he had exchanged his cruelty-van for it—by the way, as arrant a bone-setter as ever unfortunate got into, but which he, with the predilection all men have for their own, pronounced to be a "monstrous nice carriage." On their turning off the rough pavement on to the quiet smooth Macadamised road leading to Waterloo Bridge, his dissertation was interrupted by a loud horse-laugh raised by two or three toll-takers and boys lounging about the gate.

"I say, Tom, twig this 'ere machine," said one. "Dash my buttons, I never seed such a thing in all my life." "What's to pay?" inquired Jorrocks, pulling up with great dignity, their observations not having penetrated the cloak collar which encircled his ears. "To pay!" said the toll-taker—"vy, vot do ye call your consarn?" "Why, a phaeton," said Jorrocks. "My eyes! that's a good 'un," said another. "I say, Jim—he calls this 'ere thing a phe-a-ton!" "A phe-a-ton!—vy, it's more like a fire-engine," said Jim. "Don't be impertinent," said Jorrocks, who had pulled down his collar to hear what he had to pay—"but tell me what's to pay?" "Vy, it's a phe-a-ton drawn by von or more 'orses," said the toll-taker; "and containing von or more asses," said Tom. "Sixpence-halfpenny, sir," "You are a saucy fellow," said Jorrocks. "Thank ye, master, you're another," said the toll-taker; "and now that you have had your say, vot do ye ax for your mouth?" "I say, sir, do you belong to the Phenix? Vy don't you show your badge?" "I say, Tom, that 'ere fire-engine has been painted by some house-painter, it's never been in the hands of no coach-maker. Do you shave by that 'ere glazed castor of yours?" "I'm blowed it I wouldn't get you a shilling a week to shove your face in sand, to make moulds for brass knockers." "Ay, get away!—make haste, or the fire will be out," bawled out another, as Jorrocks whipped on, and rattled out of hearing.

"Now, you see," said he, resuming the thread of his discourse, as if nothing had happened, "this back seat turns down and makes a box, so that when Mrs. J—— goes to her mother's at Tooting, she can take all her things with her, instead of sending half of them by the coach as she used to do; and if we are heavy, there is a pole belonging to it, so that we can have two horses; and then there is a seat draws out here (pulling a stool from between his legs) which anybody can sit on." "Yes, anybody that is small enough," said the Yorkshireman, "but you would cut a queer figure on it, I reckon." The truth was, that the "fire-engine" was one of those useless affairs built by some fool upon a plan of his own, with the idea of combining every possible comfort and advantage, and in reality not possessing one. Friend Jorrocks had seen it at a second-hand shop in Fore Street, and became the happy owner of it, in exchange for the cruelty-van and seventeen pounds.—Their appearance on the road created no small sensation, and many were the jokes passed upon the "fire-engine." One said they were mountebanks; another that it was a horse-break; a third asked if it was one of Gurney's steam-carriages, while a fourth swore it was a new convict-cart going to Brixton. Jorrocks either did not or would not hear their remarks, and kept expatiating upon the different purposes to which the machine might be converted, and the stoutness of the horse that was drawing it.

As they approached the town of Croydon, he turned his cloak over his legs in a very workman-like manner, and was instantly hailed by some brother sportsmen;—one complimented him on his looks, another on his breeches, a third praised his horse, a fourth abused the fire-engine, and a fifth inquired where he got his glazed hat. He had an answer for them all, and a nod or a wink for every pretty maid that showed at the windows; for though past the grand climacteric, he still has a spice of the devil in him—and, as he says, "there is no harm in looking." The "Red Lion" at Smitham Bottom was the rendezvous of the day. It is a small inn on the Brighton road, some three or four miles below Croydon. On the left of the road stands the inn, on the right is a small training-ground, and the country about is open common and down. There was an immense muster about the inn, and also on the training-ground, consisting of horsemen, gig-men, post-chaise-men, footmen,—Jorrocks and the Yorkshireman made the firemen.

"Here's old Jorrocks, I do declare", exclaimed one, as Jorrocks drove the fire-engine up at as quick a pace as his horse would go. "Why, what a concern he's in", said another, "why, the old man's mad, surely".—"He's good for a subscription," added another, addressing him. "I say, Jorrocks, old boy, you'll give us ten pound for our hounds won't you?—that's a good fellow." "Oh yes, Jorrocks promised us a subscription last year," observed another, "and he is a man of his word—arn't you old leather breeches?" "No, gentlemen," said Jorrocks, standing up in the fire-engine, and sticking the whip into its nest, "I really cannot—I wish I could, but I really cannot afford it. Times really are so bad, and I have my own pack to subscribe to, and I must be 'just before I am generous.'" "Oh, but ten pounds is nothing in your way, you know, Jorrocks—adulterate a chest of tea. Old——here will give you all the leaves off his ash-trees." "No," said Jorrocks, "I really cannot—ten pounds is ten pounds, and I must cut my coat according to my cloth." "By Jove, but you must have had plenty of cloth when you cut that coat you've got on, old boy. Why there's as much cloth in the laps as would make a pair of horse-sheets." "Never mind," said Jorrocks, "I wear it, and not you." "Now," said Jorrocks in an undertone to the Yorkshireman, "you see what an unconscionable set of dogs these stag-'unters are. They're at every man for a subscription, and talk about guineas as if they grew upon gooseberry-bushes. Besides, they are such a rubbishing set—all drafts from the fox'ounds.—Now there's a chap on a piebald just by the trees— he goes into the *Gazette* reglarly once in three years, and yet to see him out, you'd fancy all the country round belonged to him. And there's a buck with his bearing-rein so tight that he can hardly move his neck," pointing to a gentleman in scarlet, with a tremendous stiff blue cravat—"he lives by keeping a mad-house and being werry high, consequential sort of a cock, they calls him the 'Lord High Keeper!'—I'll tell ye a joke about that fellow," said he, pointing to a man alighting from a red-wheeled buggy—"he's a werry shabby screw, and is always trying to save a penny.—Well, he hires a young half-witted hawbuck for a servant, who didn't clean his boots to his liking, so he began reading the Riot Act one day, and concluded by saying, 'I'm blowed if I couldn't clean them better myself with a little pump-water.'—The next day, up came the boots duller than ever.—'Bless my soul,' exclaimed he, 'why, they are worse than before, how's this, sir?'—'Please, sir, you said you could clean them better with a little pump-water, so I tried it, and I do think they are worse!' Haw! haw! haw!—Yon chap in the black plush breeches and Hessians, standing by the ginger-pop tray, is the only man what ever got the better of me in the 'oss-dealing line, and he certainlie did bite me uncommon 'andsomely. I gave him three and twenty pounds, a strong violin case with patent hinges, lined with superfine green baize, and an uncut copy of Middleton's *Cicero*, for an 'oss that the blacksmith really declared wasn't worth shoeing.—Howsomever, I paid him off, for I christened the 'oss Barabbas—who, you knows, was a robber—and the seller has gone by the name of Barabbas ever since."

"Well, but tell me, gentlemen, where do we dine?" inquired Jorrocks, turning to a group who had just approached the fire-engine. "We don't know yet," said a gentleman in scarlet, "the deer has not come yet; but yonder he is," pointing up the road to a covered cart, "and there are the hounds just coming over the hill at the back." The covered cart approached, and several went to meet it. The cry of "Oh, it's old Tunbridge," was soon heard. "Well, we shall have a good dinner," said Jorrocks, "if that is the case. Is it Tunbridge?" inquired he eagerly of one of the party who returned from the deer-cart. "Yes, it's old Tunbridge, and Snooks has ordered dinner at the Wells for sixteen at five o'clock, so the first sixteen that get there had better look out." "Here, bouy," said Jorrocks in an undertone to his servant, who was leading his screws about on the green, "take this 'oss out of the carriage, and give him a feed of corn, and then go on to Tunbridge Wells, and tell Mr. Pegg, at the Sussex Arms, that I shall be there with a friend to the dinner, and bid him write 'Jorrocks' upon two plates and place them together.—Nothing like making sure," said he, chuckling at his own acuteness.

"Now to 'orse—to 'orse!" exclaimed he, suiting the action to the word, and climbing on to his great chestnut, leaving the Yorkshireman to mount the rat-tail brown. "Let's have a look at the 'ounds", turning his horse in the direction in which they were coming. Jonathan Griffin[16] took off his cap to Jorrocks, as he approached, who waved his hand in the most patronising manner possible, adding "How are you, Jonathan?" "Pretty well, thank you, Mister Jorrocks, hope you're the same." "No, not the same, for I'm werry well, which makes all the difference—haw! haw! haw! You seem to have but a shortish pack, I think—ten, twelve, fourteen couple—'ow's that? We always take nine and twenty with the Surrey". "Why, you see, Mister Jorrocks, stag-hunting and fox-hunting are very different. The scent of the deer is very ravishing, and then we have no drawing for our game. Besides, at this season, there are always bitches to put back—but we have plenty of hounds for sport.—I suppose we may be after turning out," added Jonathan, looking at his watch—"it's past eleven."

On hearing this, a gentleman off with his glove and began collecting, or

---

[16] Poor Jonathan, one of the hardest riders and drinkers of his day, exists, like his pack, but in the recollection of mankind. He was long huntsman to the late Lord Derby, who, when he gave up his staghounds, made Jonathan a present of them, and for two or three seasons he scratched on in an indifferent sort of way, until the hounds were sold to go abroad—to Hungary, we believe.

capping, prior to turning out—it being the rule of the hunt to make sure of the money before starting, for fear of accidents. "Half a crown, if you please, sir." "Now I'll take your half a crown." "Mr. Jorrocks, shall I trouble you for half a crown?" "Oh, surely," said Jorrocks, pulling out a handful of great five-shilling pieces; "here's for this gentleman and myself," handing one of them over, "and I shan't even ask you for discount for ready money." The capping went round, and a goodly sum was collected. Meanwhile the deer-cart was drawn to the far side of a thick fence, and the door being opened, a lubberly-looking animal, as big as a donkey, blobbed out, and began feeding very composedly. "That won't do," said Jonathan Griffin, eyeing him—"ride on, Tom, and whip him away." Off went the whip, followed by a score of sportsmen whose shouts, aided by the cracking of their whips, would have frightened the devil himself; and these worthies, knowing the hounds would catch them up in due time, resolved themselves into a hunt for the present, and pursued the animal themselves. Ten minutes having expired and the hounds seeming likely to break away, Jonathan thought it advisable to let them have their wicked will, and accordingly they rushed off in full cry to the spot where the deer had been uncarted. Of course, there was no trouble in casting for the scent; indeed they were very honest, and did not pretend to any mystery; the hounds knew within an inch where it would be, and the start was pretty much like that for a hunter's plate in four-mile heats. A few dashing blades rode before the hounds at starting, but otherwise the field was tolerably quiet, and was considerably diminished after the three first leaps. The scent improved, as did the pace, and presently they got into a lane along which they rattled for five miles as hard as ever they could lay legs to the ground, throwing the mud into each other's faces, until each man looked as if he was roughcast. A Kentish wagon, drawn by six oxen, taking up the whole of the lane, had obliged the dear animal to take to the fields again, where, at the first fence, most of our high-mettled racers stood still. In truth, it was rather a nasty place, a yawning ditch, with a mud bank and a rotten landing. "Now, who's for it? Go it, Jorrocks, you're a fox-hunter," said one, who, erecting himself in his stirrups, was ogling the opposite side. "I don't like it," said Jorrocks; "is never a gate near?" "Oh yes, at the bottom of the field," and away they all tore for it. The hounds now had got out of sight, but were heard running in cover at the bottom of the turnip-field into which they had just passed, and also the clattering of horses' hoofs on the highway. The hounds came out several times on to the road, evidently carrying the scent, but as often threw up and returned into the cover. The huntsman was puzzled at last; and quite convinced that the deer was not in the wood, he called them out, and proceeded to make a cast, followed by the majority of the field. They trotted about at a brisk pace, first to the right, then to the left, afterwards to the north, and then to the south, over grass, fallow, turnips, potatoes, and flints, through three farmyards, round two horse-ponds, and at the back of a small village or hamlet, without a note, save those of a few babblers. Everyone seemed to consider it a desperate job. They were all puzzled; at last they heard a terrible holloaing about a quarter of a mile to the south, and immediately after was espied a group of horsemen, galloping along the road at full speed, in the centre of which was Jorrocks; his green coat wide open, with the tails flying a long way behind that of his horse, his right leg was thrust out, down the side of which he kept applying his ponderous hunting whip, making a most terrible clatter. As they approached, he singled himself out from the group, and was the first to reach the field. He immediately burst out into one of his usual hunting energetic strains. "Oh Jonathan Griffin! Jonathan Griffin!" said he, "here's a lamentable occurrence—a terrible disaster! Oh dear, oh dear—we shall never get to Tunbridge—that unfortunate deer has escaped us, and we shall never see nothing more of him—rely upon it, he's killed before this." "Why, how's that?" inquired Griffin, evidently in a terrible perturbation. "Why," said Jorrocks, slapping the whip down his leg again, "there's a little girl tells me, that as she was getting water at the well just at the end of the wood, where we lost him, she saw what she took to be a donkey jump into a return post-chaise from the 'Bell', at Seven Oaks, that was passing along the road with the door swinging wide open! and you may rely upon it, it was the deer. The landlord of the 'Bell' will have cut his throat before this, for, you know, he vowed wengeance against us last year, because his wife's pony-chaise was upset, and he swore that we did it." "Oh, but that's a bad job", said the huntsman; "what shall we do?" "Here, Tom," calling to the whipper-in, "jump on to the Hastings coach" (which just came up), "and try if you can't overtake him, and bring him back, chaise and all, and I'll follow slowly with the hounds." Tom was soon up, the coach bowled on, and Jonathan and the hounds trotted gently forward till they came to a public-house. Here, as they stopped lamenting over their unhappy fate, and consoling themselves with some cold sherry negus, the post-chaise appeared in sight, with the deer's head sticking out of the side window with all the dignity of a Lord Mayor. "Huzza! huzza! huzza!" exclaimed Jorrocks, taking off his hat, "here's old Tunbridge come back again, huzza! huzza!" "But who's to pay me for the po-chay," said the driver, pulling up; "I must be paid before I let him out." "How much?" says Jonathan. "Why, eighteen-pence a mile, to be sure, and three-pence a mile to the driver." "No," says Jorrocks, "that won't do, yours is a return chay; however, here's five shillings for you, and now, Jonathan, turn him out again—he's quite fresh after his ride—and see, he's got some straw in the bottom."

Old Tunbridge was again turned out, with his head towards the town from whence he took his name, and after a quarter of an hour's law, the pack was again laid on. He was not, however, in very good wind, and it was necessary to divide the second chase into two heats, for which purpose the hounds were whipped off about the middle, while the deer took a cold bath, after which he was again set a-going. By half-past three they had accomplished the run; and Mr. Pegg, of the "Sussex Arms," having mounted his Pegasus, found them at the appointed place by the Medway, where old Tunbridge's carriage was waiting, into which having handed him, they repaired to the inn, and at five o'clock eighteen of them sat down to a dinner consisting of every delicacy of the season, the Lord High Keeper in the chair. Being all "hungry as hunters," little conversation passed until after the removal of the cloth, when after the King and his Majesty's Ministers had been drunk, the President gave "The noble, manly sport of stag-hunting," which he eulogised as the most legitimate and exhilarating of all sports, and sketched its progress from its wild state of infancy when the unhappy sportsmen had to range the fields and forests for their uncertain game, to the present state of luxurious ease and elaborate refinement, when they not only brought their deer to the meet, but by selecting the proper animal, could insure a finish at the place they most wished to dine at—all of which was most enthusiastically applauded; and on the speaker's ending, "Stag-hunting," and the "Surrey staghounds," and "Long life to all stag-hunters," were drank in brimming and overflowing bumpers. Fox-hunting, hare-hunting, rabbit-hunting, cat-hunting, rat-catching, badger-baiting—all wild, seasonable, and legitimate sports followed; and the chairman having run through his list, and thinking Jorrocks was getting rather mellow, resolved to try the soothing system on him for a subscription, the badgering of the morning not having answered. Accordingly, he called on the company to charge their glasses, as he would give them a bumper toast, which he knew they would have great pleasure in drinking.—"He wished to propose the health of his excellent friend on his right—MR. JORROCKS (applause), a gentleman whose name only required mentioning in any society of hunters to insure it a hearty and enthusiastic reception. He did not flatter his excellent friend when he said he was a man for the imitation of all, and he was sure that when the present company recollected the liberal support he gave to the Surrey foxhounds, together with the keenness with which he followed that branch of amusement, they would duly appreciate, not only the honour he had conferred upon them by his presence in the field that morning, and at the table that day, but the disinterested generosity which had prompted him voluntarily to declare his intention of contributing to the future support of the Surrey staghounds (immense cheers). He therefore thought the least they could do was to drink the health of Mr. Jorrocks, and success to the Surrey foxhounds, with three times three," which was immediately responded to with deafening cheers.

Old Jorrocks, after the noise had subsided, got on his legs, and with one hand rattling the five-shilling pieces in his breeches-pocket, and the thumb of the other thrust into the arm-hole of his waistcoat, thus began to address them.— "Gentlemen," said he, "I'm no orator, but I'm an honest man—(hiccup)—I feels werry (hiccup) much obliged to my excellent friend the Lord High Keeper (shouts of laughter), I begs his pardon—my friend Mr. Juggins—for the werry flattering compliment he has paid me in coupling my name (hiccup) with the Surrey fox'ounds—a pack, I may say, without wanity (hiccup), second to none. I'm a werry old member of the 'unt, and when I was a werry poor man (hiccup) I always did my best to support them (hiccup), and now that I'm a werry rich man (cheers) I shan't do no otherwise. About subscribing to the staggers, I doesn't recollect saying nothing whatsomever about it (hiccup), but as I'm werry friendly to sporting in all its ramifications (hiccup), I'll be werry happy to give ten pounds to your 'ounds."— Immense cheers followed this declaration, which lasted for some seconds. When they had subsided, Jorrocks put his finger on his nose and, with a knowing wink of his eye, added: "Prowided my friend the Lord High Keep—I begs his pardon—Juggins—will give ten pounds to ours!"

V
THE TURF: MR. JORROCKS AT NEWMARKET

"A muffin—and the *Post*, sir," said George to the Yorkshireman,—on one of the fine fresh mornings that gently usher in the returning spring, and draw from the town-pent cits sighs for the verdure of the fields,—as he placed the above mentioned articles on his usual breakfast table in the coffee-room of the "Piazza."

With the calm deliberation of a man whose whole day is unoccupied, the Yorkshireman sweetened his tea, drew the muffin and a select dish of prawns to his elbow, and turning sideways to the table, crossed his legs and prepared to con the contents of the paper. The first page as usual was full of advertisements.—Sales by auction—Favour of your vote and interest—If the next of kin—Reform your tailor's bills—Law— Articled clerk—An absolute reversion—Pony phaeton—Artificial teeth—Messrs. Tattersall—Brace of pointers—Dog lost—Boy found—Great sacrifice—No advance in coffee— Matrimony—A single gentleman—Board and lodging in an airy situation—To omnibus proprietors—Steam to Leith and Hull—Stationery—Desirable investment for a small capital—The fire reviver or lighter.

Then turning it over, his eye ranged over a whole meadow of type, consisting of the previous night's debate, followed on by City news, Police reports, Fashionable arrivals and departures, Dinners given, Sporting intelligence, Newmarket Craven meeting. "That's more in my way," said the Yorkshireman to himself as he laid down the paper and took a sip of his tea. "I've a great mind to go, for I may just as well be at Newmarket as here, having nothing particular to do in either place. I came to stay a hundred pounds in London it's true, but if I stay ten of it at Newmarket, it'll be all the same, and I can go home from there just as well as from here"; so saying, he took another turn at the tea. The race list was a tempting one, Riddlesworth, Craven Stakes, Column Stakes, Oatlands, Port, Claret, Sherry, Madeira, and all other sorts. A good week's racing in fact, for the saintly sinners who frequent the Heath had not then discovered any greater impropriety in travelling on a Sunday, then in cheating each other on the Monday. The tea was good, as were the prawns and eggs, and George brought a second muffin, at the very moment that the Yorkshireman had finished the last piece of the first, so that by the time he had done his breakfast and drawn on his boots, which were dryer and pleasanter than the recent damp weather had allowed of their being, he felt completely at peace with himself and all the world, and putting on his hat, sallied forth with the self-satisfied air of a man who had eat a good breakfast, and yet not too much.

Newmarket was still uppermost in his mind, and as he sauntered along in the direction of the Strand, it occurred to him that perhaps Mr. Jorrocks might have no objection to accompany him. On entering that great thoroughfare of humanity, he turned to the east, and having examined the contents of all the caricature shops in the line, and paid threepence for a look at the *York Herald*, in the Chapter Coffee-house, St. Paul's Churchyard, about noon he reached the corner of St. Botolph Lane. Before Jorrocks & Co.'s warehouse, great bustle and symptoms of brisk trade were visible. With true city pride, the name on the door-post was in small dirty-white letters, sufficiently obscure to render it apparent that Mr. Jorrocks considered his house required no sign; while, as a sort of contradiction, the covered errand-cart before it, bore "JORROCKS & Co.'s WHOLESALE TEA WAREHOUSE," in great gilt letters on each side of the cover, so large that "he who runs might read," even though the errand-cart were running too. Into this cart, which was drawn by the celebrated rat-tail hunter, they were pitching divers packages for town delivery, and a couple of light porters nearly upset the Yorkshireman, as they bustled out with their loads. The warehouse itself gave evident proof of great antiquity. It was not one of your fine, light, lofty, mahogany-countered, banker-like establishments of modern times, where the stock-in-trade often consists of books and empty canisters, but a large, roomy, gloomy, dirty, dingy sort of cellar above ground, full of hogsheads, casks, flasks, sugar-loaves, jars, bags, bottles, and boxes.

The floor was half an inch thick, at least, with dirt, and was sprinkled with rice, currants, and raisins, as though they had been scattered for the purpose of growing. A small corner seemed to have been cut off, like the fold of a Leicestershire grazing-ground, and made into an office in the centre of which was a square or two of glass that commanded a view of the whole warehouse. "Is Mr. Jorrocks in?" inquired the Yorkshireman of a porter, who was busy digging currants with a wooden spade. "Yes, sir, you'll find him in the counting-house," was the answer; but on looking in, though his hat and gloves were there, no Jorrocks was visible. At the farther end of the warehouse a man in his shirt-sleeves, with a white apron round his waist and a brown paper cap on his head, was seen under a very melancholy-looking skylight, holding his head over something, as if his nose were bleeding. The Yorkshireman groped his way up to him, and asking if Mr. Jorrocks was in, found he was addressing the grocer himself. He had been leaning over a large trayful of little white cups—with teapots to match—trying the strength, flavour, and virtue of a large purchase of tea, and the beverage was all smoking before him. "My vig," exclaimed he, holding out his hand, "who'd have thought of seeing you in the city, this is something unkimmon! However, you're werry welcome in St. Botolph Lane, and as this is your first wisit, why, I'll make you a present of some tea—wot do you drink?—black or green, or perhaps both—four pounds of one and two of t'other. Here, Joe!" summoning his foreman, "put up four pounds of that last lot of black that came in, and two pounds of superior green, and this gentleman will tell you where to leave it.—And when do you think of starting?" again addressing the Yorkshireman—"egad this is fine weather for the country—have half a mind to have a jaunt myself—makes one quite young—feel as if I'd laid full fifty years aside, and were again a boy—when did you say you start?" "Why, I don't know exactly," replied the Yorkshireman, "the weather's so fine that I'm half tempted to go round by Newmarket." "Newmarket!" exclaimed Jorrocks, throwing his arm in the air, while his paper cap fell from his head with the

jerk—"by Newmarket! why, what in the name of all that's impure, have you to
do at Newmarket?"

"Why, nothing in particular; only, when there's neither hunting nor shooting
going on, what is a man to do with himself?—I'm sure you'd despise me if I
were to go fishing." "True," observed Mr. Jorrocks somewhat subdued, and
jingling the silver in his breeches-pocket. "Fox-'unting is indeed the prince of
sports. The image of war, without its guilt, and only half its danger. I confess
that I'm a martyr to it—a perfect wictim—no one knows wot I suffer from my
ardour.—If ever I'm wisited with the last infirmity of noble minds, it will be
caused by my ingovernable passion for the chase. The sight of a saddle makes
me sweat. An 'ound makes me perfectly wild. A red coat throws me into a
scarlet fever. Never throughout life have I had a good night's rest before an
'unting morning. But werry little racing does for me; Sadler's Wells is well
enough of a fine summer evening—especially when they plump the clown over
head in the New River cut, and the ponies don't misbehave in the Circus,—but
oh! Newmarket's a dreadful place, the werry name's a sickener. I used to hear a
vast about it from poor Will Softly of Friday Street. It was the ruin of him—and
wot a fine business his father left him, both wholesale and retail, in the tripe and
cow-heel line—all went in two years, and he had nothing to show at the end of
that time for upwards of twenty thousand golden sovereigns, but a
hundredweight of children's lamb's-wool socks, and warrants for thirteen
hogsheads of damaged sherry in the docks. No, take my adwice, and have
nothing to say to them—stay where you are, or, if you're short of swag, come to
Great Coram Street, where you shall have a bed, wear-and-tear for your teeth,
and all that sort of thing found you, and, if Saturday's a fine day, I'll treat you
with a jaunt to Margate."

"You are a regular old trump," said the Yorkshireman, after listening
attentively until Mr. Jorrocks had exhausted himself, "but, you see, you've never
been at Newmarket, and the people have been hoaxing you about it. I can assure
you from personal experience that the people there are quite as honest as those
you meet every day on 'Change, besides which, there is nothing more
invigorating to the human frame—nothing more cheering to the spirits, than the
sight and air of Newmarket Heath on a fine fresh spring morning like the
present. The wind seems to go by you at a racing pace, and the blood canters up
and down the veins with the finest and freest action imaginable. A stranger to
the race-course would feel, and almost instinctively know, what turf he was
treading, and the purpose for which that turf was intended".

"There's a magic in the web of it."

"Oh, I knows you are a most persuasive cock," observed Mr. Jorrocks
interrupting the Yorkshireman, "and would conwince the devil himself that
black is white, but you'll never make me believe the Newmarket folks are
honest, and as to the fine hair (air) you talk of, there's quite as good to get on
Hampstead Heath, and if it doesn't make the blood canter up and down your

weins, you can always amuse yourself by watching the donkeys cantering up and down with the sweet little children—haw! haw! haw!—But tell me what is there at Newmarket that should take a man there?" "What is there?" rejoined the Yorkshireman, "why, there's everything that makes life desirable and constitutes happiness, in this world, except hunting. First there is the beautiful, neat, clean town, with groups of booted professors, ready for the rapidest march of intellect; then there are the strings of clothed horses—the finest in the world— passing indolently at intervals to their exercise,—the flower of the English aristocracy residing in the place. You leave the town and stroll to the wide open heath, where all is brightness and space; the white rails stand forth against the dear blue sky—the brushing gallop ever and anon startles the ear and eye; crowds of stable urchins, full of silent importance, stud the heath; you feel elated and long to bound over the well groomed turf and to try the speed of the careering wind. All things at Newmarket train the mind to racing. Life seems on the start, and dull indeed were he who could rein in his feelings when such inspiring objects meet together to madden them!"

"Bravo!" exclaimed Jorrocks, throwing his paper cap in the air as the Yorkshireman concluded.—"Bravo!—werry good indeed! You speak like ten Lord Mayors—never heard nothing better. Dash my vig, if I won't go. By Jove, you've done it. Tell me one thing—is there a good place to feed at?"

"Capital!" replied the Yorkshireman, "beef, mutton, cheese, ham, all the delicacies of the season, as the sailor said"; and thereupon the Yorkshireman and Jorrocks shook hands upon the bargain.

Sunday night arrived, and with it arrived, at the "Belle Sauvage," in Ludgate Hill, Mr. Jorrocks's boy "Binjimin," with Mr. Jorrocks's carpet-bag; and shortly after Mr. Jorrocks, on his chestnut hunter, and the Yorkshireman, in a hack cab, entered the yard. Having consigned his horse to Binjimin; after giving him a very instructive lesson relative to the manner in which he would chastise him if he heard of his trotting or playing any tricks with the horse on his way home, Mr. Jorrocks proceeded to pay the remainder of his fare in the coach office. The mail was full inside and out, indeed the book-keeper assured him he could have filled a dozen more, so anxious ware all London to see the Riddlesworth run. "Inside," said he, "are you and your friend, and if it wern't that the night air might give you cold, Mr. Jorrocks" (for all the book-keepers in London know him), "I should have liked to have got you outsides, and I tried to make an exchange with two black-legs, but they would hear of nothing less than two guineas a head, which wouldn't do, you know. Here comes another of your passengers—a great foreign nobleman, they say—Baron something—though he looks as much like a foreign pickpocket as anything else."

"Vich be de voiture?" inquired a tall, gaunt-looking foreigner, with immense moustache, a high conical hat with a bright buckle, long, loose, blueish-blackish frock-coat, very short white waistcoat, baggy brownish striped trousers, and long-footed Wellington boots, with a sort of Chinese turn up at the toe. "Vich be de Newmarket Voiture?" said he, repeating the query, as he entered the office and deposited a silk umbrella, a camlet cloak, and a Swiss knapsack on the counter. The porter, without any attempt at an answer, took his goods and walked off to the mail, followed closely by the Baron, and after depositing the cloak inside, so that the Baron might ride with his "face to the horses," as the saying is, he turned the knapsack into the hind boot, and swung himself into the office till it was time to ask for something for his exertions. Meanwhile the Baron made a tour of the yard, taking a lesson in English from the lettering on the various coaches, when, on the hind boot of one, he deciphered the word Cheapside.—"Ah, Cheapside!" said he, pulling out his dictionary and turning to the letter C. "Chaste, chat, chaw,—cheap, dat be it. Cheap,—to be had at a low price—small value. Ah! I hev (have) it," said he, stamping and knitting his brows, "sacré-e-e-e-e nom de Dieu," and the first word being drawn out to its usual longitude, three strides brought him and the conclusion of the oath into the office together. He then opened out upon the book-keeper, in a tremendous volley of French, English and Hanoverian oaths, for he was a cross between the first and last named countries, the purport of which was "dat he had paid de best price, and he be dem if he vod ride on de Cheapside of de coach." In vain the clerks and book-keepers tried to convince him he was wrong in his interpretation. With the full conviction of a foreigner that he was about to be cheated, he had his cloak shifted to the opposite side of the coach, and the knapsack placed on the roof. The fourth inside having cast up, the outside passengers mounted, the insides took their places, three-pences and sixpences were pulled out for the porters, the guard twanged his horn, the coachman turned out his elbow, flourished his whip, caught the point, cried "All right! sit tight!" and trotted out of the yard.

Jorrocks and the Yorkshireman sat opposite each other, the Baron and old Sam Spring, the betting man, did likewise. Who doesn't know old Sam, with his curious tortoiseshell-rimmed spectacles, his old drab hat turned up with green, careless neckcloth, flowing robe, and comical cut? He knew Jorrocks—though—tell it not in Coram Street, he didn't know his name; but concluded from the disparity of age between him and his companion, that Jorrocks was either a shark or a shark's jackal, and the Yorkshireman a victim. With due professional delicacy, he contented himself with scrutinising the latter through his specs. The Baron's choler having subsided, he was the first to break the ice of silence. "Foine noight," was the observation, which was thrown out promiscuously to see who would take it up. Now Sam Spring, though he came late, had learned from the porter that there was a Baron in the coach, and being a great admirer of the nobility, for whose use he has a code of signals of his own, consisting of one finger to his hat for a Baron Lord as he calls them, two for a Viscount, three for an Earl, four for a Marquis, and the whole hand for a Duke, he immediately responded with "Yes, my lord," with a fore-finger to his hat. There is something sweet in the word "Lord" which finds its way home to the heart of an Englishman. No sooner did Sam pronounce it, than the Baron became transformed in Jorrocks's eyes into a very superior sort of person, and forthwith he commences ingratiating himself by offering him a share of a large paper of sandwiches, which the Baron accepted with the greatest condescension, eating what he could and stuffing the remainder into his hat. His lordship was a better hand at eating than speaking, and the united efforts of the party could not extract from him the precise purport of his journey. Sam threw out two or three feasible offers in the way of bets, but they fell still-born to the bottom of the coach, and Jorrocks talked to him about hunting and had the conversation all to himself, the Baron merely replying with a bow and a stare, sometimes diversified with, or "I tank you—vare good." The conversation by degrees resolved itself into a snore, in which they were all indulging, when the raw morning air rushed in among them, as a porter with a lanthorn opened the door and announced their arrival at Newmarket. Forthwith they turned into the street, and the outside passengers having descended, they all commenced straddling, yawning, and stretching their limbs while the guard and porters sorted their luggage. The Yorkshireman having an eye to a bed, speedily had Mr. Jorrocks's luggage and his own on the back of a porter on its way to the "Rutland Arms," while that worthy citizen followed in a sort of sleepy astonishment at the smallness of the place, inquiring if they were sure they had not stopped at some village by mistake. Two beds had been ordered for two gentlemen who could not get two seats by the mail, which fell to the lot of those who did, and into these our heroes trundled, having arranged to be called by the early exercising hour.

Whether it was from want of his usual night-cap of brandy and water, or the fatigues of travelling, or what else, remains unknown, but no sooner was Mr. Jorrocks left alone with his candle, than all at once he was seized with a sudden fit of trepidation, on thinking that he should have been inveigled to such a place as Newmarket, and the tremor increasing as he pulled four five-pound bank-notes out of his watch-pocket, besides a vast of silver and his great gold watch, he was resolved, should an attempt be made upon his property, to defend it with his life, and having squeezed the notes into the toe of his boots, and hid the silver in the wash-hand stand, he very deliberately put his watch and the poker under the pillow, and set the heavy chest of drawers with two stout chairs and a table against the door, after all which exertions he got into bed and very soon fell sound asleep.

Most of the inmates of the house were up with the lark to the early exercises, and the Yorkshireman was as early as any of them. Having found Mr. Jorrocks's door, he commenced a loud battery against it without awaking the grocer; he then tried to open it, but only succeeded in getting it an inch or two from the post, and after several holloas of "Jorrocks, my man! Mr. Jorrocks! Jorrocks, old boy! holloa, Jorrocks!" he succeeded in extracting the word "Wot?" from the worthy gentleman as he rolled over in his bed. "Jorrocks!" repeated the Yorkshireman, "it's time to be up." "Wot?" again was the answer. "Time to get up. The morning's breaking." "Let it break," replied he, adding in a mutter, as he turned over again, "it owes me nothing."

Entreaties being useless, and a large party being on the point of setting off, the Yorkshireman joined them, and spent a couple of hours on the dew-bespangled heath, during which time they not only criticised the figure and action of every horse that was out, but got up tremendous appetites for breakfast. In the meantime Mr. Jorrocks had risen, and having attired himself with his usual care, in a smart blue coat with metal buttons, buff waistcoat, blue stocking-netted tights, and Hessian boots, he turned into the main street of Newmarket, where he was lost in astonishment at the insignificance of the place. But wiser men than Mr. Jorrocks have been similarly disappointed, for it enters into the philosophy of few to conceive the fame and grandeur of Newmarket compressed into the limits of the petty, outlandish, Icelandish place that bears the name. "Dash my vig," said Mr. Jorrocks, as he brought himself to bear upon Rogers's shop-window, "this is the werry meanest town I ever did see. Pray, sir," addressing himself to a groomish-looking man in a brown cut-away coat, drab shorts and continuations, who had just emerged from the shop with a race list in his hand, "Pray, sir, be this your principal street?" The man eyed him with a mixed look of incredulity and contempt. At length, putting his thumbs into the arm-holes of his waistcoat, he replied, "I bet a crown you know as well as I do." "Done," said Mr. Jorrocks holding out his hand. "No—I won't do that," replied the man, "but I'll tell you what I'll do with you,—I'll lay you two to one, in fives or fifties if you like, that you knew before you axed, and that Thunderbolt don't win the Riddlesworth." "Really," said Mr. Jorrocks, "I'm not a betting man." "Then, wot the 'ell business have you at Newmarket?" was all the answer he got. Disgusted with such inhospitable impertinence, Mr. Jorrocks turned on his heel and walked away. Before the "White Hart" Inn was a smartish pony phaeton, in charge of a stunted stable lad. "I say, young chap," inquired Jorrocks, "whose is that?" "How did you know that I was a young chap?" inquired the abortion turning round. "Guessed it," replied Jorrocks, chuckling at his own wit. "Then guess whose it is."

"Pray, are your clocks here by London time?" he asked of a respectable elderly-looking man whom he saw turn out of the entry leading to the Kingston rooms, and take the usual survey first up the town and then down it, and afterwards compose his hands in his breeches-pockets, there to stand to see the "world." [17]"Come now, old 'un—none o' your tricks here—you've got a match on against time, I suppose," was all the answer he could get after the man (old R—n the ex-flagellator) had surveyed him from head to foot.

We need hardly say after all these rebuffs that when Mr. Jorrocks met the Yorkshireman, he was not in the best possible humour; indeed, to say nothing of the extreme sharpness and suspicion of the people, we know of no place where a man, not fond of racing, is so completely out of his element as at Newmarket, for with the exception of a little "elbow shaking" in the evening, there is literally and truly nothing else to do. It is "Heath," "Ditch in," "Abingdon mile," "T.Y.C. Stakes," "Sweepstakes," "Handicaps," "Bet," "Lay," "Take," "Odds," "Evens," morning, noon and night.

Mr. Jorrocks made bitter complaints during the breakfast, and some invidious comparisons between racing men and fox-hunters, which, however,

---

[17] Newmarket or London—it's all the same—"The world" is but composed of one's own acquaintance.

became softer towards the close, as he got deeper in the delicacy of a fine Cambridge brawn. Nature being at length appeased, he again thought of turning out, to have a look, as he said, at the shows on the course, but the appearance of his friend the Baron opposite the window, put it out of his head, and he sallied forth to join him. The Baron was evidently incog.: for he had on the same short dirty-white waistcoat, Chinese boots, and conical hat, that he travelled down in, and being a stranger in the land, of course he was uncommonly glad to pick up Jorrocks, so after he had hugged him a little, called him a "bon garçon," and a few other endearing terms, he run his great long arm through his, and walked him down street, the whole peregrinations of Newmarket being comprised in the words "up street" and "down." He then communicated in most unrepresentable language, that he was on his way to buy "an 'oss," and Jorrocks informing him that he was a perfect connoisseur in the article, the Baron again assured him of his distinguished consideration. They were met by Joe Rogers the trainer with a ring-key in his hand, who led the way to the stable, and having unlocked a box in which was a fine slapping four-year old, according to etiquette he put his hat in a corner, took a switch in one hand, laid hold of the horse's head with the other, while the lad in attendance stripped off its clothes. The Baron then turned up his wrists, and making a curious noise in his throat, proceeded to pass his hand down each leg, and along its back, after which he gave it a thump in the belly and squeezed its throat, when, being as wise as he was at starting, he stuck his thumb in his side, and took a mental survey of the whole.—"Ah," said he at length—"foin 'oss,—foin 'oss; vot ears he has?" "Oh," said Rogers, "they show breeding." "Non, non, I say vot ears he has?" "Well, but he carries them well," was the answer. "Non, non," stamping, "I say vot ears (years) he has?" "Oh, hang it, I twig—four years old." Then the Baron took another long look at him. At length he resumed, "I vill my wet." "What's that?" inquired Rogers of Jorrocks. "His wet—why, a drink to be sure," and thereupon Rogers went to the pump and brought a glass of pure water, which the Baron refused with becoming indignation. "Non, non," said he stamping, "I vill my wet." Rogers looked at Jorrocks, and Jorrocks looked at Rogers, but neither Rogers nor Jorrocks understood him. "I vill my wet," repeated the Baron with vehemence. "He must want some brandy in it," observed Mr. Jorrocks, judging of the Baron by himself, and thereupon the lad was sent for three-penn'orth. When it arrived, the Baron dashed it out of his hand with a prolonged sacré-e-e-e—! adding "I vill von wet-tin-nin-na-ary surgeon." The boy was dispatched for one, and on his arrival the veterinary surgeon went through the process that the Baron had attempted, and not being a man of many words, he just gave the Baron a nod at the end. "How moch?" inquked the Baron of Rogers. "Five hundred," was the answer. "Vot, five hundred livre?" "Oh d——n it, you may take or leave him, just as you like, but you won't get him for less." The "vet" explained that the Baron wished to know whether it was five hundred francs (French ten-pences), or five hundred guineas English money, and being informed that it was the latter, he gave his conical hat a thrust on his brow, and bolted out of the box.

But race hour approaches, and people begin to assemble in groups before the "rooms," while tax-carts, pony-gigs, post-chaises, the usual aristocratical accompaniments of Newmarket, come dribbling at intervals into the town. Here is old Sam Spring in a spring-cart, driven by a ploughboy in fustian, there the Earl of—— on a ten-pound pony, with the girths elegantly parted to prevent the saddle slipping over its head, while Miss——, his jockey's daughter, dashes by him in a phaeton with a powdered footman, and the postilion in scarlet and leathers, with a badge on his arm. Old Crockey puts on his greatcoat, Jem Bland draws the yellow phaeton and greys to the gateway of the "White Hart," to take up his friend Crutch Robinson; Zac, Jack and another, have just driven on in a fly. In short, it's a brilliant meeting! Besides four coronetted carriages with post-horses, there are three phaetons-and-pair; a thing that would have been a phaeton if they'd have let it; General Grosvenor's dog-carriage, that is to say, his carriage with a dog upon it; Lady Chesterfield and the Hon. Mrs. Anson in a pony phaeton with an out-rider (Miss—— will have one next meeting instead of the powdered footman); Tattersall in his double carriage driving without bearing-reins; Old Theobald in leather breeches and a buggy; five Bury butchers in a tax-cart; Young Dutch Sam on a pony; "Short-odds Richards" on a long-backed crocodile-looking rosinante; and no end of pedestrians.

But where is Mr. Jorrocks all this time? Why eating brawn in the "Rutland Arms" with his friend the Baron, perfectly unconscious that all these passers-by were not the daily visables of the place. "Dash my vig," said he, as he bolted another half of the round, "I see no symptoms of a stir. Come, my lord, do me the honour to take another glass of sherry." His lordship was nothing loath, so by mutual entreaties they finished the bottle, besides a considerable quantity of porter. A fine, fat, chestnut, long-tailed Suffolk punch cart mare—fresh from the plough—having been considerately provided by the Yorkshireman for Mr. Jorrocks, with a cob for himself, they proceeded to mount in the yard, when Mr. Jorrocks was concerned to find that the Baron had nothing to carry him. His lordship, too, seemed disconcerted, but it was only momentary; for walking up to the punch mare, and resting his elbow on her hind quarter to try if she kicked, he very coolly vaulted up behind Mr. Jorrocks. Now Jorrocks, though proud of the patronage of a lord, did not exactly comprehend whether he was in earnest or not, but the Baron soon let him know; for thrusting his conical hat on his brow, he put his arm round Jorrocks's waist, and gave the old mare a touch in the flank with the Chinese boot, crying out—"Along me, brave *garçon*, along *ma cher*," and the owner of the mare living at Kentford, she went off at a brisk trot in that direction, while the Yorkshireman slipped down the town unperceived. The sherry had done its business on them both; the Baron, and who, perhaps was the most "cut" of the two, chaunted the *Marsellaise* hymn of liberty with as much freedom as though he were sitting in the saddle. Thus they proceeded laughing and singing until the Bury pay-gate arrested their progress, when it occurred to the steersman to ask if they were going right. "Be this the vay to Newmarket races?" inquired Jorrocks of the pike-keeper. The man dived into the small pocket of his white apron for a ticket and very coolly replied, "Shell out, old 'un." "How much?" said Jorrocks. "Tuppence," which having got, he said, "Now, then, you may turn, for the heath be over yonder," pointing back, "at least it was there this morning, I know." After a volley of abuse for his impudence, Mr. Jorrocks, with some difficulty got the old mare pulled round, for she had a deuced hard mouth of her own, and only a plain snaffle in it; at last, however, with the aid of a boy to beat her with a furze-bush, they got her set a-going again, and, retracing their steps, they trotted "down street," rose the hill, and entered the spacious wide-extending flat of Newmarket Heath. The races were going forward on one of the distant courses, and a slight, insignificant, black streak, swelling into a sort of oblong (for all the world like an overgrown tadpole), was all that denoted the spot, or interrupted the verdant aspect of the quiet extensive plain. Jorrocks was horrified, having through life pictured Epsom as a mere drop in the ocean compared with the countless multitude of Newmarket, while the Baron, who was wholly indifferent to the matter, nearly had old Jorrocks pitched over the mare's head by applying the furze-bush (which he had got from the boy) to her tail while Mr. Jorrocks was sitting loosely, contemplating the barrenness of the prospect. The sherry was still alive, and being all for fun, he shuffled back into the saddle as soon as the old mare gave over kicking; and giving a loud tally-ho, with some minor "hunting noises," which were responded to by the Baron in notes not capable of being set to music, and aided by an equally indescribable accompaniment from the old mare at every application of the bush, she went off at score over the springy turf, and bore them triumphantly to the betting-post just as the ring was in course of formation, a fact which she announced by a loud neigh on viewing her companion of the plough, as well as by unsetting some half-dozen black-legs as she rushed through the crowd to greet her. Great was the hubbub, shouting, swearing, and laughing,—for though the Newmarketites are familiar with most conveyances, from a pair of horses down to a pair of shoes, it had not then fallen to their lot to see two men ride into the ring on the same horse,—certainly not with such a hat between them as the Baron's.

The gravest and weightiest matters will not long distract the attention of a black-leg, and the laughter having subsided without Jorrocks or the Baron being in the slightest degree disconcerted, the ring was again formed; horses' heads again turn towards the post, while carriages, gigs, and carts form an outer circle. A solemn silence ensues. The legs are scanning the list. At length one gives tongue. "What starts? Does Lord Eldon start?" "No, he don't," replies the owner. "Does Trick, by Catton?" "Yes, and Conolly rides—but mind, three pounds over." "Does John Bull?" "No John's struck out." "Polly Hopkins does, so does Talleyrand, also O, Fy! out of Penitence; Beagle and Paradox also—and perhaps Pickpocket."

Another pause, and the pencils are pulled from the betting-books. The legs and lords look at each other, but no one likes to lead off. At length a voice is heard offering to take nine to one he names the winner. "It's short odds, doing it cautiously. I'll take eight then," he adds—"sivin!" but no one bites. "What will anyone lay about Trick, by Catton?" inquires Jem Bland. "I'll lay three to two again him. I'll take two to one—two ponies to one, and give you a suv. for laying it." "Carn't" is the answer. "I'll do it, Jem," cries a voice. "No, you won't," from Bland, not liking his customer. Now they are all at it, and what a hubbub there is! "I'll back the field—I'll lay—I'll take—I'll bet—ponies—fifties—hundreds— five hundred to two." "What do you want, my lord?" "Three to one against Trick, by Catton." "Carn't afford it—the odds really arn't that in the ring." "Take two—two hundred to one." "No." "Crockford, you'll do it for me?" "Yes, my lord. Twice over if you like. Done, done." "Do it again?" "No, thank you."

"Trick, by Catton, don't start!" cries a voice. "Impossible!" exclaim his backers. "Quite true, I'm just from the weighing-house, and——told me so himself." "Shame! shame!" roar those who have backed him, and "honour— rascals—rogues—thieves—robbery—swindle—turf-ruined"—fly from tongue to tongue, but they are all speakers with never a speaker to cry order. Meanwhile the lads have galloped by on their hacks with the horses' cloths to the rubbing-house, and the horses have actually started, and are now visible in the distance sweeping over the open heath, apparently without guide or beacon.

The majority of the ring rush to the white judge's box, and have just time to range themselves along the rude stakes and ropes that guard the run in, and the course-keeper in a shooting-jacket on a rough pony to crack his whip, and cry to half a dozen stable-lads to "clear the course," before the horses come flying towards home. Now all is tremor; hope and fear vacillating in each breast. Silence stands breathless with expectation—all eyes are riveted—the horses come within descrying distance—"beautiful!" three close together, two behind. "Clear the course! clear the course! pray clear the course!" "Polly Hopkins! Polly Hopkins!" roar a hundred voices as they near. "O, Fy! O, Fy!" respond an equal number. "The horse! the horse!" bellow a hundred more, as though their yells would aid his speed, as Polly Hopkins, O, Fy! and Talleyrand rush neck-and-neck along the cords and pass the judge's box. A cry of "dead heat!" is heard. The bystanders see as suits their books, and immediately rush to the judge's box, betting, bellowing, roaring, and yelling the whole way. "What's won? what's won? what's won?" is vociferated from a hundred voices. "Polly Hopkins! Polly Hopkins! Polly Hopkins!" replies Mr. Clark with judicial dignity. "By how much? by how much?" "Half a head—half a head," [18]replies the same functionary. "What's second?" "O, Fy!" and so, amid the song of "Pretty, pretty Polly Hopkins," from the winners, and curses and execrations long, loud, and deep, from the losers, the scene closes.

The admiring winners follow Polly to the rubbing-house, while the losing horses are left in the care of their trainers and stable-boys, who console themselves with hopes of "better luck next time."

After a storm comes a calm, and the next proceeding is the wheeling of the judge's box, and removal of the old stakes and ropes to another course on a

---

[18] No judge ever gave a race as won by half a head; but we let the whole passage stand as originally written.—EDITOR.

different part of the heath, which is accomplished by a few ragged rascals, as rude and uncouth as the furniture they bear. In less than half an hour the same group of anxious careworn countenances are again turned upon each other at the betting-post, as though they had never separated. But see! the noble owner of Trick, by Catton, is in the crowd, and Jem Bland eyeing him like a hawk. "I say, Waggey," cries he (singling out a friend stationed by his lordship), "had you ought on Trick, by Catton?" "No, Jem," roars Wagstaff, shaking his head, "I knew my man too well." "Why now, Waggey, do you know I wouldn't have done such a thing for the world! no, not even to have been made a Markiss!" a horse-laugh follows this denunciation, at which the newly created marquis bites his livid lips.

The Baron, who appears to have no taste for walking, still sticks to the punch mare, which Mr. Jorrocks steers to the newly formed ring aided by the Baron and the furze-bush. Here they come upon Sam Spring, whose boy has just brought his spring-cart to bear upon the ring formed by the horsemen, and thinking it a pity a nobleman of any county should be reduced to the necessity of riding double, very politely offers to take one into his carriage. Jorrocks accepts the offer, and forthwith proceeds to make himself quite at home in it. The chorus again commences, and Jorrocks interrogates Sam as to the names of the brawlers. "Who be that?" said he, "offering to bet a thousand to a hundred." Spring, after eyeing him through his spectacles, with a grin and a look of suspicion replies, "Come now—come—let's have no nonsense—you know as well as I." "Really," replies Mr. Jorrocks most earnestly, "I don't." "Why, where have you lived all your life?" "First part of it with my grandmother at Lisson Grove, afterwards at Camberwell, but now I resides in Great Coram Street, Russell Square—a werry fashionable neighbourhood." "Oh, I see," replies Sam, "you are one of the reg'lar city coves, then—now, what brings you here?" "Just to say that I have been at Newmarket, for I'm blowed if ever you catch me here again." "That's a pity," replied Sam, "for you look like a promising man—a handsome-bodied chap in the face—don't you sport any?" "O a vast!—'unt regularly—I'm a member of the Surrey 'unt—capital one it is too—best in England by far." "What do you hunt?" inquired Sam. "Foxes, to be sure." "And are they good eating?" "Come," replied Jorrocks, "you know, as well as I do, we don't eat 'em." The dialogue was interrupted by someone calling to Sam to know what he was backing.

"The Bedlamite colt, my lord," with a forefinger to his hat. "Who's that?" inquired Jorrocks. "That's my Lord L——, a baron-lord—and a very nice one— best baron-lord I know—always bets with me—that's another baron-lord next him, and the man next him is a baron-knight, a stage below a baron-lord— something between a nobleman and a gentleman." "And who be that stout, good-looking man in a blue coat and velvet collar next him, just rubbing his chin with the race card—he'll be a lord too, I suppose?" "No,—that's Mr. Gully, as honest a man as ever came here,—that's Crockford before him. The man on the right is Mr. C——, who they call the 'cracksman,' because formerly he was a professional housebreaker, but he has given up that trade, and turned gentleman, bets, and keeps a gaming-table. This little ugly black-faced chap, that looks for all the world like a bilious Scotch terrier, has lately come among us. He was a tramping pedlar—sold worsted stockings—attended country courses, and occasionally bet a pair. Now he bets thousands of pounds, and keeps racehorses. The chaps about him all covered with chains and rings and brooches, were in the duffing line—sold brimstoned sparrows for canary-birds, Norwich shawls for real Cashmere, and dried cabbage-leaves for cigars. Now each has a first-rate house, horses and carriages, and a play-actress among them. Yon chap, with the extravagantly big mouth, is a cabinet-maker at Cambridge. He'll bet you a thousand pounds as soon as look at you."

"The chap on the right of the post with the red tie, is the son of an ostler. He commenced betting thousands with a farthing capital. The man next him, all teeth and hair, like a rat-catcher's dog, is an Honourable by birth, but not very honourable in his nature." "But see," cried Mr. Jorrocks, "Lord—— is talking to the Cracksman." "To be sure," replies Sam, "that's the beauty of the turf. The lord and the leg are reduced to an equality. Take my word for it, if you have a turn for good society, you should come upon the turf.—I say, my Lord Duke!" with all five fingers up to his hat, "I'll lay you three to two on the Bedlamite colt." "Done, Mr. Spring," replies his Grace, "three ponies to two." "There!" cried Mr. Spring, turning to Jorrocks, "didn't I tell you so?" The riot around the post increases. It is near the moment of starting, and the legs again become clamorous for what they want. Their vehemence increases. Each man is *in extremis*. "They are off!" cries one. "No, they are not," replies another. "False start," roars a third. "Now they come!" "No, they don't!" "Back again." They are off at last, however, and away they speed over the flat. The horses come within descrying distance. It's a beautiful race—run at score the whole way, and only two tailed off within the cords. Now they set to—whips and spurs go, legs leap, lords shout, and amid the same scene of confusion, betting, galloping, cursing, swearing, and bellowing, the horses rush past the judge's box.

But we have run our race, and will not fatigue our readers with repetition. Let us, however, spend the evening, and then the "Day at Newmarket" will be done.

Mr. Spring, with his usual attention to strangers, persuades Mr. Jorrocks to make one of a most agreeable dinner-party at the "White Hart" on the assurance of spending a delightful evening. Covers are laid for sixteen in the front room downstairs, and about six o'clock that number are ready to sit down. Mr. Badchild, the accomplished keeper of an oyster-room and minor hell in Pickering Place, is prevailed upon to take the chair, supported on his right by Mr. Jorrocks, and on his left by Mr. Tom Rhodes, of Thames Street, while the stout, jolly, portly Jerry Hawthorn fills—in the fullest sense of the word—the vice-chair. Just as the waiters are removing the covers, in stalks the Baron, in his conical hat, and reconnoitres the viands. Sam, all politeness, invites him to join the party. "I tank you," replies the Baron, "but I have my wet in de next room." "But bring your wet with you," rejoins Sam, "we'll all have our wet together after dinner," thinking the Baron meant his wine.

The usual inn grace—"For what we are going to receive, the host expects to be paid",—having been said with great feeling and earnestness, they all set to at the victuals, and little conversation passed until the removal of the cloth, when Mr. Badchild, calling upon his vice, observed that as in all probability there were gentlemen of different political and other opinions present, perhaps the best way would be to give a comprehensive toast, and so get over any debatable ground,—he therefore proposed to drink in a bumper "The king, the queen, and all the royal family, the ministry, particularly the Master of the Horse, the Army, the Navy, the Church, the State, and after the excellent dinner they had eaten, he would include the name of the landlord of the White Hart" (great applause). Song from Jerry Hawthorn—"The King of the Cannibal Islands".—The chairman then called upon the company to fill their glasses to a toast upon which there could be no difference of opinion. "It was a sport which they all enjoyed, one that was delightful to the old and to the young, to the peer and to the peasant, and open to all. Whatever might be the merits of other amusements, he had never yet met any man with the hardihood to deny that racing was at once the noblest and the most legitimate" (loud cheers, and thumps on the table, that set all the glasses dancing), "not only was it the noblest and most legitimate, but it was the most profitable; and where was the man of high and honourable principle who did not feel when breathing the pure atmosphere of that Heath, a lofty self-satisfaction at the thought, that though he might have left those who were near and dear to him in a less genial atmosphere, still he was not selfishly enjoying himself, without a thought for their welfare; for racing, while it brought health and vigour to the father, also brought what was dearer to the mind of a parent—the means of promoting the happiness and prosperity of his family—(immense cheers). With these few observations he should simply propose 'The Turf,' and may we long be above it"—(applause and, on the motion of Mr. Spring, three cheers for Mrs. Badchild and all the little Badchildren were called for and given). When the noise had subsided. Mr. Jorrocks very deliberately got up, amid whispers and inquiries as to who he was. "Gentlemen," said he, with an indignant stare, and a thump on the table, "Gentlemen, I say, in much of what has fallen from our worthy chairman, I go-in-sides, save in what he says about racing—I insists that 'unting is the sport of sports" (immense laughter, and cries of "wot an old fool!") "Gentlemen may laugh, but I say it's a fact, and though I doesn't wish to create no displeasancy whatsomever, yet I should despise myself most confoundedly—should consider myself unworthy of the great and distinguished 'unt to which I have the honour to belong, if I sat quietly down without sticking up for the chase (laughter).—I say, it's one of the balances of the constitution (laughter).—I say, it's the sport of kings! the image of war without its guilt (hisses and immense laughter). He would fearlessly propose a bumper toast—he would give them 'fox-hunting.'" There was some demur about drinking it, but on the interposition of Sam Spring, who assured the company that Jorrocks was one of the right sort, and with an addition proposed by Jerry Hawthorn, which made the toast more comprehensible, they swallowed it, and the chairman followed it up with "The

Sod",—which was drunk with great applause. Mr. Cox of Blue Hammerton returned thanks. "He considered cock-fighting the finest of all fine amusements. Nothing could equal the rush between two prime grey-hackles—that was his colour. The chairman had said a vast for racing, and to cut the matter short, he might observe that cock-fighting combined all the advantages of making money, with the additional benefit of not being interfered with by the weather. He begged to return his best thanks for himself and brother sods, and only regretted he had not been taught speaking in his youth, or he would certainly have convinced them all, that 'cocking' was the sport." "Coursing" was the next toast—for which Arthur Pavis, the jockey, returned thanks. "He was very fond of the 'long dogs,' and thought, after racing, coursing was the true thing. He was no orator, and so he drank off his wine to the health of the company." "Steeplechasing" followed, for which Mr. Coalman of St. Albans returned thanks, assuring the company that it answered his purpose remarkably well. Then the Vice gave the "Chair," and the Chair gave the "Vice"; and by way of a finale, Mr. Badchild proposed the game of "Chicken-hazard," observing in a whisper to Mr. Jorrocks, that perhaps he would like to subscribe to a joint-stock purse for the purpose of going to hell. To which Mr. Jorrocks, with great gravity, replied; "Sir, I'm d——d if I do."

VI
A WEEK AT CHELTENHAM: THE CHELTENHAM DANDY

MR. Jorrocks had been very poorly indeed of indigestion, as he calls it, produced by tucking in too much roast beef and plum pudding at Christmas, and prolonging the period of his festivities a little beyond the season allowed by Moore's *Almanack*, and having in vain applied the usual remedies prescribed on such occasions, he at length consented to try the Cheltenham waters, though altogether opposed to the element, he not having "astonished his stomach," as he says, for the last fifteen years with a glass of water.

Having established himself and the Yorkshireman in a small private lodging in High Street, consisting of two bedrooms and a sitting-room, he commenced his visits to the royal spa, and after a few good drenches, picked up so rapidly, that to whatever inn they went to dine, the landlords and waiters were astounded at the consumption of prog, and in a very short time he was known from the "Royal Hotel" down to Hurlston's Commercial Inn, as the great London Cormorant. At first, however, he was extremely depressed in spirits, and did nothing the whole day after his arrival, but talk about the arrangement of his temporal affairs; and the first symptom he gave of returning health was one day at dinner at the "Plough," by astonishing two or three scarlet-coated swells, who as usual were disporting themselves in the coffee-room, by bellowing to the waiter for some Talli-ho "sarce" to his fish. Before this he had never once spoken of his favourite diversion, and the sportsmen cantered by the window to cover in the morning, and back in the afternoon, without eliciting a single observation from him. The morning after this change for the better, he addressed his companion at breakfast as follows: "Blow me tight, Mr. York, if I arn't regularly renowated. I'm as fresh as an old hat after a shower of rain. I really thinks I shall get over this terrible illness, for I dreamt of 'unting last night, and, if you've a mind, we'll go and see my Lord Segrave's reynard dog, and then start from this 'ere corrupt place, for, you see, it's nothing but a town, and what's the use of sticking oneself in a little pokey lodging like this 'ere, where there really is not room to swing a cat, and paying the deuce knows how much tin, too, when one has a splendid house in Great Coram Street going on all the time, with a rigler establishment of servants and all that sort of thing. Now, you knows, I doesn't grudge a wisit to Margate, though that's a town too, but then, you see, one has the sea to look at, whereas here, it's nothing but a long street with shops, not so good as those in Red Lion Street, with a few small streets branching off from it, and as to the prommenard, as they calls it, aside the spa, with its trees and garden stuff, why, I'm sure, to my mind, the Clarence Gardens up by the Regent's Park, are quite as fine. It's true the doctor says I must remain another fortnight to perfect the cure, but then them 'ere M.D.'s, or whatever you calls them, are such rum jockeys, and I always thinks they say one word for the patient and two for themselves. Now, my chap said, I must only take half a bottle o' black strap a day at the werry most, whereas I have never had less than a whole one—his half first, as I say, and my own after—and because I tells him

I take a pint, he flatters himself his treatment is capital, and that he is a wonderful M.D.; but as a man can't be better than well, I think we'll just see what there's to be seen in the neighbourhood, and then cut our sticks, and, as I said before, I should like werry much to see my Lord Segrave's hounds, in order that I may judge whether there is anything in the wide world to be compared to the Surrey, for if I remember right, Mr. Nimrod described them as werry, werry fine, indeed."

Having formed this resolution, Jorrocks stamped on the floor (for the bell was broken) for the little boy who did the odd jobs of the house, to bring up his Hessian boots, into which having thrust his great calves, and replaced the old brown great-coat which he uses for a dressing-gown by a superfine Saxony blue, with metal buttons and pockets outside, he pulled his wig straight, stuck his white hat with the green flaps knowingly on his head, and sallied forth for execution as stout a man as ever. Knowing that the kennel is near the Winchcourt road, they proceeded in that direction, but after walking about a mile, came upon a groom on a chestnut horse, who, returning from the chase, was wetting his whistle at the appropriate sign of the "Fox and Hounds," and who informed them that they had passed the turning for the kennel, but that the hounds were out, and then in a wood which he pointed out on the hillside about two miles off, into which they had just brought their fox. Looking in that direction, they presently saw the summit of one of the highest of the range of hills that encircle the town of Cheltenham, covered with horsemen and pedestrians, who kept moving backwards and forwards on the "mountain's brow," looking in the distance more like a flock of sheep than anything else. Jorrocks, being all right again and up to anything, proposed a start to the wood, and though he thought they should hardly reach it before the hounds either killed their fox or he broke away again, they agreed to take the chance, and away they went, "best leg first" as the saying is. The cover (Queen Wood by name, and, as Jorrocks found out from somebody, the property of Lord Ellenborough) being much larger than it at first appeared and the fox but a bad one, they were in lots of time, and having toiled to the top of the wood, Jorrocks swaggered in among the horsemen with all the importance of an alderman. For full an hour after they got there the hounds kept running in cover, the fox being repeatedly viewed and the pack continually pressing him. Once or twice he came out, but after skirting the cover's edge a few yards turned in again. Indeed, there were two foxes on foot, one being a three-legged one, and it was extraordinary how he went and stood before hounds, going apparently very cautiously and stopping every now and then to listen. At last a thundering old grey-backed fellow went away before the whole field, making for the steep declivities that lead into the downs, and though the brow of the hill was covered with foot-people who holloa'd and shouted enough to turn a lion, he would make his point, and only altering his course so as to avoid running right among the mob, he gained the summit of the hill and disappeared. This hill, being uncommonly steep, was a breather for hounds that had been running so long as they had, in a thick cover too, and neither they nor the horses went at it with any great dash. The fox was not a fellow to be caught very easily, and nothing but a good start could have given them any chance, but the hounds never got well settled to the scent, and after a fruitless cast his lordship gave it up, and Jorrocks and Co. trudged back to Cheltenham, J—— highly delighted at so favourable an opportunity of seeing the hounds. Indeed, so pleased was he with the turn-out and the whole thing, that finding from Skinner, one of the whippers-in, that they met on the following morning at Purge Down-turnpike, in their best country, forgetting all about his indigestion and the royal spa, he went to Newman and Longridge, the horse dealers and livery stable keepers and engaged a couple of nags "to look at the hounds upon," as he impressed upon their minds, which he ordered to be ready at nine o'clock.

This day he proposed to give the landlord of the "George Inn," in the High Street, the benefit of his rapacious appetite, and about five o'clock (his latest London hour) they sat down to dinner. The "George" is neither exactly a swell house like the "Royal Hotel" or the "Plough," nor yet a commercial one, but something betwixt and between. The coffee-room is very small, consequently all the frequenters are drawn together, and if a conversation is started a man must be deuced unsociable that does not join in the cry.

As three or four were sitting round the fire chatting over their tipple, and Jorrocks was telling some of his best bouncers, the door opened and a waiter bowed a fresh animal into the cage, who, after eyeing the party, took off his hat and forthwith proceeded to pull off divers neckcloths, cloaks, great-coats, muffitees, until he reduced himself to about half the size he was on entering. He was a little square-built old man, with white hair and plenty of it, a long stupid red face with little pig eyes, a very long awkward body, and very short legs. He was dressed in a blue coat, buff waistcoat, a sort of baggy grey or thunder-and-lightning trousers, over which he had buttoned a pair of long black gaiters. Having "peeled," he rubbed his hands and blew upon them, as much as to say, "Now, gentlemen, won't you let me have a smell of the fire?" and, accordingly, by a sort of military revolution, they made a place for him right in the centre.

"Coldish night I reckon, sir," said Jorrocks, looking him over.

"Very cold indeed, very cold indeed," answered he, rubbing his elbows against his ribs, and stamping with his feet. "I've just got off the top of the Liverpool coach, and, I can assure you, it's very cold riding outside a coach all day long—however, I always say that it's better than being inside, though, indeed, it's very little that I trouble coaches at all in the course of the year—generally travel in my own carriage, only my family have it with them in Bristol now, where I'm going to join them; but I'm well used to the elements, hunting, shooting, and fishing, as I do constantly."

This later announcement made Jorrocks rouse up, and finding himself in the company of a sportsman and one, too, who travelled in his own carriage, he assumed a different tone and commenced on a fresh tack—"and pray, may I make bold to inquire what country you hunts in, sir?" said he.

"Oh! I live in Cheshire—Mainwaring's country, but Melton's the place I chiefly hunt at,—know all the fellows there; rare set of dogs, to be sure,—only country worth hunting in, to my mind."

Jorrocks. Rigler swells, though, the chaps, arn't they? Recollect one swell of a fellow coming with his upper lip all over fur into our country, thinking to astonish our weak minds, but I reckon we told him out.

Stranger. What! you hunt, do you?

Jorrocks. A few—you've perhaps heard tell of the Surrey 'unt?

Stranger. Cocktail affair, isn't it?

Jorrocks. No such thing, I assure you. Cocktail indeed! I likes that.

Stranger. Well, but it's not what we calls a fast-coach.

Jorrocks. I doesn't know wot you calls a fast-coach, but if you've a mind to make a match, I'll bet you a hat, ay, or half a dozen hats, that I'll find a fellow to take the conceit out o' any your Meltonians.

Stranger. Oh! I don't doubt but you have some good men among you; I'm sure I didn't mean anything offensive, by asking if it was a cocktail affair, but we Meltonians certainly have a trick, I must confess, of running every other country down; come, sir, I'll drink the Surrey hunt with all my heart, said he, swigging off the remains of a glass of brandy-and-water which the waiter had brought him shortly after entering.

Jorrocks. Thank you, sir, kindly. Waiter, bring me a bottom o' brandy, cold, without—and don't stint for quantity, if you please. Doesn't you think these inns werry expensive places, sir? I doesn't mean this in particular, but inns in general.

Stranger. Oh! I don't know, sir. We must expect to pay. "Live and let live," is my motto. I always pay my inn bills without looking them over. Just cast my eyes at the bottom to see the amount, then call for pen and ink, add so much for waiter, so much for chambermaid, so much for boots, and if I'm travelling in my own carriage so much for the ostler for greasing. That's the way I do business, sir.

Jorrocks. Well, sir, a werry pleasant plan too, especially for the innkeeper— and all werry right for a gentleman of fortune like you. My motto, however, is "Waste not, want not," and my wife's father's motto was "Wilful waste brings woeful want," and I likes to have my money's worth.—Now, said he, pulling out a handful of bills, at some places that I go to they charges me six shillings a day for my dinner, and when I was ill and couldn't digest nothing but the lightest and plainest of breakfasts, when a fork breakfast in fact would have made a stiff 'un of me, and my muffin mill was almost stopped, they charged me two shillings for one cake, and sixpence for two eggs.—Now I'm in the tea trade myself, you must know, and I contend that as things go, or at least as things went before the Barbarian eye, as they call Napier, kicked up a row with the Hong merchants, it's altogether a shameful imposition, and I wonder people put up with it.

Stranger. Oh, sir, I don't know. I think that it is the charge all over the country. Besides, it doesn't do to look too closely at these things, and you must allow something for keeping up the coffee-room, you know—fire, candles, and so on.

Jorrocks. But blow me tight, you surely don't want a candle to breakfast by?

However, I contends that innkeepers are great fools for making these sort of charges, for it makes people get out of their houses as quick as ever they can, whereas they might be inclined to stay if they could get things moderate.—For my part I likes a coffee-room, but having been used to commercial houses when I travelled, I knows what the charges ought to be. Now, this room is snug enough though small, and won't require no great keeping up.

Stranger. No—but this room is smaller than the generality of them, you know. They frequently have two fires in them, besides no end of oil burning.—I know the expense of these things, for I have a very large house in the country, and rely upon it, innkeepers have not such immense profits as many people imagines—but, as I said before, "live and let live."

Jorrocks. So says I, "live and let live"—but wot I complains of is, that some innkeepers charge so much that they won't let people live. No man is fonder of eating than myself, but I don't like to pay by the mouthful, or yet to drink tea at so much a thimbleful. By the way, Sar, if you are not previously engaged, I should be werry happy to supply you with red Mocho or best Twankay at a very reasonable figure indeed for cash?

Stranger. Thank you, sir, thank you. Those are things I never interfere with—leave all these things to my people. My housekeeper sends me in her book every quarter day, with an account of what she pays. I just look at the amount—add so much for wages, and write a cheque—"live and let live!" say I. However, added he, pulling out his watch, and ringing the bell for the chambermaid, "I hate to get up very early, so I think it is time to go to bed, and I wish you a very good night, gentlemen all."

Jorrocks gets up, advances half-way to the door, makes him one of his most obsequious bows, and wishes him a werry good night. Having heard him tramp upstairs and safely deposited in his bedroom, they pulled their chairs together again, and making a smaller circle round the fire, proceeded to canvass their departed friend. Jorrocks began—"I say, wot a regular swell the chap is—a Meltonian, too.—I wonders who the deuce he is. Wish Mr. Nimrod was among us, he could tell us all about him, I dare say. I'm blowed if I didn't take him for a commercial gentleman at first, until he spoke about his carriages. I likes to see gentlemen of fortune making themselves sociable by coming into the coffee-room, instead of sticking themselves up in private sitting-rooms, as if nobody was good enough for them. You know Melton, Mr. York; did you ever see the gentleman out?"

"I can't say that I ever did," said his friend, "but people look so different in their red coats to what they do in mufti, that there's no such thing as recognising them unless you had a previous acquaintance with them. The fields in Leicestershire are sometimes so large that it requires a residence to get anything like a general knowledge of the hunt, and, you know, Northamptonshire's the country for my money, after Surrey, of course."

"I don't think he is a gentleman," observed a thin sallow-complexioned young man, who, sitting on one side of the fire, had watched the stranger very narrowly without joining in the conversation. "He gives me more the idea of a gentleman's servant, acting the part of master, than anything else."

Jorrocks. Oh! he is a gentleman, I'm sure—besides, a servant wouldn't travel in a carriage you know, and he talked about greasing the wheels and all that sort of thing, which showed he was familiar with the thing.

"That's very true," replied the youth—"but a servant may travel in the rumble and pay for greasing the wheels all the same, or perhaps have to grease them himself."

"Well, I should say he's a foolish purse-proud sort of fellow," observed another, "who has come into money unexpectedly, and who likes to be the cock of his party, and show off a little."

Jorrocks. I'll be bound to say you're all wrong—you are not fox-hunters, you see, or you would know that that is a way the sportsmen have—we always make ourselves at home and agreeable—have a word for everybody in fact, and no reserve; besides, you see, there was nothing gammonacious, as I calls it, about his toggery, no round-cut coats with sporting buttons, or coaches and four, or foxes for pins in his shirt.

"I don't care for that," replied the sallow youth, "dress him as you will, court suit, bag wig, and sword, you'll make nothing better of him—he's a SNOB."

Jorrocks, getting up, runs to the table on which the hats were standing, saying, "I wonder if he's left his castor behind him? I've always found a man's hat will tell a good deal. This is yours, Mr. York, with the loop to it, and here's mine—I always writes Golgotha in mine, which being interpreted, you know, means the place of a skull. These are yours, I presume, gentlemen?" said he, taking up two others. "Confound him, he's taken his tile with him—however, I'm quite positive he's a gentleman—lay you a hat apiece all round he is, if you like!"

"But how are we to prove it?" inquired the youth.

Jorrocks. Call in the waiter.

Youth. He may know nothing about him, and a waiter's gentleman is always the man who pays him most.

Jorrocks. Trust the waiter for knowing something about him, and if he doesn't, why, it's only to send a purlite message upstairs, saying that two gentlemen in the coffee-room have bet a trifle that he is some nobleman—Lord Maryborough, for instance,—he's a little chap—but we must make haste, or the gentleman will be asleep.

"Well, then, I'll take your bet of a hat," replied the youth, "that he is not what I call a gentleman."

Jorrocks. I don't know what you calls a gentleman. I'll lay you a hat, a guinea one, either white or black, whichever you like, but none o' your dog hairs or gossamers, mind—that he's a man of dibs, and doesn't follow no trade or calling, and if that isn't a gentleman, I don't know wot is. What say you, Mr. York?

"Suppose we put it thus—You bet this gentleman a hat that he's a Meltonian, which will comprise all the rest."

Jorrocks. Werry well put. Do you take me, sir? A guinea hat against a guinea hat.

"I do," said the youth.

Jorrocks. Then DONE—now ring the bell for the waiter—I'll pump him.

Enter waiter.

Jorrocks. Snuff them candles, if you please, and bring me another bottom o' brandy-cold, without—and, waiter! here, pray who is that gentleman that came in by the Liverpool coach to-night? The little gentleman in long black gaiters who sat in this chair, you know, and had some brandy-and-water.

Waiter. I know who you mean, sir, quite well, the gentleman who's gone to bed. Let me see, what's his name? He keeps that large Hotel in—— Street, Liverpool—what's the—Here an immense burst of laughter drowned the remainder of the sentence.

Jorrocks rose in a rage. "No! you double-distilled blockhead," said he, "no such thing—you're thinking of someone else. The gentleman hunts at Melton Mowbray, and travels in his own carriage."

Waiter. I don't know nothing about Melton Mowbray, sir, but the last time he came through here on his road to Bristol, he was in one of his own rattle-trap yellows, and had such a load—his wife, a nurse, and eight children inside; himself, his son, and an apple-tree on the dickey—that the horses knocked up half-way and...

Jorrocks. Say no more—say no more—d——n his teeth and toe-nails—and that's swearing—a thing I never do but on the most outrageous occasions. Confounded humbug, I'll be upsides with him, however. Waiter, bring the bill and no more brandy. Never was so done in all my life—a gammonacious fellow! "There, sir, there's your one pound one," said he, handing a sovereign and a shilling to the winner of the hat. "Give me my tile, and let's mizzle.—Waiter, I can't wait; must bring the bill up to my lodgings in the morning if it isn't ready.—Come away, come away—I shall never get over this as long as ever I live. 'Live and let live,' indeed! no wonder he stuck up for the innkeepers—a publican and a sinner as he is. Good night, gentlemen, good night."

Exit Jorrocks.

VII
AQUATICS: MR. JORROCKS AT MARGATE

THE shady side of Cheapside had become a luxury, and footmen in red plush breeches objects of real commiseration, when Mr. Jorrocks, tired of the heat and "ungrateful hurry of the town," resolved upon undertaking an aquatic excursion. He was sitting, as is "his custom always in the afternoon," in the arbour at the farther end of his gravel walk, which he dignifies by the name of "garden," and had just finished a rough mental calculation, as to whether he could eat more bread spread with jam or honey, when the idea of the jaunt entered his imagination. Being a man of great decision, he speedily winnowed the project over in his mind, and producing a five-pound note from the fob of his small clothes, passed it in review between his fingers, rubbed out the creases, held it up to the light, refolded and restored it to his fob. "Batsay," cried he, "bring my castor—the white one as hangs next the blue cloak;" and forthwith a rough-napped, unshorn-looking, white hat was transferred from the peg to Mr. Jorrocks's head. This done, he proceeded to the "Piazza," where he found the Yorkshireman exercising himself up and down the spacious coffee-room, and, grasping his hand with the firmness of a vice, he forthwith began unburthening himself of the object of his mission. "'Ow are you?" said he, shaking his arm like the handle of a pump. "'Ow are you, I say?—I'm so delighted to see you, ye carn't think—isn't this charming weather! It makes me feel like a butterfly—really think the 'air is sprouting under my vig." Here he took off his wig and rubbed his hand over his bald head, as though he were feeling for the shoots.

"Now to business—Mrs. J—— is away at Tooting, as you perhaps knows, and I'm all alone in Great Coram Street, with the key of the cellar, larder, and all that sort of thing, and I've a werry great mind to be off on a jaunt—what say you?" "Not the slightest objection," replied the Yorkshireman, "on the old principle of you finding cash, and me finding company." "Why, now I'll tell you, werry honestly, that I should greatly prefer your paying your own shot; but, however, if you've a mind to do as I do, I'll let you stand in the half of a five-pound note and whatever silver I have in my pocket," pulling out a great handful as he spoke, and counting up thirty-two and sixpence. "Very good," replied the Yorkshireman when he had finished, "I'm your man;—and not to be behindhand in point of liberality, I've got threepence that I received in change at the cigar divan just now, which I will add to the common stock, so that we shall have six pounds twelve and ninepence between us." "Between us!" exclaimed Mr. Jorrocks, "now that's so like a Yorkshireman. I declare you Northerns seem to think all the world are asleep except yourselves;—howsomever, I von't quarrel with you—you're a goodish sort of chap in your way, and so long as I keep the swag, we carn't get far wrong. Well, then, to-morrow at two we'll start for Margate—the most delightful place in all the world, where we will have a rare jollification, and can stay just as long as the money holds out. So now good-bye—I'm off home again to see about wittles for the woyage."

It were almost superfluous to mention that the following day was a

Saturday—for no discreet citizen would think of leaving town on any other. It dawned with uncommon splendour, and the cocks of Coram Street and adjacent parts seemed to hail the morn with more than their wonted energy. Never, save on a hunting morning, did Mr. Jorrocks tumble about in bed with such restless anxiety as cock after cock took up the crow in every gradation of noise from the shrill note of the free street-scouring chanticleer before the door, to the faint response of the cooped and prisoned victims of the neighbouring poulterer's, their efforts being aided by the flutterings and impertinent chirruping of swarms of town-bred sparrows.

At length the boy, Binjimin, tapped at his master's door, and, depositing his can of shaving-water on his dressing-table, took away his coat and waistcoat, under pretence of brushing them, but in reality to feel if he had left any pence in the pockets. With pleasure Mr. Jorrocks threw aside the bed-clothes, and bounded upon the floor with a bump that shook his own and adjoining houses. On this day a few extra minutes were devoted to his toilet, one or two of which were expended in adjusting a gold foxhead pin in a conspicuous part of his white tie, and in drawing on a pair of new dark blue stocking-net pantaloons, made so excessively tight, that at starting, any of his Newmarket friends would have laid three to two against his ever getting into them at all. When on, however, they fully developed the substantial proportions of his well-rounded limbs, while his large tasselled Hessians showed that the bootmaker had been instructed to make a pair for a "great calf." A blue coat, with metal buttons, ample laps, and pockets outside, with a handsome buff kerseymere waistcoat, formed his costume on this occasion. Breakfast being over, he repaired to St. Botolph Lane, there to see his letters and look after his commercial affairs; in which the reader not being interested, we will allow the Yorkshireman to figure a little.

About half-past one this enterprising young man placed himself in Tommy Sly's wherry at the foot of the Savoy stairs, and not agreeing in opinion with Mr. Jorrocks that it is of "no use keeping a dog and barking oneself," he took an oar and helped to row himself down to London Bridge. At the wharf below the bridge there lay a magnificent steamer, painted pea-green and white, with flags flying from her masts, and the deck swarming with smart bonnets and bodices. Her name was the *Royal Adelaide*, from which the sagacious reader will infer that this excursion was made during the late reign. The Yorkshireman and Tommy Sly having wormed their way among the boats, were at length brought up within one of the vessels, and after lying on their oars a few seconds, they were attracted by, "Now, sir, are you going to sleep there?" addressed to a rival nautical whose boat obstructed the way, and on looking up on deck what a sight burst upon the Yorkshireman's astonished vision!—Mr. Jorrocks, with his coat off, and a fine green velvet cap or turban, with a broad gold band and tassel, on his head, hoisting a great hamper out of the wherry, rejecting all offers of assistance, and treating the laughter and jeers of the porters and bystanders with ineffable contempt. At length he placed the load to his liking, and putting on his coat, adjusted his hunting telescope, and advanced to the side, as the Yorkshireman mounted the step-ladder and came upon deck. "Werry near being over late," said he, pulling out his watch, just at which moment the last bell rang, and a few strokes of the paddles sent the vessel away from the quay. "A miss is as good as a mile," replied the Yorkshireman; "but pray what have you got in the hamper?"

"In the 'amper! Why, wittles to be sure. You seem to forget we are going a woyage, and 'ow keen the sea hair is. I've brought a knuckle of weal, half a ham, beef, sarsingers, chickens, sherry white, and all that sort of thing, and werry acceptable they'll be by the time we get to the Nore, or may be before."

"Ease her! Stop her!" cried the captain through his trumpet, just as the vessel was getting into her stride in mid-stream, and, with true curiosity, the passengers flocked to the side, to see who was coming, though they could not possibly have examined half they had on board. Mr. Jorrocks, of course, was not behindhand in inquisitiveness, and proceeded to adjust his telescope. A wherry was seen rowing among the craft, containing the boatman, and a gentleman in a woolly white hat, with a bright pea-green coat, and a basket on his knee. "By jingo, here's Jemmy Green!" exclaimed Mr. Jorrocks, taking his telescope from his eye, and giving his thigh a hearty slap. "How unkimmon lucky! The werry man of all others I should most like to see. You know James Green, don't you?" addressing the Yorkshireman—"young James Green, junior, of Tooley Street—everybody knows him—most agreeable young man in Christendom—fine warbler—beautiful dancer—everything that a young man should be."

"How are you James?" cried Jorrocks, seizing him by the hand as his friend stepped upon deck; but whether it was the nervousness occasioned by the rocking of the wherry, or the shaking of the step-ladder up the side of the steamer, or Mr. Jorrocks's new turban cap, but Mr. Green, with an old-maidish reserve, drew back from the proffered embrace of his friend. "You have the adwantage of me, sir," said he, fidgeting back as he spoke, and eyeing Mr. Jorrocks with unmeasured surprise—"Yet stay—if I'm not deceived it's Mr. Jorrocks—so it is!" and thereupon they joined hands most cordially, amid exclamations of, "'Ow are you, J——?" "'Ow are you, G——?" "'Ow are you, J——?" "So glad to see you, J——" "So glad to see you, G——" "So glad to see you, J——" "And pray what may you have in your basket?" inquired Mr. Jorrocks, putting his hand to the bottom of a neat little green-and-white willow woman's basket, apparently for the purpose of ascertaining its weight. "Only my clothes, and a little prowision for the woyage. A baked pigeon, some cold maccaroni, and a few pectoral lozenges. At the bottom are my Margate shoes, with a comb in one, and a razor in t'other; then comes the prog, and at the top, I've a dickey and a clean front for to-morrow. I abominates travelling with much luggage. Where, I ax, is the use of carrying nightcaps, when the innkeepers always prowide them, without extra charge? The same with regard to soap. Shave, I say, with what you find in your tray. A wet towel makes an excellent tooth-brush, and a pen-knife both cuts and cleans your nails. Perhaps you'll present your friend to me," added he in the same breath, with a glance at the Yorkshireman, upon whose arm Mr. Jorrocks was resting his telescope hand. "Much pleasure," replied Mr. Jorrocks, with his usual urbanity. "Allow me to introduce Mr. Stubbs, Mr. Green, Mr. Green, Mr. Stubbs: now pray shake hands," added he, "for I'm sure you'll be werry fond of each other"; and thereupon Jemmy, in the most patronising manner, extended his two forefingers to the Yorkshireman, who presented him with one in return. For the information of such of our readers as may never have seen Mr. James Green, senior junior, either in Tooley Street, Southwark, where the patronymic name abounds, or at Messrs. Tattersall's, where he generally exhibits on a Monday afternoon, we may premise, that though a little man in stature, he is a great man in mind and a great swell in costume. On the present occasion, as already stated, he had on a woolly white hat, his usual pea-green coat, with a fine, false, four-frilled front to his shirt, embroidered, plaited, and puckered, like a lady's habit-shirt. Down the front were three or four different sorts of studs, and a butterfly brooch, made of various coloured glasses, sat in the centre. His cravat was of a yellow silk with a flowered border, confining gills sharp and pointed that looked up his nostrils; his double-breasted waistcoat was of red and yellow tartan with blue glass post-boy buttons; and his trousers, which were very wide and cut out over the foot of rusty-black chamois-leather opera-boots, were of a broad blue stripe upon a white ground. A curly, bushy, sandy-coloured wig protruded from the sides of his woolly white hat, and shaded a vacant countenance, which formed the frontispiece of a great chuckle head. Sky-blue gloves and a stout cane, with large tassels, completed the rigging of this borough dandy. Altogether he was as fine as any peacock, and as vain as the proudest.

"And 'ow is Mrs. J——?" inquired Green with the utmost affability—"I hopes she's uncommon well—pray, is she of your party?" looking round. "Why, no," replied Mr. Jorrocks, "she's off at Tooting at her mother's, and I'm just away, on the sly, to stay a five-pound at Margate this delightful weather. 'Ow long do you remain?" "Oh, only till Monday morning—I goes every Saturday; in fact," added he in an undertone, "I've a season ticket, so I may just as well use it, as stay poking in Tooley Street with the old folks, who really are so uncommon glumpy, that it's quite refreshing to get away from them."

"That's a pity," replied Mr. Jorrocks, with one of his benevolent looks. "But 'ow comes it, James, you are not married? You are not a bouy now, and should be looking out for a home of your own." "True, my dear J——, true," replied Mr. Green; "and I'll tell you wot, our principal book-keeper and I have made many calculations on the subject, and being a man of literature like yourself, he gave it as his opinion the last time we talked the matter over, that it would only be avoiding Silly and running into Crab-beds; which I presume means Quod or the Bench. Unless he can have a wife 'made to order,' he says he'll never wed. Besides, the women are such a bothersome encroaching set. I declare I'm so pestered with them that I don't know vich vay to turn. They are always tormenting of me. Only last week one sent me a specification of what she'd marry me for, and I declare her dress, alone, came to more than I have to find myself in clothes, ball-and concert-tickets, keep an 'oss, go to theatres, buy lozenges, letter-paper, and everything else with. There were bumbazeens, and challies, and merinos, and crape, and gauze, and dimity, and caps, bonnets, stockings, shoes, boots, rigids, stays, ringlets; and, would you believe it, she had the unspeakable audacity to include a bustle! It was the most monstrous specification and proposal I ever read, and I returned it by the twopenny post, axing her if she hadn't forgotten to include a set of false teeth. Still, I confess, I'm tired of Tooley Street. I feel that I have a soul above hemp, and was intended for a brighter sphere; but vot can one do, cooped up at home without men of henergy for companions? No prospect of improvement either; for I left our old gentleman alarmingly well just now, pulling about the flax and tow, as though his dinner depended upon his exertions. I think if the women would let me alone, I might have some chance, but it worries a man of sensibility and refinement to have them always tormenting of one.—I've no objection to be led, but, dash my buttons, I von't be driven." "Certainly not," replied Mr. Jorrocks, with great gravity, jingling the silver in his breeches-pocket. "It's an old saying, James, and times proves it true, that you may take an 'oss to the water but you carn't make him drink—and talking of 'osses, pray, how are you off in that line?" "Oh, werry well—uncommon, I may say—a thoroughbred, bang tail down to the hocks, by Phantom, out of Baron Munchausen's dam—gave a hatful of money for him at Tatts'.—five fives—a deal of tin as times go. But he's a perfect 'oss, I assure you—bright bay with four black legs, and never a white hair upon him. He's touched in the vind, but that's nothing—I'm not a fox-hunter, you know, Mr. Jorrocks; besides, I find the music he makes werry useful in the streets, as a warning to the old happle women to get out of the way. Pray, sir," turning to the Yorkshireman with a jerk, "do you dance?"—as the boat band, consisting of a harp, a flute, a lute, a long horn, and a short horn, struck up a quadrille,—and, without waiting for a reply, our hero sidled past, and glided among the crowd that covered the deck.

"A fine young man, James," observed Mr. Jorrocks, eyeing Jemmy as he elbowed his way down the boat—"fine young man—wants a little of his father's ballast, but there's no putting old heads on young shoulders. He's a beautiful dancer," added Mr. Jorrocks, putting his arm through the Yorkshireman's, "let's go and see him foot it." Having worked their way down, they at length got near the dancers, and mounting a ballast box had a fine view of the quadrille. There were eight or ten couple at work, and Jemmy had chosen a fat, dumpy, red-faced girl, in a bright orange-coloured muslin gown, with black velvet Vandyked flounces, and green boots—a sort of walking sunflower, with whom he was pointing his toe, kicking out behind, and pirouetting with great energy and agility. His male *vis-à-vis* was a waistcoatless young Daniel Lambert, in white ducks, and a blue dress-coat, with a carnation in his mouth, who with a damsel in ten colours, reel'd to and fro in humble imitation. "Green for ever!" cried Mr. Jorrocks, taking off his velvet cap and waving it encouragingly over his head: "Green for ever! Go it Green!" and, accordingly, Green went it with redoubled vigour. "Wiggins for ever!" responded a female voice opposite, "I say, Wiggins!" which was followed by a loud clapping of hands, as the fat gentleman made an astonishing step. Each had his admiring applauders, though Wiggins "had the call" among the ladies—the opposition voice that put him in nomination proceeding from the mother of his partner, who, like her daughter, was a sort of walking pattern book. The spirit of emulation lasted throughout the quadrille, after which, sunflower in hand, Green traversed the deck to receive the compliments of the company.

"You must be 'ungry," observed Mr. Jorrocks, with great politeness to the lady, "after all your exertions," as the latter stood mopping herself with a coarse linen handkerchief—"pray, James, bring your partner to our 'amper, and let me offer her some refreshment," which was one word for the Sunflower and two for himself, the sea breeze having made Mr. Jorrocks what he called "unkimmon peckish." The hamper was speedily opened, the knuckle of veal, the half ham, the aitch bone of beef, the Dorking sausages (made in Drury Lane), the chickens, and some dozen or two of plovers' eggs were exhibited, while Green, with disinterested generosity, added his baked pigeon and cold maccaroni to the common stock. A vigorous attack was speedily commenced, and was kept up, with occasional interruptions by Green running away to dance, until they hove in sight of Herne Bay, which caused an interruption to a very interesting lecture on wines, that Mr. Jorrocks was in the act of delivering, which went to prove that port and sherry were the parents of all wines, port the father, and sherry the mother; and that Bluecellas, hock, Burgundy, claret, Teneriffe, Madeira, were made by the addition of water, vinegar, and a few chemical ingredients, and that of all "humbugs," pale sherry was the greatest, being neither more nor less than brown sherry watered. Mr. Jorrocks then set to work to pack up the leavings in the hamper, observing as he proceeded, that wilful waste brought woeful want, and that "waste not, want not," had ever been the motto of the Jorrocks family.

It was nearly eight o'clock ere the *Royal Adelaide* touched the point of the far-famed Margate Jetty, a fact that was announced as well by the usual bump, and scuttle to the side to get out first, as by the band striking up *God save the King*, and the mate demanding the tickets of the passengers. The sun had just dropped beneath the horizon, and the gas-lights of the town had been considerably lighted to show him to bed, for the day was yet in the full vigour of life and light.

Two or three other cargoes of cockneys having arrived before, the whole place was in commotion, and the beach swarmed with spectators as anxious to watch this last disembarkation as they had been to see the first. By a salutary regulation of the sages who watch over the interests of the town, "all manner of persons," are prohibited from walking upon the jetty during this ceremony, but the platform of which it is composed being very low, those who stand on the beach outside the rails, are just about on a right level to shoot their impudence cleverly into the ears of the new-comers who are paraded along two lines of gaping, quizzing, laughing, joking, jeering citizens, who fire volleys of wit and satire upon them as they pass. "There's leetle Jemmy Green again!" exclaimed a nursery-maid with two fat, ruddy children in her arms, "he's a beauty without paint!" "Hallo, Jorrocks, my hearty! lend us your hand," cried a brother member of the Surrey Hunt. Then there was a pointing of fingers and cries of "That's Jorrocks! that's Green!" "That's Green! that's Jorrocks!" and a murmuring titter, and exclamations of "There's Simpkins! how pretty he is!" "But there's Wiggins, who's much nicer." "My eye, what a cauliflower hat Mrs. Thompson's got!" "What a buck young Snooks is!" "What gummy legs that girl in green has!" "Miss Trotter's bustle's on crooked!" from the young ladies at Miss Trimmer's seminary who were drawn up to show the numerical strength of the academy, and act the part of walking advertisements. These observations were speedily drowned by the lusty lungs of a flyman bellowing out, as Green passed, "Hallo! my young brockley-sprout, are you here again?—now then for the tizzy you owe me,—I have been waiting here for it ever since last Monday morning." This salute produced an irate look and a shake of his cane from Green, with a mutter of something about "imperance," and a wish that he had his big fighting foreman there to thrash him. When they got to the gate at the end, the tide of fashion became obstructed by the kissings of husbands and wives, the greetings of fathers and sons, the officiousness of porters, the cries of flymen, the importunities of innkeepers, the cards of bathing-women, the salutations of donkey drivers, the programmes of librarians, and the rush and push of the inquisitive; and the waters of "comers" and "stayers" mingled in one common flood of indescribable confusion.

Mr. Jorrocks, who, hamper in hand, had elbowed his way with persevering resignation, here found himself so beset with friends all anxious to wring his digits, that, fearful of losing either his bed or his friends, he besought Green to step on to the "White Hart" and see about accommodation. Accordingly Green ran his fingers through the bushy sides of his yellow wig, jerked up his gills, and with a *négligé* air strutted up to that inn, which, as all frequenters of Margate know, stands near the landing-place, and commands a fine view of the harbour. Mr. Creed, the landlord, was airing himself at the door, or, as Shakespeare has it, "taking his ease at his inn," and knowing Green of old to be a most unprofitable customer, he did not trouble to move his position farther than just to draw up one leg so as not wholly to obstruct the passage, and looked at him as much as to say "I prefer your room to your company." "Quite full here, sir," said he, anticipating Green's question. "Full, indeed?" replied Jemmy, pulling up his gills—"that's werry awkward, Mr. Jorrocks has come down with myself and a friend, and we want accommodation." "Mr. Jorrocks, indeed!" replied Mr. Creed, altering his tone and manner; "I'm sure I shall be delighted to receive Mr. Jorrocks—he's one of the oldest customers I have—and one of the best—none of your 'glass of water and toothpick' gentleman—real downright, black-strap man, likes it hot and strong from the wood—always pays like a gentleman—never fights about three-pences, like some people I know," looking at Jemmy. "Pray, what rooms may you require?" "Vy, there's myself, Mr. Jorrocks, and Mr. Jorrocks's other friend—three in all, and we shall want three good, hairy bedrooms." "Well, I don't know," replied Mr. Creed, laughing, "about their hairiness, but I can rub them with bear's grease for you." Jemmy pulled up his gills and was about to reply, when Mr. Jorrocks's appearance interrupted the dialogue. Mr. Creed advanced to receive him, blowing up his porters for not having been down to carry up the hamper, which he took himself and bore to the coffee-room, amid protestations of his delight at seeing his worthy visitor.

Having talked over the changes of Margate, of those that were there, those that were not, and those that were coming, and adverted to the important topic of supper, Mr. Jorrocks took out his yellow and white spotted handkerchief and proceeded to flop his Hessian boots, while Mr. Creed, with his own hands, rubbed him over with a long billiard-table brush. Green, too, put himself in form by the aid of the looking-glass, and these preliminaries being adjusted, the trio sallied forth arm-in-arm, Mr. Jorrocks occupying the centre. It was a fine, balmy summer evening, the beetles and moths still buzzed and flickered in the air, and the sea rippled against the shingly shore, with a low indistinct murmur that scarcely sounded among the busy hum of men. The shades of night were drawing on—a slight mist hung about the hills, and a silvery moon shed a broad brilliant ray upon the quivering waters "of the dark blue sea," and an equal light over the wide expanse of the troubled town. How strange that man should leave the quiet scenes of nature, to mix in myriads of those they profess to quit cities to avoid! One turn to the shore, and the gas-lights of the town drew back the party like moths to the streets, which were literally swarming with the population. "Cheapside, at three o'clock in the afternoon," as Mr. Jorrocks observed, was never fuller than Margate streets that evening. All was lighted up—all brilliant and all gay—care seemed banished from every countenance, and pretty faces and smart gowns reigned in its stead. Mr. Jorrocks met with friends and acquaintances at every turn, most of whom asked "when he came?" and "when he was going away?" Having perambulated the streets, the sound of music attracted Jemmy Green's attention, and our party turned into a long, crowded and brilliantly lighted bazaar, just as the last notes of a barrel-organ at the far end faded away, and a young woman in a hat and feathers, with a swan's-down muff and tippet, was handed by a very smart young man in dirty white Berlin gloves, and an equally soiled white waistcoat, into a sort of orchestra above where, after the plaudits of the company had subsided, she struck-up:

"If I had a donkey vot vouldn't go."

At the conclusion of the song, and before the company had time to disperse, the same smart young gentleman,—having rehanded the young lady from the orchestra and pocketed his gloves,—ran his fingers through his hair, and announced from that eminence, that the spirited proprietors of the Bazaar were then going to offer for public competition in the enterprising shape of a raffle, in tickets, at one shilling each, a most magnificently genteel, rosewood, general perfume box fitted up with cedar and lined with red silk velvet, adorned with cut-steel clasps at the sides, and a solid, massive, silver name-plate at the top, with a best patent Bramah lock and six chaste and beautifully rich cut-glass bottles, and a plate-glass mirror at the top—a box so splendidly perfect, so beautifully unique, as alike to defy the powers of praise and the critiques of the envious; and thereupon he produced a flashy sort of thing that might be worth three and sixpence, for which he modestly required ten subscribers, at a shilling each, adding, "that even with that number the proprietors would incur a werry heavy loss, for which nothing but a boundless sense of gratitude for favours past could possibly recompense them." The youth's eloquence and the glitter of the box reflecting, as it did at every turn, the gas-lights both in its steel and glass, had the desired effect—shillings went down, and tickets went off rapidly, until only three remained. "Four, five, and ten, are the only numbers now remaining," observed the youth, running his eye up the list and wetting his pencil in his mouth. "Four, five and ten! ten, four, five! five, four, ten! are the only numbers now vacant for this werry genteel and magnificent rosewood perfume-box, lined with red velvet, cut-steel clasps, a silver plate for the name, best patent Bramah lock, and six beautiful rich cut-glass bottles, with a plate glass mirror in the lid— and only four, five, and ten now vacant!" "I'll take ten," said Green, laying down a shilling. "Thank you, sir—only four and five now wanting, ladies and gentlemen—pray, be in time—pray, be in time! This is without exception the most brilliant prize ever offered for public competition. There were only two of these werry elegant boxes made,—the unfortunate mechanic who executed them being carried off by that terrible malady, the cholera morbus,—and the other is now in the possession of his most Christian Majesty the King of the French. Only four and five wanting to commence throwing for this really perfect specimen of human ingenuity—only four and five!" "I'll take them," cried Green, throwing down two shillings more—and then the table was cleared—the dice box produced, and the crowd drew round. "Number one!—who holds number one?" inquired the keeper, arranging the paper, and sucking the end of his pencil. A young gentleman in a blue jacket and white trousers owned the lot, and, accordingly, led off the game. The lottery-keeper handed the box, and put in the dice—rattle, rattle, rattle, rattle, rattle, rattle, plop, and lift up—"seven and four are eleven"—"now again, if you please, sir," putting the dice into the box— rattle, rattle, rattle, rattle, rattle, rattle, plop, and lift up—a loud laugh—"one and two make three"—the youth bit his lips;—rattle, rattle, rattle, rattle, rattle, rattle, rattle, plop—a pause—and lift up—"threes!"—"six, three, and eleven, are twenty." "Now who holds number two?—what lady or gentleman holds number two? Pray, step forward!" The Sunflower drew near—Green looked confused— she fixed her eye upon him, half in fear, half in entreaty—would he offer to throw for her? No, by Jove, Green was not so green as all that came to, and he let her shake herself. She threw twenty-two, thereby putting an extinguisher on the boy, and raising Jemmy's chance considerably. "Three" was held by a youngster in nankeen petticoats, who would throw for himself, and shook the box violently enough to be heard at Broadstairs. He scored nineteen, and, beginning to cry immediately, was taken home. Green was next, and all eyes turned upon him, for he was a noted hand. He advanced to the table with great sangfroid, and, turning back the wrists of his coat, exhibited his beautiful sparkling paste shirt buttons, and the elegant turn of his taper hand, the middle finger of which was covered with massive rings. He took the box in a *négligé* manner, and without condescending to shake it, slid the dice out upon the table by a gentle sideway motion—"sixes!" cried all, and down the marker put twelve. At the second throw, he adopted another mode. As soon as the dice were in, he just chucked them up in the air like as many halfpence, and down they came five and six—"eleven," said the marker. With a look of triumph Green held the box for the third time, which he just turned upside down, and lo, on uncovering, there stood two—"ones!" A loud laugh burst forth, and Green looked confused. "I'm so glad!" whispered a young lady, who had made an unsuccessful "set" at Jemmy the previous season, in a tone loud enough for him to hear. "I hope he'll lose," rejoined a female friend, rather louder. "That Jemmy Green is my absolute abhorrence," observed a third. "'Orrible man, with his nasty vig," observed the mamma of the first speaker—"shouldn't have my darter not at no price." Green, however, headed the poll, having beat the Sunflower, and had still two lots in reserve. For number five, he threw twenty-five, and was immediately outstripped, amid much laughter and clapping of hands from the ladies, by number six, who in his turn fell a prey to number seven. Between eight and nine there was a very interesting contest who should be lowest, and hopes and fears were at their altitude, when Jemmy Green again turned back his coat-wrist to throw for number ten. His confidence had forsaken him a little, as indicated by a slight quivering of the under-lip, but he managed to conceal it from all except the ladies, who kept too scrutinising an eye upon him. His first throw brought sixes, which raised his spirits amazingly; but on their appearance a second time, he could scarcely contain himself, backed as he was by the plaudits of his friend Mr. Jorrocks. Then came the deciding throw—every eye was fixed on Jemmy, he shook the box, turned it down, and lo! there came seven.

"Mr. James Green is the fortunate winner of this magnificent prize!" exclaimed the youth, holding up the box in mid-air, and thereupon all the ladies crowded round Green, some to congratulate him, others to compliment him on his looks, while one or two of the least knowing tried to coax him out of his box. Jemmy, however, was too old a stager, and pocketed the box and other compliments at the same time.

Another grind of the organ, and another song followed from the same young lady, during which operation Green sent for the manager, and, after a little beating about the bush, proposed singing a song or two, if he would give him lottery-tickets gratis. He asked three shilling-tickets for each song, and finally closed for five tickets for two songs, on the understanding that he was to be announced as a distinguished amateur, who had come forward by most particular desire.

Accordingly the manager—a roundabout, red-faced, consequential little cockney—mounted the rostrum, and begged to announce to the company that that "celebrated wocalist, Mr. James Green, so well known as a distinguished amateur and conwivialist, both at Bagnigge Wells, and Vite Conduit House, LONDON, had werry kindly consented, in order to promote the hilarity of the evening, to favour the company with a song immediately after the drawing of the next lottery," and after a few high-flown compliments, which elicited a laugh from those who were up to Jemmy's mode of doing business, he concluded by offering a *papier-maché* tea-caddy for public competition, in shilling lots as before.

As soon as the drawing was over, they gave the organ a grind, and Jemmy popped up with a hop, step, and a jump, with his woolly white hat under his arm, and presented himself with a scrape and a bow to the company. After a few preparatory "hems and haws," he pulled up his gills and spoke as follows: "Ladies and gentlemen! hem"—another pull at his gills—"ladies and gentlemen—my walued friend, Mr. Kitey Graves, has announced that I will entertain the company with a song; though nothing, I assure you—hem—could be farther from my idea—hem—when my excellent friend asked me,"— "Hookey Walker!" exclaimed someone who had heard Jemmy declare the same thing half a dozen times—"and, indeed, ladies and gentlemen—hem—nothing but the werry great regard I have for Mr. Kitey Graves, who I have known and loved ever since he was the height of sixpennorth of coppers" a loud laugh followed this allusion, seeing that eighteenpenny-worth would almost measure out the speaker. On giving another "hem," and again pulling up his gills, an old Kentish farmer, in a brown coat and mahogany-coloured tops, holloaed out, "I say, sir! I'm afear'd you'll be catching cold!" "I 'opes not," replied Jemmy in a fluster, "is it raining? I've no umbrella, and my werry best coat on!" "No! raining, no!" replied the farmer, "only you've pulled at your shirt so long that I think you must be bare behind! Haw! haw! haw!" at which all the males roared with laughter, and the females hid their faces in their handkerchiefs, and tittered and giggled, and tried to be shocked. "ORDER! ORDER!" cried Mr. Jorrocks, in a loud and sonorous voice, which had the effect of quelling the riot and drawing all eyes upon himself. "Ladies and gentlemen," said he, taking off his cap with great gravity, and extending his right arm,

> Immodest words admit of no defence,
> For want of decency is want of sense;

a couplet so apropos, and so well delivered, as to have the immediate effect of restoring order and making the farmer look foolish. Encouraged by the voice of his great patron, Green once more essayed to finish his speech, which he did by a fresh assurance of the surprise by which he had been taken by the request of his friend, Kitey Graves, and an exhortation for the company to make allowance for any deficiency of "woice," inasmuch as how as labouring under "a wiolent 'orseness," for which he had long been taking pectoral lozenges. He then gave his gills another pull, felt if they were even, and struck up:

> "Bid me discourse,"

in notes, compared to which the screaming of a peacock would be perfect melody. Mr. Jorrocks having taken a conspicuous position, applauded long, loudly, and warmly, at every pause—approbation the more deserved and disinterested, inasmuch as the worthy gentleman suffers considerably from music, and only knows two tunes, one of which, he says, "is *God save the King*, and the other isn't."

Having seen his protégé fairly under way, Mr. Jorrocks gave him a hint that he would return to the "White Hart," and have supper ready by the time he was done; accordingly the Yorkshireman and he withdrew along an avenue politely formed by the separation of the company, who applauded as they passed.

An imperial quart and a half of Mr. Creed's stoutest draft port, with the orthodox proportion of lemon, cloves, sugar, and cinnamon, had almost boiled itself to perfection under the skilful superintendence of Mr. Jorrocks, on the coffee-room fire, and a table had been handsomely decorated with shrimps, lobsters, broiled bones, fried ham, poached eggs, when just as the clock had finished striking eleven, the coffee-room door opened with a rush, and in tripped Jemmy Green with his hands crammed full of packages, and his trousers' pockets sticking out like a Dutch burgomaster's. "Vell, I've done 'em brown to-night, I think," said he, depositing his hat and half a dozen packages on the sideboard, and running his fingers through his curls to make them stand up. "I've won nine lotteries, and left one undrawn when I came away, because it did not seem likely to fill. Let me see," said he, emptying his pockets,—"there is the beautiful rosewood box that I won, ven you was there; the next was a set of crimping-irons, vich I von also; the third was a jockey-vip, which I did not want and only stood one ticket for and lost; the fourth was this elegant box, with a view of Margate on the lid; then came these six sherry labels with silver rims; a snuff-box with an inwisible mouse; a coral rattle with silver bells; a silk yard measure in a walnut-shell; a couple of West India beetles; a humming-bird in a glass case, which I lost; and then these dozen bodkins with silver eyes—so that altogether I have made a pretty good night's work of it. Kitey Graves wasn't in great force, so after I had sung *Bid me Discourse*, and *I'd be a Butterfly*, I cut my stick and went to the hopposition shop, where they used me much more genteelly; giving me three tickets for a song, and introducing me in more flattering terms to the company—don't like being considered one of the nasty 'reglars,' and they should make a point of explaining that one isn't. Besides, what business had Kitey to say anything about Bagnigge Vells? a hass!—Now, perhaps, you'll favour me with some supper."

"Certainly," replied Mr. Jorrocks, patting Jemmy approvingly on the head—"you deserve some. It's only no song, no supper, and you've been singing like a nightingale;" thereupon they set to with vigorous determination.

A bright Sunday dawned, and the beach at an early hour was crowded with men in dressing-gowns of every shape, hue, and material, with buff slippers—the "regulation Margate shoeing," both for men and women. As the hour of eleven approached, and the church bells began to ring, the town seemed to awaken suddenly from a trance, and bonnets the most superb, and dresses the most extravagant, poured forth from lodgings the most miserable. Having shaved and dressed himself with more than ordinary care and attention, Mr. Jorrocks walked his friends off to church, assuring them that no one need hope to prosper throughout the week who did not attend it on the Sunday, and he marked his own devotion throughout the service by drowning the clerk's voice with his responses. After this spiritual ablution Mr. Jorrocks bethought himself of having a bodily one in the sea; and the day being excessively hot, and the tide about the proper mark, he pocketed a couple of towels out of his bedroom and went away to bathe, leaving Green and the Yorkshireman to amuse themselves at the "White Hart."

This house, as we have already stated, faces the harbour, and is a corner one, running a considerable way up the next street, with a side door communicating, as well as the front one, with the coffee-room. This room differs from the generality of coffee-rooms, inasmuch as the windows range the whole length of the room, and being very low they afford every facility for the children and passers-by to inspect the interior. Whether this is done to show the Turkey carpet, the pea-green cornices, the bright mahogany slips of tables, the gay trellised geranium-papered room, or the aristocratic visitors who frequent it, is immaterial—the description is as accurate as if George Robins had drawn it himself. In this room then, as the Yorkshireman and Green were lying dozing on three chairs apiece, each having fallen asleep to avoid the trouble of talking to the other, they were suddenly roused by loud yells and hootings at the side door, and the bursting into the coffee-room of what at first brush they thought must be a bull. The Yorkshireman jumped up, rubbed his eyes, and lo! before him stood Mr. Jorrocks, puffing like a stranded grampus, with a bunch of sea-weed under his arm and the dress in which he had started, with the exception of the dark blue stocking-net pantaloons, the place of which were supplied by a flowing white linen kilt, commonly called a shirt, in the four corners of which were knotted a few small pebbles—producing, with the Hessian boots and one thing and another, the most laughable figure imaginable. The blood of the Jorrockses was up, however, and throwing his hands in the air, he thus delivered himself. "Oh gentlemen! gentlemen!—here's a lamentable occurrence—a terrible disaster—oh dear! oh dear!—I never thought I should come to this. You know, James Green," appealing to Jemmy, "that I never was the man to raise a blush on the cheek of modesty; I have always said that 'want of decency is want of sense,' and see how I am rewarded! Oh dear! oh dear! that I should ever have trusted my pantaloons out of my sight." While all this, which was the work of a moment, was going forward, the mob, which had been shut out at the side door on Jorrocks's entry, had got round to the coffee-room window, and were all wedging their faces in to have a sight of him. It was principally composed of children, who kept up the most discordant yells, mingled with shouts of "there's old cutty shirt!"—"who's got your breeches, old cock?"—"make a scramble!"— "turn him out for another hunt!"—"turn him again!"—until, fearing for the respectability of his house, the landlord persuaded Mr. Jorrocks to retire into the bar to state his grievances. It then appeared that having travelled along the coast, as far as the first preventive stationhouse on the Ramsgate side of Margate, the grocer had thought it a convenient place for performing his intended ablutions, and, accordingly, proceeded to do what all people of either sex agree upon in such cases—namely to divest himself of his garments; but before he completed the ceremony, observing some females on the cliffs above, and not being (as he said) a man "to raise a blush on the cheek of modesty," he advanced to the water's edge in his aforesaid unmentionables, and forgetting that it was not yet high tide, he left them there, when they were speedily covered, and the pockets being full of silver and copper, of course they were "swamped." After dabbling about in the water and amusing himself with picking up sea-weed for about ten minutes, Mr. Jorrocks was horrified, on returning to the spot where he thought he had left his stocking-net pantaloons, to find that they had disappeared; and after a long fruitless search, the unfortunate gentleman was compelled to abandon the pursuit, and render himself an object of chase to all the little boys and girls who chose to follow him into Margate on his return without them.

Jorrocks, as might be expected, was very bad about his loss, and could not get over it—it stuck in his gizzard, he said—and there it seemed likely to remain. In vain Mr. Creed offered him a pair of trousers—he never had worn a pair. In vain he asked for the loan of a pair of white cords and top-boots, or even drab shorts and continuations. Mr. Creed was no sportsman, and did not keep any. The bellman could not cry the lost unmentionables because it was Sunday, and even if they should be found on the ebbing of the tide, they would take no end of time to dry. Mr. Jorrocks declared his pleasure at an end, and forthwith began making inquiries as to the best mode of getting home. The coaches were all gone, steamboats there were none, save for every place but London, and posting, he said, was "cruelly expensive." In the midst of his dilemma, "Boots," who is always the most intelligent man about an inn, popped in his curly head, and informed Mr. Jorrocks that the Unity hoy, a most commodious vessel, neat, trim, and water-tight, manned by his own maternal uncle, was going to cut away to London at three o'clock, and would land him before he could say "Jack Robinson." Mr. Jorrocks jumped at the offer, and forthwith attiring himself in a pair of Mr. Creed's loose inexpressibles, over which he drew his Hessian boots, he tucked the hamper containing the knuckle of veal and other etceteras under one arm, and the bunch of sea-weed he had been busy collecting, instead of watching his clothes, under the other, and, followed by his friends, made direct for the vessel.

Everybody knows, or ought to know, what a hoy is—it is a large sailing-boat, sometimes with one deck, sometimes with none; and the Unity, trading in bulky goods, was of the latter description, though there was a sort of dog-hole at the stern, which the master dignified by the name of a "state cabin," into which he purposed putting Mr. Jorrocks, if the weather should turn cold before they arrived. The wind, however, he said, was so favourable, and his cargo—"timber and fruit," as he described it, that is to say, broomsticks and potatoes—so light, that he warranted landing him at Blackwall at least by ten o'clock, where he could either sleep, or get a short stage or an omnibus on to Leadenhall Street. The vessel looked anything but tempting, neither was the captain's appearance prepossessing, still Mr. Jorrocks, all things considered, thought he would chance it; and depositing his hamper and sea-weed, and giving special instructions about having his pantaloons cried in the morning—recounting that besides the silver, and eighteen-pence in copper, there was a steel pencil-case with "J.J." on the seal at the top, an anonymous letter, and two keys—he took an affectionate leave of his friends, and stepped on board, the vessel was shoved off and stood out to sea.

Monday morning drew the cockneys from their roosts betimes, to take their farewell splash and dive in the sea. As the day advanced, the bustle and confusion on the shore and in the town increased, and everyone seemed on the move. The ladies paid their last visits to the bazaars and shell shops, and children extracted the last ounce of exertion from the exhausted leg-weary donkeys. Meanwhile the lords of the creation strutted about, some in dressing-gowns, others, "full puff," with bags and boxes under their arms—while sturdy porters were wheeling barrows full of luggage to the jetty. The bell-man went round dressed in a blue and red cloak, with a gold hatband. Ring-a-ding, ring-a-ding, ring-a-ding, dong, went the bell, and the gaping cockneys congregated around. He commenced—"To be sould in the market-place a quantity of fresh ling." Ring-a-ding, ring-a-ding, dong: "The *Royal Adelaide*, fast and splendid steam-packet, Capt. Whittingham, will leave the pier this morning at nine o'clock precisely, and land the passengers at London Bridge Steam-packet Wharf—fore cabin fares and children four shillings—saloon five shillings." Ring-a-ding, ring-a-ding, dong: "The superb and splendid steam-packet, the *Magnet*, will leave the pier this morning at nine o'clock precisely, and land the passengers at the St. Catherine Docks—fore-cabin fares and children four shillings—saloon five shillings." Ring-a-ding, ring-a-ding, dong: "Lost at the back of James Street—a lady's black silk—black lace wale—whoever has found the same, and will bring it to the cryer, shall receive one shilling reward." Ring-a-ding, ring-a-ding, dong: "Lost, last night, between the jetty and the York Hotel, a little boy, as answers to the name of Spot, whoever has found the same, and will bring him to the cryer, shall receive a reward of half-a-crown." Ring-a-ding, ring-a-ding, dong: "Lost, stolen, or strayed, or otherwise conveyed, a brown-and-white King Charles's setter as answers to the name of Jacob Jones. Whoever has found the same, or will give such information as shall lead to the detection and conversion of the offender or offenders shall be handsomely rewarded." Ring-a-ding, ring-a-ding, dong: "Lost below the prewentive sarvice station by a gentleman of great respectability—a pair of blue knit pantaloons, containing eighteen penny-worth of copper—a steel pencil-case—a werry anonymous letter, and two keys. Whoever will bring the same to the cryer shall receive a reward.—*God save the King!*"

Then, as the hour of nine approached, what a concourse appeared! There were fat and lean, and short and tall, and middling, going away, and fat and lean, and short and tall, and middling, waiting to see them off; Green, as usual, making himself conspicuous, and canvassing everyone he could lay hold of for the *Magnet* steamer. At the end of the jetty, on each side, lay the *Royal Adelaide* and the *Magnet*, with as fierce a contest for patronage as ever was witnessed. Both decks were crowded with anxious faces—for the Monday's steamboat race is as great an event as a Derby, and a cockney would as lieve lay on an outside horse as patronise a boat that was likely to let another pass her. Nay, so high is the enthusiasm carried, that books are regularly made on the occasion, and there is as much clamour for bets as in the ring at Epsom or Newmarket. "Tomkins,

I'll lay you a dinner—for three—*Royal Adelaide* against the *Magnet*," bawled Jenkins from the former boat. "Done," cries Tomkins. "The *Magnet* for a bottle of port," bawled out another. "A whitebait dinner for two, the *Magnet* reaches Greenwich first." "What should you know about the *Magnet*?" inquires the mate of the *Royal Adelaide*. "Vy, I think I should know something about nauticals too, for Lord St. Wincent was my godfather." "I'll bet five shillings on the *Royal Adelaide*." "I'll take you," says another. "I'll bet a bottom of brandy on the *Magnet*," roars out the mate. "Two goes of Hollands', the *Magnet's* off Herne Bay before the *Royal Adelaide*." "I'll lay a pair of crimping-irons against five shillings, the *Magnet* beats the *Royal Adelaide*," bellowed out Green, who having come on board, had mounted the paddle-box. "I say, Green, I'll lay you an even five if you like." "Well, five pounds," cries Green. "No, shillings," says his friend. "Never bet in shillings," replies Green, pulling up his shirt collar. "I'll bet fifty pounds," he adds,-getting valiant. "I'll bet a hundred ponds—a thousand pounds—a million pounds—half the National Debt, if you like."

Precisely as the jetty clock finishes striking nine, the ropes are slipped, and the rival steamers stand out to sea with beautiful precision, amid the crying, the kissing of hands, the raising of hats, the waving of handkerchiefs, from those who are left for the week, while the passengers are cheered by adverse tunes from the respective bands on board. The *Magnet*, having the outside, gets the breeze first hand, but the *Royal Adelaide* keeps well alongside, and both firemen being deeply interested in the event, they boil up a tremendous gallop, without either being able to claim the slightest advantage for upwards of an hour and a half, when the *Royal Adelaide* manages to shoot ahead for a few minutes, amid the cheers and exclamations of her crew. The *Magnet's* fireman, however, is on the alert, and a few extra pokes of the fire presently bring the boats together again, in which state they continue, nose and nose, until the stiller water of the side of the Thames favours the *Magnet*, and she shoots ahead amid the cheers and vociferations of her party, and is not neared again during the voyage.

This excitement over, the respective crews sink into a sort of melancholy sedateness, and Green in vain endeavours to kick up a quadrille. The men were exhausted and the women dispirited, and altogether they were a very different set of beings to what they were on the Saturday. Dull faces and dirty-white ducks were the order of the day.

The only incident of the voyage was, that on approaching the mouth of the Medway, the *Royal Adelaide* was hailed by a vessel, and the Yorkshireman, on looking overboard, was shocked to behold Mr. Jorrocks sitting in the stern of his hoy in the identical position he had taken up the previous day, with his bunch of sea-weed under his elbow, and the remains of the knuckle of veal, ham, and chicken, spread on the hamper before him. "Stop her?" cried the Yorkshireman, and then hailing Mr. Jorrocks he holloaed out, "In the name of the prophet, Figs, what are you doing there?" "Oh, gentlemen! gentlemen!" exclaimed Mr. Jorrocks, brightening up as he recognised the boat, "take compassion on a most misfortunate indiwidual—here have I been in this 'orrid 'oy, ever since three o'clock yesterday afternoon and here I seem likely to end my days—for blow me tight if I couldn't swim as fast as it goes." "Look sharp, then," cried the mate of the steamer, "and chuck us up your luggage." Up went the sea-weed, the hamper, and Mr. Jorrocks; and before the hoyman awoke out of a nap, into which he had composed himself on resigning the rudder to his lad, our worthy citizen was steaming away a mile before his vessel, bilking him of his fare.

Who does not recognise in this last disaster, the truth of the old adage?

"Most haste, least speed."

VIII
THE ROAD: ENGLISH AND FRENCH

"JORROCKS'S France, in three wolumes, would sound werry well," observed our worthy citizen, one afternoon, to his confidential companion the Yorkshireman, as they sat in the veranda in Coram Street, eating red currants and sipping cold whiskey punch; "and I thinks I could make something of it. They tells me that at the 'west end' the booksellers will give forty pounds for anything that will run into three wolumes, and one might soon pick up as much matter as would stretch into that quantity."

The above observation was introduced in a long conversation between Mr. Jorrocks and his friend, relative to an indignity that had been offered him by the rejection by the editor of a sporting periodical of a long treatise on eels, which, independently of the singularity of diction, had become so attenuated in the handling, as to have every appearance of filling three whole numbers of the work; and Mr. Jorrocks had determined to avenge the insult by turning author on his own account. The Yorkshireman, ever ready for amusement, cordially supported Mr. Jorrocks in his views, and a bargain was soon struck between them, the main stipulations of which were, that Mr. Jorrocks should find cash, and the Yorkshireman should procure information.

Accordingly, on the Saturday after, the nine o'clock Dover heavy drew up at the "Bricklayers' Arms," with Mr. Jorrocks on the box seat, and the Yorkshireman imbedded among the usual heterogeneous assembly—soldiers, sailors, Frenchmen, fishermen, ladies' maids, and footmen—that compose the cargo of these coaches. Here they were assailed with the usual persecution from the tribe of Israel, in the shape of a hundred merchants, proclaiming the virtues of their wares; one with black-lead pencils, twelve a shilling, with an invitation to "cut 'em and try 'em"; another with a good pocket-knife, "twelve blades and saw, sir"; a third, with a tame squirrel and a piping bullfinch, that could whistle *God save the King* and the *White Cockade*—to be given for an old coat. "Buy a silver guard-chain for your vatch, sir!" cried a dark eyed urchin, mounting the fore-wheel, and holding a bunch of them in Mr. Jorrocks's face; "buy pocketbook, memorandum-book!" whined another. "Keepsake—Forget-me-not—all the last year's annuals at half-price!" "Sponge cheap, sponge! take a piece, sir— take a piece." "Patent leather straps." "Barcelona nuts. Slippers. *Morning Hurl* (*Herald*). Rhubarb. 'Andsome dog-collar, sir, cheap!—do to fasten your wife up with!"

"Stand clear, ye warmints!" cries the coachman, elbowing his way among them—and, remounting the box, he takes the whip and reins out of Mr. Jorrocks's hands, cries "All right behind? sit tight!" and off they go.

The day was fine, and the hearts of all seemed light and gay. The coach, though slow, was clean and smart, the harness bright and well-polished, while the sleek brown horses poked their heads about at ease, without the torture of the bearing-rein. The coachman, like his vehicle, was heavy, and had he been set on all fours, a party of six might have eat off his back. Thus they proceeded at a good steady substantial sort of pace; trotting on level ground, walking up hills, and dragging down inclines. Nor among the whole party was there a murmur of discontent at the pace. Most of the passengers seemed careless which way they went, so long as they did but move, and they rolled through the Garden of England with the most stoical indifference. We know not whether it has ever struck the reader, but the travellers by Dover coaches are less captious about pace than those on most others.

And now let us fancy our friends up, and down, Shooter's Hill, through Dartford, Northfleet, and Gravesend—at which latter place, the first foreign symptom appears, in words, "Poste aux Chevaux," on the door-post of the inn; and let us imagine them bowling down Rochester Hill at a somewhat amended pace, with the old castle, by the river Medway, the towns of Chatham, Strood and Rochester full before them, and the finely wooded country extending round in pleasing variety of hill and dale. As they reach the foot of the hill, the guard commences a solo on his bugle, to give notice to the innkeeper to have the coach dinner on the table. All huddled together, inside and out, long passengers and short ones, they cut across the bridge, rattle along the narrow street, sparking the mud from the newly-watered streets on the shop windows and passengers on each side, and pull up at the "Pig and Crossbow," with a jerk and a dash as though they had been travelling at the rate of twelve miles an hour. Two other coaches are "dining," while some few passengers, whose "hour is not yet come," sit patiently on the roof, or pace up and down the street with short and hurried turns, anxious to see the horses brought out that are to forward them on their journey. And what a commotion this new arrival creates! From the arched doorway of the inn issue two chamber-maids, one in curls the other in a cap; Boots, with both curls and a cap, and a ladder in his hand; a knock-kneed waiter, with a dirty duster, to count noses, while the neat landlady, in a spruce black silk gown and clean white apron, stands smirking, smiling, and rubbing her hands down her sides, inveigling the passengers into the house, where she will turn them over to the waiters to take their chance the instant she gets them in. About the door the usual idlers are assembled.—A coachman out of place, a beggar out at the elbows, a sergeant in uniform, and three recruits with ribbons in their hats; a captain with his boots cut for corns, the coachman that is to drive to Dover, a youth in a straw hat and a rowing shirt, the little inquisitive old man of the place—who sees all the midday coaches change horses, speculates on the passengers and sees who the parcels are for—and, though last but not least, Mr. Bangup, the "varmint" man, the height of whose ambition is to be taken for a coachman. As the coach pulled up, he was in the bar taking a glass of cold sherry "without" and a cigar, which latter he brings out lighted in his mouth, with his shaved white hat stuck knowingly on one side, and the thumbs of his brown hands thrust into the arm-holes of his waistcoat, throwing back his single breasted fancy buttoned green coat, and showing a cream coloured cravat, fastened with a gold coach-and-four pin, which, with a buff waistcoat and tight drab trousers buttoning over the boot, complete his "toggery," as he would call it. His whiskers are large and riotous in the extreme, while his hair is clipped as close as a charity schoolboy's. The coachman and he are on the best of terms, as the outward twist of their elbows and jerks of the head on meeting testify. His conversation is short and slangy, accompanied with the correct nasal twang. After standing and blowing a few puffs, during which time the passengers have all alighted, and the coachman has got through the thick of his business, he takes the cigar out of his mouth, and, spitting on the flags, addresses his friend with, "Y've got the old near-side leader back from Joe, I see." "Yes, Mr. Bangup, yes," replies his friend, "but I had some work first— our gov'rnor was all for the change—at last, says I to our 'osskeeper, says I, it arn't no use your harnessing that 'ere roan for me any more, for as how I von't drive him, so it's not to no use harnessing of him, for I von't be gammon'd out of my team not by none on them, therefore it arn't to never no use harnessing of him again for me." "So you did 'em," observes Mr. Bangup. "Lord bless ye, yes! it warn't to no use aggravising about it, for says I, I von't stand it, so it warn't to no manner of use harnessing of him again for me." "Come, Smith, what are you chaffing there about?" inquires the landlord, coming out with the wide-spread way-bill in his hands, "have you two insides?" "No, gov'rnor, I has but von, and that's precious empty, haw! haw! haw!" "Well, but now get Brown to blow his horn early, and you help to hurry the passengers away from my grub, and may be I'll give you your dinner for your trouble," replies the landlord, reckoning he would save both his meat and his horses by the experiment. "Ay, there goes the dinner!" added he, just as Mr. Jorrocks's voice was heard inside the "Pig and Crossbow," giving a most tremendous roar for his food.—"Pork at the top, and pork at the bottom," the host observes to the waiter in passing, "and mind, put the joints before the women—they are slow carvers."

While the foregoing scene was enacting outside, our travellers had been driven through the passage into a little, dark, dingy room at the back of the house, with a dirty, rain-bespattered window, looking against a whitewashed blank wall. The table, which was covered with a thrice-used cloth, was set out with lumps of bread, knives, and two and three pronged forks laid alternately. Altogether it was anything but inviting, but coach passengers are very complacent; and on the Dover road it matters little if they are not. The bustle of preparation was soon over. Coats No. 1, No. 2, and No. 3, are taken off in succession, for some people wear top-coats to keep out the "heat"; chins are released from their silken jeopardy, hats are hid in corners, and fur caps thrust into pockets of the owners. Inside passengers eye outside ones with suspicion, while a deaf gentleman, who has left his trumpet in the coach, meets an acquaintance whom he has not seen for seven years, and can only shake hands and grin to the movements of the lips of the speaker. "You find it very warm inside, I should think, sir?" "Thank ye, thank ye, my good friend; I'm rayther deaf, but I presume you're inquiring after my wife and daughters—they are very well, I thank ye." "Where will you sit at dinner?" rejoins the first speaker, in hopes of a more successful hit. "It is two years since I saw him." "No; where will you sit, sir? I said." "Oh, John? I beg your pardon—I'm rayther deaf—he's in Jamaica with his regiment." "Come, waiter, BRING DINNER!" roared Mr.

Jorrocks, at the top of his voice, being the identical shout that was heard outside, and presently the two dishes of pork, a couple of ducks, and a lump of half-raw, sadly mangled, cold roast beef, with waxy potatoes and overgrown cabbages, were scattered along the table. "What a beastly dinner!" exclaims an inside dandy, in a sable-collared frock-coat—"the whole place reeks with onions and vulgarity. Waiter, bring me a silver fork!" "Allow me to duck you, ma'am?" inquires an outside passenger, in a facetious tone, of a female in a green silk cloak, as he turns the duck over in the dish. "Thank you, sir, but I've some pork coming." "Will you take some of this thingumbob?" turning a questionable-looking pig's countenance over in its pewter bed. "You are in considerable danger, my friend—you are in considerable danger," drawls forth the superfine insider to an outsider opposite. "How's that?" inquires the former in alarm. "Why, you are eating with your knife, and you are in considerable danger of cutting your mouth".—What is the matter at the far end of the table?—a lady in russet brown, with a black velvet bonnet and a feather, in convulsions. "She's choking by Jove! hit her on the back—gently, gently—she's swallowed a fish-bone." "I'll lay five to two she dies," cries Mr. Bolus, the sporting doctor of Sittingbourne. She coughs—up comes a couple of tooth-picks, she having drunk off a green glass of them in mistake.

"Now hark'e, waiter! there's the guard blowing his horn, and we have scarcely had a bite apiece," cries Mr. Jorrocks, as that functionary sounded his instrument most energetically in the passage; "blow me tight, if I stir before the full half-hour's up, so he may blow till he's black in the face." "Take some cheese, sir?" inquires the waiter. "No, surely not, some more pork, and then some tarts". "Sorry, sir, we have no tarts we can recommend. Cheese is partiklar good." [Enter coachman, peeled down to a more moderate-sized man.]

"Leaves ye here, if you please, sur." "With all my heart, my good friend." "Please to remember the coachman—driv ye thirty miles." "Yes, but you'll recollect how saucy you were about my wife's bonnet-box there's sixpence between us for you." "Oh, sur! I'm sure I didn't mean no unpurliteness. I 'opes you'll forget it; it was werry aggravising, certainly, but driv ye thirty miles. 'Opes you'll give a trifle more, thirty miles." "No, no, no more; so be off." "Please to remember the coachman, ma'am, thirty miles!" "Leaves ye here, sir, if you please; goes no further, sir; thirty miles, ma'am; all the vay from Lunnun, sir."

A loud flourish on the bugle caused the remainder of the gathering to be made in dumb show, and having exhausted his wind, the guard squeezed through the door, and, with an extremely red face, assured the company that "time was hup" and the "coach quite ready." Then out came the purses, brown, green, and blue, with the usual inquiry, "What's dinner, waiter?" "Two and six, dinner, beer, three,—two and nine yours," replied the knock-kneed caitiff to the first inquirer, pushing a blue-and-white plate under his nose; "yours is three and six, ma'am;—two glasses of brandy-and-water, four shillings, if you please sir—a bottle of real Devonshire cider."—"You must change me a sovereign," handing one out. "Certainly, sir," upon which the waiter, giving it a loud ring upon the table, ran out of the room. "Now, gentlemen and ladies! pray, come, time's hup—carn't wait—must go"—roars the guard, as the passengers shuffle themselves into their coats, cloaks, and cravats, and Joe "Boots" runs up the passage with the ladder for the lady. "Now, my dear Mrs. Sprat, good-bye.— God bless you, and remember me most kindly to your husband and dear little ones —and pray, write soon," says an elderly lady, as she hugs and kisses a youngish one at the door, who has been staying with her for a week, during which time they have quarrelled regularly every night. "Have you all your things, dearest? three boxes, five parcels, an umbrella, a parasol, the cage for Tommy's canary, and the bundle in the red silk handkerchief—then good-bye, my beloved, step up—and now, Mr. Guard, you know where to set her down." "Good-bye, dearest Mrs. Jackson, all right, thank you," replies Mrs. Sprat, stepping up the ladder, and adjusting herself in the gammon board opposite the guard, the seat the last comer generally gets.—"But stay! I've forgot my reticule—it's on the drawers in the bedroom—stop, coachman! I say, guard!" "Carn't wait, ma'am—time's hup"—and just at this moment a two-horse coach is heard stealing up the street, upon which the coachman calls to the horse-keepers to "stand clear with their cloths, and take care no one pays them twice over," gives a whistling hiss to his leaders, the double thong to his wheelers, and starts off at a trot, muttering something about, "cuss'd pair-'oss coach,— convict-looking passengers," observing confidentially to Mr. Jorrocks, as he turned the angle of the street, "that he would rather be hung off a long stage, than die a natural death on a short one," while the guard drowns the voices of the lady who has left her reticule, and of the gentleman who has got no change for his sovereign, in a hearty puff of:

Rule Britannia,—Britannia rule the waves.
Britons, never, never, never, shall be slaves!

Blithely and merrily, like all coach passengers after feeding, our party rolled steadily along, with occasional gibes at those they met or passed, such as telling waggoners their linch-pins were out; carters' mates, there were nice pocket-knives lying on the road; making urchins follow the coach for miles by holding up shillings and mock parcels; or simple equestrians dismount in a jiffy on telling them their horses' shoes were not all on "before." [19]Towards the decline of the day, Dover heights appeared in view, with the stately castle guarding the Channel, which seen through the clear atmosphere of an autumnal evening, with the French coast conspicuous in the distance, had more the appearance of a wide river than a branch of the sea.

The coachman mended his pace a little, as he bowled along the gentle descents or rounded the base of some lofty hill, and pulling up at Lydden took a glass of soda-water and brandy, while four strapping greys, with highly-polished, richly-plated harness, and hollyhocks at their heads, were put to, to trot the last

---

[19] This is more of a hunting-field joke than a road one. "Have I all my shoes on?" "They are not all on before."

few miles into Dover. Paying-time being near, the guard began to do the amiable—hoped Mrs. Sprat had ridden comfortable; and the coachman turned to the gentleman whose sovereign was left behind to assure him he would bring his change the next day, and was much comforted by the assurance that he was on his way to Italy for the winter. As the coach approached Charlton Gate, the guard flourished his bugle and again struck up *Rule Britannia*, which lasted the whole breadth of the market-place, and length of Snargate Street, drawing from Mr. Muddle's shop the few loiterers who yet remained, and causing Mr. Le Plastrier, the patriotic moth-impaler, to suspend the examination of the bowels of a watch, as they rattled past his window.

At the door of the "Ship Hotel" the canary-coloured coach of Mr. Wright, the landlord, with four piebald horses, was in waiting for him to take his evening drive, and Mrs. Wright's pony phaeton, with a neat tiger in a blue frock-coat and leathers, was also stationed behind to convey her a few miles on the London road. Of course the equipages of such important personages could not be expected to move for a common stage-coach, consequently it pulled up a few yards from the door. It is melancholy to think that so much spirit should have gone unrewarded, or in other words, that Mr. Wright should have gone wrong in his affairs.—Mrs. Ramsbottom said she never understood the meaning of the term, "The Crown, and Bill of Rights (Wright's)," until she went to Rochester. Many people, we doubt not, retain a lively recollection of the "bill of Wright's of Dover." But to our travellers.

"Now, sir! this be Dover, that be the Ship, I be the coachman, and we goes no further," observed the amphibious-looking coachman, in a pea-jacket and top-boots, to Mr. Jorrocks, who still kept his seat on the box, as if he expected, that because they booked people "through to Paris," at the coach office in London, that the vehicle crossed the Channel and conveyed them on the other side. At this intimation, Mr. Jorrocks clambered down, and was speedily surrounded by touts and captains of vessels soliciting his custom. "*Bonjour*, me Lor'," said a gaunt French sailor in ear-rings, and a blue-and-white jersey shirt, taking off a red nightcap with mock politeness, "you shall be cross." "What's that about?" inquires Mr. Jorrocks—"cross! what does the chap mean?" "Ten shillin', just, me Lor'," replied the man. "Cross for ten shillings," muttered Mr. Jorrocks, "vot does the Mouncheer mean? Hope he hasn't picked my pocket." "I—you—vill," said the sailor slowly, using his fingers to enforce his meaning, "take to France," pointing south, "for ten shillin' in my *bateau*, me Lor'," continued the sailor, with a grin of satisfaction as he saw Mr. Jorrocks began to comprehend him. "Ah! I twig—you'll take me across the water." said our citizen chuckling at the idea of understanding French and being called a Lord—"for ten shillings—half-sovereign in fact." "Don't go with him, sir," interrupted a Dutch-built English tar; "he's got nothing but a lousy lugger that will be all to-morrow in getting over, if it ever gets at all; and the *Royal George*, superb steamer, sails with a King's Messenger and dispatches for all the foreign courts at half-past ten, and must be across by twelve, whether it can or not." "Please take a card for the *Brocklebank*—quickest steamer out of Dover—wind's made expressly to suit her, and she can beat the *Royal George* like winking. Passengers never sick in the most uproarious weather," cried another tout, running the corner of his card into Mr. Jorrocks's eye to engage his attention. Then came the captain of the French mail-packet, who was dressed much like a new policeman, with an embroidered collar to his coat, and a broad red band round a forage cap which he raised with great politeness, as he entreated Mr. Jorrocks's patronage of his high-pressure engine, "vich had beat a balloon, and vod take him for half less than noting." A crowd collected, in the centre of which stood Mr. Jorrocks perfectly unmoved, with his wig awry and his carpet-bag under his arm. "Gentlemen," said he, extending his right hand, "you seem to me to be desperately civil—your purliteness appears to know no bounds—but, to be candid with you, I beg to say that whoever will carry me across the herring pond cheapest shall have my custom, so now begin and bid downwards." "Nine shillings," said an Englishman directly—"eight" replied a Frenchman—"seven and sixpence"—"seven shillings"—"six and sixpence"—"six shillings"—"five and sixpence"; at last it came down to five shillings, at which there were two bidders, the French captain and the tout of the *Royal George*,—and Mr. Jorrocks, like a true born Briton, promised his patronage to the latter, at which the Frenchmen shrugged up their shoulders, and burst out a-laughing, one calling him, "my Lor' Ros-bif," and the other "Monsieur God-dem," as they walked off in search of other victims.

None but the natives of Dover can tell what the weather is, unless the wind comes directly off the sea, and it was not until Mr. Jorrocks proceeded to embark after breakfast the next morning, that he ascertained there was a heavy swell on, so quiet had the heights kept the gambols of Boreas. Three steamers were simmering into action on the London-hotel side of the harbour, in one of which—the *Royal George*—two britzkas and a barouche were lashed ready for sea, while the custom-house porters were trundling barrows full of luggage under the personal superintendence of a little shock-headed French commissionnaire of Mr. Wright's in a gold-laced cap, and the other gentry of the same profession from the different inns. As the *Royal George* lay nearly level with the quay, Mr. Jorrocks stepped on board without troubling himself to risk his shins among the steps of a ladder that was considerately thrust into the place of embarkation; and as soon as he set foot upon deck, of course he was besieged by the usual myriad of land sharks. First came Monsieur the Commissionnaire with his book, out of which he enumerated two portmanteaus and two carpet-bags, for each of which he made a specific charge leaving his own gratuity optional with his employer; then came Mr. Boots to ask for something for showing them the way; after him the porter of the inn for carrying their cloaks and great-coats, all of which Mr. Jorrocks submitted to, most philosophically, but when the interpreter of the deaf and dumb ladder man demanded something for the use of the ladder, his indignation got the better of him and he exclaimed loud enough to be heard by all on deck, "Surely you wouldn't charge a man for what he has not enjoyed!"

A voyage is to many people like taking an emetic—they look at the medicine and wish it well over, and look at the sea and wish themselves well over. Everything looked bright and gay at Dover—the cliffs seemed whiter than ever—the sailors had on clean trousers, and the few people that appeared in the streets were dressed in their Sunday best. The cart-horses were seen feeding leisurely on the hills, and there was a placid calmness about everything on shore, which the travellers would fain have had extended to the sea. They came slowly and solemnly upon deck, muffled up in cloaks and coats, some with their passage money in their hands, and took their places apparently with the full expectation of being sick.

The French packet-boat first gave symptoms of animation, in the shape of a few vigorous puffs from the boiler, which were responded to by the *Royal George*, whose rope was slipped without the usual tinkle of the bell, and she shot out to sea, closely followed by the Frenchman, who was succeeded by the other English boat. Three or four tremendous long protracted dives, each followed by a majestic rise on the bosom of the waves, denoted the crossing of the bar; and just as the creaking of the cordage, the flapping of the sails, and the nervous quivering of the paddles, as they lost their hold of the water, were in full vigour, the mate crossed the deck with a large white basin in his hand, the sight of which turned the stomachs of half the passengers. Who shall describe the misery that ensued? The groans and moans of the sufferers, increasing every minute, as the vessel heaved and dived, and rolled and creaked, while hand-basins multiplied as half-sick passengers caught the green countenance and fixed eye of some prostrate sufferer and were overcome themselves.

Mr. Jorrocks, what with his Margate trips, and a most substantial breakfast of beef-steaks and porter, tea, eggs, muffins, prawns, and fried ham, held out as long as anybody—indeed, at one time the odds were that he would not be sick at all; and he kept walking up and down deck like a true British tar. In one of his turns he was observed to make a full stop.—Immediately before the boiler his eye caught a cadaverous-looking countenance that rose between the top of a blue camlet cloak, and the bottom of a green travelling-cap, with a large patent-leather peak; he was certain that he knew it, and, somehow or other, he thought, not favourably. The passenger was in that happy mood just debating whether he should hold out against sickness any longer, or resign himself unreservedly to its horrors, when Mr. Jorrocks's eye encountered his, and the meeting did not appear to contribute to his happiness. Mr. Jorrocks paused and looked at him steadily for some seconds, during which time his thoughts made a rapid cast over his memory. "Sergeant Bumptious, by gum!" exclaimed he, giving his thigh a hearty slap, as the deeply indented pock-marks on the learned gentleman's face betrayed his identity. "Sergeant," said he, going up to him, "I'm werry 'appy to see ye—may be in the course of your practice at Croydon you've heard that there are more times than one to catch a thief." "Who are you?" inquired the sergeant with a growl, just at which moment the boat gave a roll, and he wound up the inquiry by a donation to the fishes. "Who am I?" replied Mr. Jorrocks, as soon as he was done, "I'll soon tell ye that—I'm Mr. JORROCKS! Jorrocks wersus Cheatum, in fact—now that you have got your bullying toggery off, I'll be 'appy to fight ye either by land or sea." "Oh-h-h-h!" groaned the sergeant at the mention of the latter word, and thereupon he put his head over the boat and paid his second subscription. Mr. Jorrocks stood eyeing him, and when the sergeant recovered, he observed with apparent mildness and compassion, "Now, my dear sergeant, to show ye that I can return good for evil, allow me to fatch you a nice 'ot mutton chop!" "Oh-h-h-h!" groaned the sergeant, as though he would die. "Or perhaps you'd prefer a cut of boiled beef with yellow fat, and a dab of cabbage?" an alternative which was too powerful for the worthy citizen himself—for, like Sterne with his captive, he had drawn a picture that his own imagination could not sustain—and, in attempting to reach the side of the boat, he cascaded over the sergeant, and they rolled over each other, senseless and helpless upon deck.

"Mew, mew," screamed the seagulls;—"creak, creak," went the cordage;—"flop, flop," went the sails; round went the white basins, and the steward with the mop; and few passengers would have cared to have gone overboard, when, at the end of three hours' misery, the captain proclaimed that they were running into still water off Boulogne. This intimation was followed by the collection of the passage money by the mate, and the jingling of a tin box by the steward, under the noses of the party, for perquisites for the crew. Jorrocks and the sergeant lay together like babes in the wood until they were roused by this operation, when, with a parting growl at his companion, Mr. Jorrocks got up; and though he had an idea in his own mind that a man had better live abroad all his life than encounter such misery as he had undergone, for the purpose of returning to England, he recollected his intended work upon France, and began to make his observations upon the town of Boulogne, towards which the vessel was rapidly steaming. "Not half so fine as Margate," said he; "the houses seem all afraid of the sea, and turn their ends to it instead of fronting it, except yon great white place, which I suppose is the baths"; and, taking his hunting telescope out of his pocket, he stuck out his legs and prepared to make an observation. "How the people are swarming down to see us!" he exclaimed. "I see such a load of petticoats—glad Mrs. J—— ain't with us; may have some fun here, I guess. Dear me, wot lovely women! wot ankles! beat the English, hollow—would give something to be a single man!" While he made these remarks, the boat ran up the harbour in good style, to the evident gratification of the multitude who lined the pier from end to end, and followed her in her passage. "Ease her! stop her!" at last cried the captain, as she got opposite a low wooden guard-house, midway down the port. A few strokes of the paddles sent her up to the quay, some ropes were run from each end of the guard-house down to the boat, within which space no one was admitted except about a dozen soldiers or custom-house officers—in green coats, white trousers, black sugar-loaf "caps," and having swords by their sides—and some thick-legged fisherwomen, with long gold ear-rings, to lower the ladder for disembarkation. The idlers, that is to say, all the inhabitants of Boulogne, range themselves outside the ropes on foot, horseback, in carriages, or anyhow, to take the chance of seeing someone they know, to laugh at the melancholy looks of those who have been sick, and to criticise the company, who are turned into the guarded space like a flock of sheep before them.

Mr. Jorrocks, having scaled the ladder, gave himself a hearty and congratulatory shake on again finding himself on terra firma, and sticking his hat jauntily on one side, as though he didn't know what sea-sickness was, proceeded to run his eye along the spectators on one side of the ropes; when presently he was heard to exclaim, "My vig, there's Thompson! He owes us a hundred pounds, and has been doing these three years." And thereupon he bolted up to a fine looking young fellow—with mustachios, in a hussar foraging cap stuck on one side of his head, dressed in a black velvet shooting-jacket, and with half a jeweller's shop about him in the way of chains, brooches, rings and buttons—who had brought a good-looking bay horse to bear with his chest against the cords. "Thompson," said Mr. Jorrocks, in a firm tone of voice, "how are you?" "How do ye do, Mister Jorrocks," drawled out the latter, taking a cigar from his mouth, and puffing a cloud of smoke over the grocer's head. "Well, I'm werry well, but I should like to have a few moments' conversation with you." "Would ye?" said Thompson, blowing another cloud. "Yes, I would; you remember that 'ere little bill you got Simpkins to discount for you one day when I was absent; we have had it by us a long time now, and it is about time you were taking it up." "You think so, do you, Mister Jorrocks; can't you renew it? I'll give you a draft on Aldgate pump for the amount." "Come, none of your funning with me, I've had enough of your nonsense: give me my pewter, or I'll have that horse from under you; for though it has got the hair rubbed off its near knee, it will do werry well to carry me with the Surrey occasionally." "You old fool," said Thompson, "you forget where you are; if I could pay you your little bill, do you suppose I would be here? You can't squeeze blood out of a turnip, can ye? But I'll tell you what, my covey, if I can't give you satisfaction in money, you shall give me the satisfaction of a gentleman, if you don't take care what you are about, you old tinker. By Jove, I'll order pistols and coffee for two to-morrow morning at Napoleon's column, and let the daylight through your carcass if you utter another syllable about the bill. Why, now, you stare as Balaam did at his ass, when he found it capable of holding an argument with him!"

And true enough, Jorrocks was dumbfounded at this sort of reply from a creditor, it not being at all in accordance with the *Lex mercatoria*, or law of merchants, and quite unknown on 'Change. Before, however, he had time to recover his surprise, all the passengers having entered the roped area, one of the green-coated gentry gave him a polite twist by the coat-tail, and with a wave of the hand and bend of his body, beckoned him to proceed with the crowd into the guard-house. After passing an outer room, they entered the bureau by a door in the middle of a wooden partition, where two men were sitting with pens ready to enter the names of the arrivers in ledgers.

"Votre nom et designation?" said one of them to Mr. Jorrocks—who, with a bad start, had managed to squeeze in first—to which Mr. Jorrocks shook his head. "Sare, what's your name, sare?" inquired the same personage. "JORROCKS," was the answer, delivered with great emphasis, and thereupon the secretary wrote "Shorrock." "—Monsieur Shorrock," said he, looking up, "votre profession, Monsieur? Vot you are, sare?" "A grocer," replied Mr. Jorrocks, which caused a titter from those behind who meant to sink the shop. "Marchand-Epicier," wrote the bureau-keeper. "Quel age avez-vous, Monsieur? How old you are, sare?" "Two pound twelve," replied Mr. Jorrocks, surprised at his inquisitiveness. "No, sare, not vot monnay you have, sare, hot old you are, sare." "Well, two pound twelve, fifty-two in fact." Mr. Jorrocks was then passed out, to take his chance among the touts and commissionaires of the various hotels, who are enough to pull passengers to pieces in their solicitations for custom. In Boulogne, however, no man with money is ever short of friends; and Thompson having given the hint to two or three acquaintances as he rode up street, there were no end of broken-down sportsmen, levanters, and gentlemen who live on the interest of what they owe other people, waiting to receive Mr. Jorrocks. The greetings on their parts were most cordial and enthusiastic, and even some who were in his books did not hesitate to hail him; the majority of the party, however, was composed of those with whom he had at various tunes and places enjoyed the sports of the field, but whom he had never missed until they met at Boulogne.

Their inquiries were business-like and familiar:—"are ye, Jorrocks?" cried one, holding out both hands. "How are ye, my lad of wax? Do you still play billiards?—Give you nine, and play you for a Nap." "Come to my house this evening, old boy, and take a hand at whist for old acquaintance sake," urged the friend on his left; "got some rare cognac, and a box of beautiful Havannahs." "No, Jorrocks,—dine with me," said a third, "and play chicken-hazard." "Don't," said a fourth, confidentially, "he'll fleece ye like fun". "Let me put your name down to our Pigeon Club; only a guinea entrance and a guinea subscription—nothing to a rich man like you." "Have you any coin to lend on unexceptionable personal security, with a power of killing and selling your man if he don't pay?" inquired another. "Are they going to abolish the law of arrest? 'twould be very convenient if they did." "Will you discount me a bill at three months?" "Is B—— out of the Bench yet?" "Who do they call Nodding Homer in your hunt?" "Oh, gentlemen, gentlemen!" cried Mr. Jorrocks, "go it gently, go it gently! Consider the day is 'ot, I'm almost out of breath, and faint for want of food. I've come all the way from Angle-tear, as we say in France, and lost my breakfast on the wogaye. Where is there an inn where I can recruit my famished frame? What's this?" looking up at a sign, "'Done a boar in a manger,' what does this mean?—where's my French dictionary? I've heard that boar is very good to eat." "Yes, but this boar is to drink," said a friend on the right; "but you must not put up at a house of that sort; come to the Hôtel d'Orleans, where all the best fellows and men of consequence go, a celebrated house in the days of the Boulogne Hunt. Ah, that was the time, Mr. Jorrocks! we lived like fighting-cocks then; you should have been among us, such a rollicking set of dogs! could hunt all day, race maggots and drink claret all night, and take an occasional by-day with the hounds on a Sunday. Can't do that with the Surrey, I guess. There's the Hôtel d'Orleans," pointing to it as they turned the corner of the street; "splendid house it is. I've no interest in taking you there, don't suppose so; but the sun of its greatness is fast setting—there's no such shaking of elbows as there used to be—the IOU system knocked that up. Still, you'll be very comfortable; a bit of carpet by your bedside, curtains to your windows, a pie-dish to wash in, a clean towel every third day, and as many friends to dine with you as ever you like—no want of company in Boulogne, I assure you. Here, Mr. W——," addressing the innkeeper who appeared at the door, "this is the very celebrated Mr. Jorrocks, of whom we have all heard so much,—take him and use him as you would your own son; and, hark ye (aside), don't forget I brought him."

"Garsoon," said Jorrocks, after having composed himself a little during which time he was also composing a French speech from his dictionary and Madame de Genlis's[20] *Manuel du Voyageur*, "A che hora [ora] si pranza?" looking at the waiter, who seemed astonished. "Oh, stop!" said he, looking again, "that's Italian—I've got hold of the wrong column. A quelle heure dine—hang me if I know how to call this chap—dine [spelling it], t'on?" "What were you wishing to say, sir?" inquired the waiter, interrupting his display of the language. "Wot, do you speak English?" asked Jorrocks in amazement. "I hope so, sir," replied the man, "for I'm an Englishman." "Then, why the devil did you not say so, you great lout, instead of putting me into a sweat this 'ot day by speaking French to you?" "Beg pardon, sir, thought you were a Frenchman." "Did you, indeed?" said Jorrocks, delighted; "then, by Jove, I do speak French! Somehow or other I thought I could, as I came over. Bring me a thundering beef-steak, and a pint of stout, directly!" The Hôtel d'Orleans being a regular roast-beef and plum-pudding sort of house, Mr. Jorrocks speedily had an immense stripe of tough beef and boiled potatoes placed before him, in the well-windowed *salle à manger*, and the day being fine he regaled himself at a table at an open window, whereby he saw the smart passers-by, and let them view him in return.

Sunday is a gay day in France, and Boulogne equals the best town in smartness. The shops are better set out, the women are better dressed, and there is a holiday brightness and air of pleasure on every countenance. Then instead of seeing a sulky husband trudging behind a pouting wife with a child in her arms, an infallible sign of a Sunday evening in England, they trip away to the rural *fête champêtre*, where with dancing, lemonade, and love, they pass away the night in temperate if not innocent hilarity. "Happy people! that once a week, at least, lay down their cares, and dance and sing, and sport away the weights of grievance, which bow down the spirit of other nations to the earth."

The voyage, though short, commenced a new era in Mr. Jorrocks's life, and he entirely forget all about Sunday and Dover dullness the moment he set foot on sprightly France, and he no more recollected it was Sunday, than if such a day had ceased to exist in the calendar. Having bolted his steak, he gave his

---

[20] For the benefit of our "tarry-at-home" readers, we should premise that Madame de Genlis's work is arranged for the convenience of travellers who do not speak any language but their own; and it consists of dialogues on different necessary subjects, with French and Italian translations opposite the English.

Hessians their usual flop with his handkerchief, combed his whiskers, pulled his wig straight, and sallied forth, dictionary in hand, to translate the signs, admire the clever little children talking French, quiz the horses, and laugh at everything he didn't understand; to spend his first afternoon, in short, as nine-tenths of the English who go "abroad" are in the habit of doing.

Early the next morning. Mr. Jorrocks and the Yorkshireman, accompanied by the commissionnaire of the Hôtel d'Orleans, repaired to the upper town, for the purpose of obtaining passports, and as they ascended the steep street called La grand Rue, which connects the two towns, they held a consultation as to what the former should be described. A "Marchand-Epicier" would obtain Mr. Jorrocks no respect, but, then, he objected to the word "Rentier." "What is the French for fox-'unter?" said he, after a thoughtful pause, turning to his dictionary. There was no such word. "Sportsman, then? Ay, Chasseur! how would that read? John Jorrocks, Esq., Chasseur,—not bad, I think," said he. "That will do," replied the Yorkshireman, "but you must sink the Esquire now, and tack 'Monsieur' before your name, and a very pretty euphonious sound 'Monsieur Jorrocks' will have; and when you hear some of the little Parisian grisettes lisp it out as you turn the garters over on their counters, while they turn their dark flashing eyes over upon you, it will be enough to rejuvenate your old frame. But suppose we add to 'Chasseur'—'Member of the Surrey Hunt?'" "By all means," replied Mr. Jorrocks, delighted at the idea, and ascending the stairs of the Consulate three steps at a time.

The Consul, Mons. De Horter, was in attendance sitting in state, with a gendarme at the door and his secretary at his elbow. "*Bonjour,* Monsieur," said he, bowing, as Mr. Jorrocks passed through the lofty folding door; to which our traveller replied, "The top of the morning to you, sir," thinking something of that sort would be right. The Consul, having scanned him through his green spectacles, drew a large sheet of thin printed paper from his portfolio, with the arms of France placed under a great petticoat at the top, and proceeded to fill up a request from his most Christian Majesty to all the authorities, both civil and military, of France, and also of all the allied "pays," "de laisser librement passer" Monsieur John Jorrocks, Chasseur and member of the Hont de Surrey, and plusieurs other Honts; and also, Monsieur Stubbs, native of Angleterre, going from Boulogne to Paris, and to give them aid and protection, "en cas de besoin," all of which Mr. Jorrocks —like many travellers before him—construed into a most flattering compliment and mark of respect, from his most Christian Majesty to himself.

Under the word "signalement" in the margin, the Consul also drew the following sketch of our hero, in order, as Mr. Jorrocks supposed, that the King of the Mouncheers might know him when he saw him:

"Age de 52 ans
Taille d'un mètre 62 centimetres
Perruque brun
Front large
Yeux gris-sanguin

Nez moyen
Barbe grisâtre
Vizage ronde
Teint rouge."

He then handed it over to Mr. Jorrocks for his signature, who, observing the words "Signature du Porteur" at the bottom, passed it on to the porter of the inn, until put right by the Consul, who, on receiving his fee, bowed him out with great politeness.

Great as had been the grocer's astonishment at the horses and carts that he had seen stirring about the streets, his amazement knew no bounds when the first Paris diligence came rolling into town with six horses, spreading over the streets as they swung about in all directions—covered with bells, sheep-skins, worsted balls, and foxes' brushes, driven by one solitary postilion on the off wheeler. "My vig," cried he, "here's Wombwell's wild-beast show! What the deuce are they doing in France? I've not heard of them since last Bartlemy-fair, when I took my brother Joe's children to see them feed. But stop—this is full of men! My eyes, so it is! It's what young Dutch Sam would call a male coach, because there are no females about it. Well, I declare, I am almost sorry I did not bring Mrs. J——. Wot would they think to see such a concern in Cheapside? Why, it holds half a township—a perfect willage on wheels. My eyes, wot a curiosity! Well, I never thought to live to see such a sight as this!—wish it was going our way that I might have a ride in it. Hope ours will be as big." Shortly after theirs did arrive, and Mr. Jorrocks was like a perfect child with delight. It was not a male coach, however, for in the different compartments were five or six ladies. "Oh, wot elegant creatures," cried he, eyeing them; "I could ride to Jerusalem with them without being tired; wot a thing it is to be a bachelor!"

The Conducteur—with the usual frogged, tagged, embroidered jacket, and fur-bound cap—having hoisted their luggage on high, the passengers who had turned out of their respective compartments to stretch their legs after their cramping from Calais, proceeded to resume their places. There were only two seats vacant in the interior, or, as Mr. Jorrocks called it, the "middle house," consequently the Yorkshireman and he crossed legs. The other four passengers had corner-seats, things much coveted by French travellers. On Mr. Stubbs's right sat an immense Englishman, enveloped in a dark blue camlet cloak, fastened with bronze lionhead clasps, a red neckcloth, and a shabby, napless, broad-brimmed, brown hat. His face was large, round, and red, without an atom of expression, and his little pig eyes twinkled over a sort of a mark that denoted where his nose should have been; in short, his head was more like a barber's wig block than anything else, and his outline would have formed a model of the dome of St. Paul's. On the Yorkshireman's left was a chattering young red-trousered dragoon, in a frock-coat and flat foraging cap with a flying tassel. Mr. Jorrocks was more fortunate than his friend, and rubbed sides with two women; one was English, either an upper nursery-maid or an under governess, but who might be safely trusted to travel by herself. She was dressed in a black beaver bonnet lined with scarlet silk, a nankeen pelisse with a blue ribbon, and pea-green boots, and she carried a sort of small fish-basket on her knee, with a "plain Christian's prayer book" on the top. The other was French, approaching to middle age, with a nice smart plump figure, good hazel-coloured eyes, a beautiful foot and ankle, and very well dressed. Indeed, her dress very materially reduced the appearance of her age, and she was what the milliners would call remarkably well "got up." Her bonnet was a pink satin, with a white blonde ruche surmounted by a rich blonde veil, with a white rose placed elegantly on one side, and her glossy auburn hair pressed down the sides of a milk-white forehead, in the Madonna style.—Her pelisse was of "violet-des-bois" figured silk, worn with a black velvet pelerine and a handsomely embroidered collar. Her boots were of a colour to match the pelisse; and a massive gold chain round her neck, and a solitary pearl ring on a middle finger, were all the jewellery she displayed. Mr. Jorrocks caught a glimpse of her foot and ankle as she mounted the steps to resume her place in the diligence, and pushing the Yorkshireman aside, he bundled in directly after her, and took up the place we have described.

The vehicle was soon in motion, and its ponderous roll enchanted the heart of the grocer. Independently of the novelty, he was in a humour to be pleased, and everything with him was *couleur de rose*. Not so the Yorkshireman's right-hand neighbour, who lounged in the corner, muffled up in his cloak, muttering and cursing at every jolt of the diligence, as it bumped across the gutters and jolted along the streets of Boulogne. At length having got off the pavement, after crushing along at a trot through the soft road that immediately succeeds, they reached the little hill near Mr. Gooseman's farm, and the horses gradually relaxed into a walk, when he burst forth with a tremendous oath, swearing that he had "travelled three hundred thousand miles, and never saw horses walk up such a bit of a bank before." He looked round the diligence in the expectation of someone joining him, but no one deigned a reply, so, with a growl and a jerk of his shoulders, he again threw himself into his corner. The dragoon and the French lady then began narrating the histories of their lives, as the French people always do, and Mr. Jorrocks and the Yorkshireman sat looking at each other. At length Mr. Jorrocks, pulling his dictionary and *Madame de Genlis* out of his pocket, observed, "I quite forgot to ask the guard at what time we dine—most important consideration, for I hold it unfair to takes one's stomach by surprise, and a man should have due notice, that he may tune his appetite accordingly. I have always thought, that there's as much dexterity required to bring an appetite to table in the full bloom of perfection, as there is in training an 'oss to run on a particular day.—Let me see," added he, turning over the pages of *de Genlis*—"it will be under the head of eating and drinking, I suppose.—Here it is—(opens and reads)—'I have a good appetite—I am hungry—I am werry hungry—I am almost starved'—that won't do—'I have eaten enough'—that won't do either—'To breakfast'—no.—But here it is, by Jingo—'Dialogue before dinner'—capital book for us travellers, this Mrs. de Genlis—(reads) 'Pray, take dinner with us to-day, I shall give you plain fare.'—That means rough and enough, I suppose," observed Mr. Jorrocks to the Yorkshireman.—"'What time do we dine to-day? French: A quelle heure dinonsnous aujourd'hui?—Italian: A che hora (ora) si prancey (pranza) oggi?"" "Ah, Monsieur, vous parlez Français à merveille," said the French lady, smiling with the greatest good nature upon him. "A marble!" said Mr. Jorrocks, "wot does that mean?" preparing to look it out in the dictionary. "Ah, Monsieur, I shall you explain—you speak French like a natif." "Indeed!" said Mr. Jorrocks, with a bow, "I feel werry proud of your praise; and your English is quite delightful.— By Jove," said he to the Yorkshireman, with a most self-satisfied grin, "you were right in what you told me about the gals calling me Monsieur.—I declare she's driven right home to my 'art—transfixed me at once, in fact."

Everyone who has done a little "voyaging," as they call it in France, knows that a few miles to the south of Samer rises a very steep hill, across which the route lies, and that diligence travellers are generally invited to walk up it. A path which strikes off near the foot of the hill, across the open, cuts off the angle, and—diligences being anything but what the name would imply,—the passengers, by availing themselves of the short cut, have ample time for striking up confabs, and inquiring into the comforts of the occupiers of the various compartments. Our friends of the "interior" were all busy jabbering and talking—some with their tongues, others with their hands and tongues—with the exception of the monster in the cloak, who sat like a sack in the corner, until the horses, having reached the well-known breathing place, made a dead halt, and the conducteur proceeded to invite the party to descend and "promenade" up the hill. "What's happened now?" cried the monster, jumping up as the door opened; "surely, they don't expect us to walk up this mountain! I've travelled three hundred thousand miles, and was never asked to do such a thing in all my life before. I won't do it; I paid for riding, and ride I will. You are all a set of infamous cheats," said he to the conducteur in good plain English; but the conducteur, not understanding the language, shut the door as soon as all the rest were out, and let him roll on by himself. Jorrocks stuck to his woman, who had a negro boy in the rotonde, dressed in baggy slate-coloured trousers, with a green waistcoat and a blue coat, with a coronet on the button, who came to hand her out, and was addressed by the heroic name of "Agamemnon." Jorrocks got a glimpse of the button, but, not understanding foreign coronets, thought it was a crest; nevertheless, he thought he might as well inquire who his friend was, so, slinking back as they reached the foot of the hill he got hold of the nigger, and asked what they called his missis. Massa did not understand, and Mr. Jorrocks, sorely puzzled how to explain, again had recourse to the *Manuel du Voyageur*; but Madame de Genlis had not anticipated such an occurrence, and there was no dialogue adapted to his situation. There was a conversation with a lacquey, however, commencing with—"Are you disposed to enter into my service?" and, in the hopes of hitting upon something that would convey his wishes, he "hark'd forward," and passing by—"Are you married?" arrived at— "What is your wife's occupation?" "Que fait votre femme?" said he, suiting the action to the word, and pointing to Madame. Agamemnon showed his ivories, as he laughed at the idea of Jorrocks calling his mistress his wife, and by signs and words conveyed to him some idea of the importance of the personage to whom he alluded. This he did most completely, for before the diligence came up, Jorrocks pulled the Yorkshireman aside, and asked if he was aware that they were travelling with a real live Countess; "Madame la Countess Benwolio, the nigger informs me," said he; "a werry grande femme, though what that means I don't know." "Oh, Countesses are common enough here," replied the Yorkshireman. "I dare say she's a stay-maker. I remember a paint-maker who had a German Baron for a colour-grinder once." "Oh," said Jorrocks, "you are jealous—you always try to run down my friends; but that won't do, I'm wide awake to your tricks"; so saying, he shuffled off, and getting hold of the Countess, helped Agamemnon to hoist her into the diligence. He was most insinuating for the next two hours, and jabbered about love and fox-hunting, admiring the fine, flat, open country, and the absence of hedges and flints; but as neither youth nor age can subsist on love alone, his confounded appetite began to trouble him, and got quite the better of him before they reached Abbeville. Every mile seemed a league, and he had his head out of the window at least twenty times before they came in sight of the town. At length the diligence got its slow length dragged not only to Abbeville, but to the sign of the "Fidèle Berger"—or "Fiddle Burgur," as Mr. Jorrocks pronounced it—where they were to dine. The door being opened, out he jumped, and with his *Manuel du Voyageur* in one hand, and the Countess Benvolio in the other, he pushed his way through the crowd of "pauvres misérables" congregated under the gateway, who exhibited every species of disease and infirmity that poor human nature is liable or heir to, and entered the hotel. The "Sally manger," as he called it, was a long brick-floored room on the basement, with a white stove at one end, and the walls plentifully decorated with a panoramic view of the Grand Nation wallopping the Spaniards at the siege of Saragossa. The diligence being a leetle behind time as usual, the soup was on the table when they entered. The passengers quickly ranged themselves round, and, with his mouth watering as the female garçon lifted the cover from the tureen, Mr. Jorrocks sat in the expectation of seeing the rich contents ladled into the plates. His countenance fell fifty per cent as the first spoonful passed before his eyes.—"My vig, why it's water!" exclaimed he—"water, I do declare, with worms[21] in it—I can't eat such stuff as that—it's not man's meat—oh dear, oh dear, I fear I've made a terrible mistake in coming to France! Never saw such stuff as this at Bleaden's or Birch's, or anywhere in the city." "I've travelled three hundred thousand miles," said the fat man, sending his plate from him in disgust, "and never tasted such a mess as this before." "I'll show them up in *The Times*," cried Mr. Jorrocks; "and, look, what stuff is here—beef boiled to rags!—well, I never, no never, saw anything like this before. Oh, I wish I was in Great Coram Street again!—I'm sure I can't live here—I wonder if I could get a return chaise—waiter—garsoon—cuss! Oh dear! I see *Madame de Genlis* is of no use in a pinch—and yet what a dialogue here is! Oh heavens! grant your poor Jorrocks but one request, and that is the contents of a single sentence. 'I want a roasted or boiled leg of

---

[21] Macaroni soup.

mutton, beef, hung beef, a quarter of mutton, mutton chops, veal cutlets, stuffed tongue, dried tongue, hog's pudding, white sausage, meat sausage, chicken with rice, a nice fat roast fowl, roast chicken with cressy, roast or boiled pigeon, a fricassee of chicken, sweet-bread, goose, lamb, calf's cheek, calf's head, fresh pork, salt pork, cold meat, hash.'—But where's the use of titivating one's appetite with reading of such luxteries? Oh, what a wife Madame de Genlis would have made for me! Oh dear, oh dear, I shall die of hunger, I see —I shall die of absolute famine—my stomach thinks my throat's cut already!" In the height of his distress in came two turkeys and a couple of fowls, and his countenance shone forth like an April sun after a shower. "Come, this is better," said he; "I'll trouble you, sir, for a leg and a wing, and a bit of the breast, for I'm really famished—oh hang! the fellow's a Frenchman, and I shall lose half the day in looking it out in my dictionary. Oh dear, oh dear, where's the dinner dialogue!—well, here's something to that purpose. 'I will send you a bit of this fowl.' 'A little bit of the fowl cannot hurt you.'—No, nor a great bit either.— 'Which do you like best, leg or wing?' 'Qu'aimez-vous le mieux, la cuisse ou l'aile?'" Here the Countess Benvolio, who had been playing a good knife and fork herself, pricked up her ears, and guessing at Jorrocks's wants, interceded with her countryman and got him a plateful of fowl. It was soon disposed of, however, and half a dish of hashed hare or cat, that was placed within reach of him shortly after, was quickly transferred into his plate. A French dinner is admirably calculated for leading the appetite on by easy stages to the grand consummation of satiety. It begins meagrely, as we have shown, and proceeds gradually through the various gradations of lights, savories, solids, and substantiate. Presently there was a large dish of stewed eels put on. "What's that?" asked Jorrocks of the man.—"Poisson," was the reply. "Poison! why, you infidel, have you no conscience?" "Fishe," said the Countess. "Oh, ay, I smell— eels—just like what we have at the Eel-pie-house at Twickenham—your ladyship, I am thirsty—'ge soif,' in fact." "Ah, bon!" said the Countess, laughing, and giving him a tumbler of claret. "I've travelled three hundred thousand miles," said the fat man, "and never saw claret drunk in that way before." "It's not werry good, I think," said Mr. Jorrocks, smacking his lips; "if it was not claret I would sooner drink port." Some wild ducks and fricandeau de veau which followed, were cut up and handed round, Jorrocks helping himself plentifully to both, as also to pommes de terre à la maitre d'hôtel, and bread at discretion. "Faith, but this is not a bad dinner, after all's said and done, when one gets fairly into it." "Fear it will be very expensive," observed the fat man. Just when Jorrocks began to think he had satisfied nature, in came a roast leg of mutton, a beef-steak, "à la G—d-dam", [22] and a dish of larks and snipes.

"Must have another tumbler of wine before I can grapple with these chaps," said he, eyeing them, and looking into Madame de Genlis's book: "'Garsoon,

---

[22] When the giraffe mania prevailed in Paris, and gloves, handkerchiefs, gowns, reticules, etc. were "à la Giraffe," an Englishman asked a waiter if they had any beef-steaks "à la Giraffe." "No, monsieur, but we have them à la G—d-dem," was the answer.

donnez-moi un verre de vin,'" holding up the book and pointing to the sentence. He again set to and "went a good one" at both mutton and snipes, but on pulling up he appeared somewhat exhausted. He had not got through it all yet, however. Just as he was taking breath, a *garçon* entered with some custards and an enormous omelette soufflée, whose puffy brown sides bagged over the tin dish that contained it. "There's a tart!" cried Mr. Jorrocks; "Oh, my eyes, what a swell!—Well, I suppose I must have a shy at it.—'In for a penny in for a pound!' as we say at the Lord Mayor's feed. Know I shall be sick, but, however, here goes," sending his plate across the table to the *garçon*, who was going to help it. The first dive of the spoon undeceived him as he heard it sound at the bottom of the dish. "Oh lauk, what a go! All puff, by Jove!—a regular humbug—a balloon pudding, in short! I won't eat such stuff—give it to Mouncheer there," rejecting the offer of a piece. "I like the solids;—will trouble you for some of that cheese, sir, and don't let it taste of the knive. But what do they mean by setting the dessert on before the cloth is removed? And here comes tea and coffee—may as well have some, I suppose it will be all the same price. And what's this?" eyeing a lot of liqueur glasses full of eau de vie. "Chasse-café, Monsieur," said the *garçon*. "Chasse calf—chasse calf—what's that? Oh, I twig—what we call 'shove in the mouth' at the Free-and-Easy. Yes, certainly, give me a glass." "You shall take some dessert," said the Countess, handing him over some peaches and biscuits. "Well, I'll try my hand at it, if it will oblege your ladyship, but I really have had almost enough." "And some abricot," said she, helping him to a couple of fine juicy ones. "Oh, thank you, my lady, thank you, my lady, I'm nearly satisfied." "Vous ne mangez pas," said she, giving him half a plate of grapes. "Oh, my lady, you don't understand me— I can't eat any more—I am regularly high and dry—chock full—bursting, in fact." Here she handed him a plate of sponge-cakes mixed with bon-bons and macaroons, saying, "Vous êtes un pauvre mangeur—vous ne mangez rien, Monsieur." "Oh dear, she does not understand me, I see.—Indeed, my lady, I cannot eat any more.—Ge woudera, se ge could-era, mais ge can-ne-ra pas!" "Well, now, I've travelled three hundred thousand miles, and never heard such a bit of French as that before," said the fat man, chuckling.

IX
MR. JORROCKS IN PARIS

AS the grey morning mist gradually dispersed, and daylight began to penetrate the cloud that dimmed the four squares of glass composing the windows of the diligence, the Yorkshireman, half-asleep and half-awake, took a mental survey of his fellow-travellers.—Before him sat his worthy friend, snoring away with his mouth open, and his head, which kept bobbing over on to the shoulder of the Countess, enveloped in the ample folds of a white cotton nightcap.—She, too, was asleep and, disarmed of all her daylight arts, dozed away in tranquil security. Her mouth also was open, exhibiting rather a moderate set of teeth, and her Madonna front having got a-twist, exposed a mixture of brown and iron-grey hairs at the parting place. Her bonnet swung from the roof of the diligence, and its place was supplied by a handsome lace cap, fastened under her chin by a broad-hemmed cambric handkerchief. Presently the sun rose, and a bright ray shooting into the Countess's corner, awoke her with a start, and after a hurried glance at the passengers, who appeared to be all asleep, she drew a small ivory-cased looking-glass from her bag, and proceeded to examine her features. Mr. Jorrocks awoke shortly after, and with an awful groan exclaimed that his backbone was fairly worn out with sitting. "Oh dear!" said he, "my behind aches as if I had been kicked all the way from Hockleyhole to Marylebone. Are we near Paris? for I'm sure I can't find seat any longer, indeed I can't. I'd rather ride two hundred miles in nine hours, like H'osbaldeston, than be shut up in this woiture another hour. It really is past bearing, and that's the long and short of the matter." This exclamation roused all the party, who began yawning and rubbing their eyes and looking at their watches. The windows also were lowered to take in fresh air, and on looking out they found themselves rolling along a sandy road, lined on each side with apple-trees, whose branches were "groaning" with fruit. They breakfasted at Beaumont, and had a regular spread of fish, beef-steak, mutton-chops, a large joint of hot roast veal, roast chickens, several yards of sour bread, grapes, peaches, pears, and plums, with vin ordinaire, and coffee au lait; but Mr. Jorrocks was off his feed, and stood all the time to ease his haunches.

Towards three in the afternoon they caught the first glimpse of the gilded dome of the Hospital of Invalids, which was a signal for all the party to brush up and make themselves agreeable. Even the three-hundred-thousand miler opened out, and began telling some wonderful anecdotes, while the Countess and Mr. Jorrocks carried on a fierce flirtation, or whatever else they pleased to call it. At last, after a deal of jargon, he broke off by appealing to the Yorkshireman to know what "inn" they should "put up at" in Paris. "I don't know, I'm sure," said he; "it depends a good deal upon how you mean to live. As you pay my shot it does not do for beggars to be choosers; but suppose we try Meurice's" "Oh no," replied Mr. Jorrocks, "her ladyship tells me it is werry expensive, for the English always pay through the nose if they go to English houses in Paris; and, as we talk French, we can put up at a French one, you know." "Well, then, we can try one of the French ones in the Rue de la Paix." "Rue de la Pay! no, by Jove, that won't do for me—the werry name is enough—no Rue de la Pay for me, at least if I have to pay the shot." "Well, then, you must get your friend there to tell you of some place, for I don't care twopence, as long as I have a bed, where it is." The Countess and he then laid their heads together again, and when the diligence stopped to change horses at St. Denis, Mr. Jorrocks asked the Yorkshireman to alight, and taking him aside, announced with great glee that her ladyship, finding they were strangers in the land, had most kindly invited them to stay with her, and that she had a most splendid house in the Rue des Mauvais-Garçons, ornamented with mirrors, musical clocks, and he didn't know what, and kept the best company in all France, marquesses, barons, viscounts, authors, etc. Before the Yorkshireman had time to reply, the conducteur came and hurried them back into the diligence, and closed the door with a bang, to be sure of having his passengers there while he and the postilion shuffled the cards and cut for a glass of *eau-de-vie* apiece.

The Countess, suspecting what they had been after, resumed the conversation as soon as Mr. Jorrocks was seated.—"You shall manger cinque fois every day," said she; "cinque fois," she repeated.—"Humph!" said Mr. Jorrocks to himself, "what can that mean?—cank four—four times five's twenty—eat twenty times a day—not possible!" "Oui, Monsieur, cinque fois," repeated the Countess, telling the number off on her fingers—"Café at nine of the matin, déjeuner à la fourchette at onze o'clock, diner at cinque heure, café at six hour, and souper at neuf hour." "Upon my word," replied Mr. Jorrocks, his eyes sparkling with pleasure, "your offer is werry inwiting. My lady," said he, bowing before her, "Je suis—I am much flattered." "And, Monsieur?" said she, looking at the Yorkshireman. He, too, assured her that he was very much flattered, and was beginning to excuse himself, when the Countess interrupted him somewhat abruptly by turning to Mr. Jorrocks and saying, "He sall be your son—n'est ce pas?" "No, my lady, I've no children," replied he, and the Countess's eyes in their turn underwent a momentary illumination.

The Parisian barrier was soon reached, and the man taken up to kick about the jaded travellers' luggage at the journey's end. While this operation was going on in the diligence yard, the Countess stuck close to Mr. Jorrocks, and having dispatched Agamemnon for a fiacre, bundled him in, luggage and all, and desiring her worthy domestic to mount the box, and direct the driver, she kissed her hand to the Yorkshireman, assuring him she would be most happy to see him, in proof of which, she drove away without telling him her number, or where the Rue des Mauvais-Garçons was.

Paris is a charming place after the heat of the summer has passed away, and the fine, clear, autumnal days arrive. Then is the time to see the Tuileries gardens to perfection, when the Parisians have returned from their châteaus, and emigrating English and those homeward bound halt to renovate on the road; then is the time that the gayest plants put forth their brightest hues, and drooping orange flowers scent the air which silvery fountains lend their aid to cool.

On a Sunday afternoon, such as we have described, our friend Mr. Stubbs (who since his arrival had been living very comfortably at the Hôtel d'Hollande, in expectation of Mr. Jorrocks paying his bill) indulged in six sous' worth of chairs—one to sit upon and one for each leg—and, John Bull-like, stretched himself out in the shade beneath the lofty trees, to view the gay groups who promenaded the alleys before him. First, there came a helmeted cuirassier, with his wife in blue satin, and a little boy in his hand in uniform, with a wooden sword, a perfect miniature of the father; then a group of short-petticoated, shuffling French women, each with an Italian greyhound in slips, followed by an awkward Englishman with a sister on each arm, all stepping out like grenadiers; then came a ribbon'd chevalier of the Legion of Honour, whose hat was oftener in his hand than on his head, followed by a nondescript looking militaire with fierce mustachios, in shining jack-boots, white leathers, and a sort of Italian military cloak, with one side thrown over the shoulder, to exhibit the wearer's leg, and the bright scabbard of a large sword, while on the hero's left arm hung a splendidly dressed woman. "What a figure!" said the Yorkshireman to himself, as they came before him, and he took another good stare.—"Yet stay—no, impossible!—Gracious Heaven! it can't be—and yet it is—by Jove, it's Jorrocks!"

"Why now, you old imbecile," cried he, jumping off his chairs and running up to him, "What are you after?" bursting into a loud laugh as he looked at Mr. Jorrocks's mustachios (a pair of great false ones). "Is there no piece of tomfoolery too great for you? What's come across you now? Where the deuce did you get these things?" taking hold of the curls at one side of his mustachios.

"How now?" roared Mr. Jorrocks with rage and astonishment. "How now! ye young scaramouch, vot do you mean by insulting a gentleman sportsman in broad daylight, in the presence of a lady of quality? By Jingo," added he, his eyes sparkling with rage, "if you are not off before I can say 'dumpling' I'll run you through the gizzard and give your miserable carcass to the dogs," suiting the action to the word, and groping under his cloak for the hilt of his sword.—A crowd collected, and the Yorkshireman perceiving symptoms of a scene, slunk out of the mêlée, and Mr. Jorrocks, after an indignant shake or two of his feathers and curl of his mustachios, pursued his course up the gardens.

This was the first time they had met since their arrival, which was above a week before; indeed, it was nine days, for the landlord of the house where the Yorkshireman lived had sent his "little bill" two days before this, it being an established rule of his house, and one which was conspicuously posted in all the rooms, that the bills were to be settled weekly; and Mr. Stubbs had that very morning observed that the hat of Monsieur l'Hote was not raised half so high from his head, nor his body inclined so much towards the ground as it was wont to be—a pretty significant hint that he wanted his cash.—Now the Yorkshireman, among his other accomplishments, had a turn for play, and unfortunately had been at the Salon the night before, when, after continuous run of ill-luck, he came away twelve francs below the amount of the hotel-keeper's bill, consequently a rumpus with Mr. Jorrocks could not have taken place at a more unfortunate moment. Thinking, however, a good night's rest or two might settle him down, and put all matters right, he let things alone until the Tuesday following, when again finding Monsieur's little "memoire" on one side of his coffeecup, and a framed copy of the "rules and regulations" of the house on the other, he felt constrained to take some decisive step towards its liquidation. Accordingly, having breakfasted, he combed his hair straight over his face, and putting on a very penitential look, called a cab, and desired the man to drive him to the Rue des Mauvais-Garçons.—After zigzagging, twisting, and turning about in various directions, they at last jingled to the end of a very narrow dirty-looking street, whose unswept pavement had not been cheered by a ray of sunshine since the houses were built. It was excessively narrow, and there were no flags on either side; but through the centre ran a dribbling stream, here and there obstructed by oyster-shells, or vegetable refuse, as the water had served as a plaything for children, or been stopped by servants for domestic purposes. The street being extremely old, of course the houses were very large, forming, as all houses do in Paris, little squares entered by folding doors, at one side of which, in a sort of lodge, lives the Porter—"Parlez au Portier"—who receives letters, parcels, and communications for the several occupiers, consisting sometimes of twenty or thirty different establishments in one house. From this functionary may be learned the names of the different tenants. Having dismissed his cab, the Yorkshireman entered the first gateway on his left, to take the chance of gaining some intelligence of the Countess. The Porter—a cobbler by trade—was hammering away, last on knee, at the sole of a shoe, and with a grin on his countenance, informed the Yorkshireman that the Countess lived next door but one. A thrill of fear came over him on finding himself so near the residence of his indignant friend, but it was of momentary duration, and he soon entered the courtyard of No. 3—where he was directed by an unshaved grisly-looking porter, to proceed "un troisième," and ring the bell at the door on the right-hand side. Obedient to his directions, the Yorkshireman proceeded to climb a wide but dirty stone staircase, with carved and gilded balusters, whose wall and steps had known no water for many years, and at length found himself on the landing opposite the very apartment which contained the redoubtable Jorrocks. Here he stood for a few seconds, breathing and cooling himself after his exertions, during which time he pictured to himself the worthy citizen immersed in papers deeply engaged in the preparation of his France in three volumes, and wished that the first five minutes of their interview were over. At length he mustered courage to grasp a greasy-looking red tassel, and give a gentle tinkle to the bell. The door was quickly opened by Agamemnon in dirty loose trousers and slippers, and without a coat. He recognised his fellow-traveller, and in answer to his inquiry if Monsieur Jorrocks was at home, grinned, and answered, "Oh oui, certainement, Monsieur le Colonel Jorrockes est ici," and motioned him to come in. The Yorkshireman entered the little ante-room—a sort of scullery, full of mops, pans, dirty shoes, dusters, candlesticks—and the first thing that caught his eye was Jorrocks's sword, which Agamemnon had been burnishing up with sandpaper and leather, lying on a table before the window. This was not very encouraging, but Agamemnon gave no time for reflection, and opening half a light salmon-coloured folding door directly opposite the one by which he entered, the Yorkshireman passed through, unannounced and unperceived by Mr. Jorrocks or the Countess, who were completely absorbed in a game of dominoes, sitting on opposite sides of a common deal table, whose rose-coloured silk cover was laid over the back of a chair. Jorrocks was sitting on a stool with his back to the door, and the Countess being very intent on the game, Mr. Stubbs had time for a hasty survey of the company and apartment before she looked up. It was about one o'clock, and of course she was still *en déshabillé*, with her nightcap on, a loose *robe de chambre* of flannel, and a flaming broad-striped red-and-black Scotch shawl thrown over her shoulders, and swan's-down-lined slippers on her feet. Mr. Jorrocks had his leather pantaloons on, with a rich blue and yellow brocade dressing-gown, and blue morocco slippers to match. His jack-boots, to which he had added a pair of regimental heel-spurs, were airing before a stove, which contained the dying embers of a small log. The room was low, and contained the usual allowance of red figured velvet-cushioned chairs, with brass nails; the window curtains were red-and-white on rings and gilded rods; a secretaire stood against one of the walls, and there was a large mirror above the marble mantelpiece, which supported a clock surmounted by a flying Cupid, and two vases of artificial flowers covered with glass, on one of which was placed an elegant bonnet of the newest and most approved fashion. The floor, of highly polished oak, was strewed about with playbills, slippers, curl-papers, boxes, cards, dice, ribbons, dirty handkerchiefs, etc.; and on one side of the deal table was a plate containing five well-picked mutton-chop bones, and hard by lay Mr. Jorrocks's mustachios and a dirty small tooth-comb.

Just as the Yorkshireman had got thus far in his survey, the Countess gave the finishing stroke to the game, and Mr. Jorrocks, jumping up in a rage, gave his leathers such a slap as sent a cloud of pipe-clay flying into his face. "Vous avez the devil's own luck"; exclaimed he, repeating the blow, when, to avoid the cloud, he turned short round, and encountered the Yorkshireman.

"How now?" roared he at the top of his voice, "who sent for you? Have you come here to insult me in my own house? I'll lay my soul to an 'oss-shoe, I'll be too many for ye! Where's my sword?"

"Now, my good Mr. Jorrocks," replied the Yorkshireman very mildly, "pray, don't put yourself into a passion—consider the lady, and don't let us have any unpleasantness in Madame la Duchesse Benvolio's house," making her a very low bow as he spoke, and laying his hand on his heart.

"D—n your displeasancies!" roared Jorrocks, "and that's swearing—a thing I've never done since my brother Joe fobbed me of my bottom piece of muffin. Out with you, I say! Out with ye! you're a nasty dirty blackguard; I'm done with you for ever. I detest the sight of you and hate ye afresh every time I see you!"

"Doucement, mon cher Colonel," interposed the Countess, "'ve sall play anoder game, and you sall had von better chance," clapping him on the back as she spoke. "I von't!" bellowed Jorrocks. "Turn this chap out first. I'll do it myself. H'Agamemnon! H'Agamemnon! happortez my sword! bring my sword! tout suite, directly!"

"Police! Police! Police!" screamed the Countess out of the window; "Police! Police! Police!" bellowed Agamemnon from the next one; "Police! Police! Police!" re-echoed the grisly porter down below; and before they had time to reflect on what had passed, a sergeant's file of the National Guard had entered the hotel, mounted the stairs, and taken possession of the apartment. The sight of the soldiers with their bright bayonets, all fixed and gleaming as they were, cooled Mr. Jorrocks's courage in an instant, and, after standing a few seconds in petrified astonishment, he made a dart at his jack-boots and bolted out of the room. The Countess Benvolio then unlocked her secretaire, in which was a plated liqueur-stand with bottles and glasses, out of which she poured the sergeant three, and the privates two glasses each of pure *eau-de-vie*, after which Agamemnon showed them the top of the stairs.

In less than ten minutes all was quiet again, and the Yorkshireman was occupying Mr. Jorrocks's stool. The Countess then began putting things a little in order, adorned the deal table with the rose-coloured cover—before doing which she swept off Mr. Jorrocks's mustachios, and thrust a dirty white handkerchief and the small tooth-comb under the cushion of a chair—while Agamemnon carried away the plate with the bones. "Ah, le pauvre Colonel," said the Countess, eyeing the bones as they passed, "he sall be von grand homme to eat—him eat toujours—all day long—Oh, him mange beaucoup—beaucoup—beaucoup. He is von varé amiable man, bot he sall not be moch patience. I guess he sall be varé rich—n'est ce pas? have many guinea?—He say he keep beaucoup des chiens—many dogs for the hont—he sail be vot dey call rom customer (rum customer) in Angleterre, I think."

Thus she went rattling on, telling the Yorkshireman all sorts of stories about the *pauvre* Colonel, whom she seemed ready to change for a younger piece of goods with a more moderate appetite; and finding Mr. Stubbs more complaisant than he had been in the diligence, she concluded by proposing that he should accompany the Colonel and herself to a *soirée-dansante* that evening at a friend of hers, another Countess, in the "Rue des Bons-Enfants."

Being disengaged as usual, he at once assented, on condition that the Countess would effect a reconciliation between Mr. Jorrocks and himself, for which purpose she at once repaired to his room, and presently reappeared arm-in-arm with our late outrageously indignant hero. The Colonel had been occupying his time at the toilette, and was *en grand costume*—finely cleaned leathers, jack-boots and brass spurs, with a spick and span new blue military frock-coat, hooking and eyeing up to the chin, and all covered with braid, frogs, tags, and buttons.

"Dere be von beau garçon!" exclaimed the Countess, turning him round after having led him into the middle of the room—"dat habit does fit you like vax." "Yes," replied Mr. Jorrocks, raising his arms as though he were going to take flight, "but it is rather tight—partiklarly round the waist—shouldn't like to dine in it. What do you think of it?" turning round and addressing the

Yorkshireman as if nothing had happened—"suppose you get one like it?" "Do," rejoined the Countess, "and some of the other things—vot you call them, Colonel?" "What—breeches?" "Yes, breeches—but the oder name—vot you call dem?" "Oh, leathers?" replied Mr. Jorrocks. "No, no, another name still." "I know no other. Pantaloons, perhaps, you mean?" "No, no, not pantaloons." "Not pantaloons?—then I know of nothing else. You don't mean these sacks of things, called trousers?" taking hold of the Yorkshireman's. "No, no, not trousers." "Then really, my lady, I don't know any other name." "Oh, yes, Colonel, you know the things I intend. Vot is it you call Davil in Angleterre?" "Oh, we have lots of names for him—Old Nick, for instance."—"Old Nick breeches," said the Countess thoughtfully; "no, dat sall not be it—vot else?" "Old Harry?" replied Mr. Jorrocks.—"Old Harry breeches," repeated the Countess in the hopes of catching the name by the ear—"no, nor dat either, encore anoder name, Colonel." "Old Scratch, then?" "Old Scratch breeches," re-echoed the Countess—"no, dat shall not do."—"Beelzebub?" rejoined Mr. Jorrocks. "Beelzebub breeches," repeated the Countess—"nor dat." "Satan, then?" said Mr. Jorrocks. "Oh oui!" responded the Countess with delight, "satan! black satan breeches—you shall von pair of black satan breeches, like the Colonel."

"And the Colonel will pay for them, I presume?" said the Yorkshireman, looking at Mr. Jorrocks.

"I carn't," said Mr. Jorrocks in an undertone; "I'm nearly cleaned out, and shall be in Short's Gardens before I know where I am, unless I hold better cards this evening than I've done yet. Somehow or other, these French are rather too sharp for me, and I've been down upon my luck ever since I came.—Lose every night, in fact, and then they are so werry anxious for me to have my rewenge, as they call it, that they make parties expressly for me every evening; but, instead of getting my rewenge, I only lose more and more money.—They seem to me always to turn up the king whenever they want him.—To-night we are going to a Countess's of werry great consequence, and, as you know écarté well, I'll back your play, and, perhaps, we may do something between us."

This being all arranged, Mr. Stubbs took his departure, and Mr. Jorrocks having girded on his sword, and the Countess having made her morning toilette, they proceed to their daily promenade in the Tuileries Gardens.

A little before nine that evening, the Yorkshireman again found himself toiling up the dirty staircase, and on reaching the third landing was received by Agamemnon in a roomy uniform of a chasseur—dark green and tarnished gold, with a cocked-hat and black feather, and a couteau de chasse, slung by a shining patent-leather belt over his shoulder. The opening of the inner door displayed the worthy Colonel sitting at his ease, with his toes on each side of the stove (for the evenings had begun to get cool), munching the last bit of crust of the fifth Périgord pie that the Countess had got him to buy.—He was extremely smart; thin black gauze-silk stockings, black satin breeches; well-washed, well-starched white waistcoat with a rolling collar, showing an amplitude of frill, a blue coat with yellow buttons and a velvet collar, while his pumps shone as bright as polished steel.

The Countess presently sidled into the room, all smirks and smiles as dressy ladies generally are when well "got up." Rouge and the milliner had effectually reduced her age from five and forty down to five and twenty. She wore a dress of the palest pink satin, with lilies of the valley in her hair, and an exquisitely wrought gold armlet, with a most Lilliputian watch in the centre.

Mr. Jorrocks having finished his pie-crust, and stuck on his mustachios, the Countess blew out her bougies, and the trio, preceeded by Agamemnon with a lanthorn in his hand, descended the stairs, whose greasy, muddy steps contrasted strangely with the rich delicacy of the Countess's beautifully slippered feet. Having handed them into the voiture, Agamemnon mounted up behind, and in less than ten minutes they rumbled into the spacious courtyard of the Countess de Jackson, in the Rue des Bons-Enfants, and drew up beneath a lofty arch at the foot of a long flight of dirty black-and-white marble stairs, about the centre of which was stationed a *lacquey de place* to show the company up to the hall. The Countess de Jackson (the wife of an English horse-dealer) lived in an *entresol au troisième*, but the hotel being of considerable dimensions, her apartment was much more spacious than the Countess Benvolio's. Indeed, the Countess de Jackson, being a *marchande des modes*, had occasion for greater accommodation, and she had five low rooms, whereof the centre one was circular, from which four others, consisting of an ante-room, a kitchen, a bedroom, and *salle à manger*, radiated.

Agamemnon having opened the door of the *fiacre*, the Countess Benvolio took the Yorkshireman's arm, and at once preceded to make the ascent, leaving the Colonel to settle the fare, observing as they mounted the stairs, that he was "von exceeding excellent man, but varé slow."

"Madame la Contesse Benvolio and Monsieur Stoops!" cried the *lacquey de place* as they reached the door of the low ante-room, where the Countess Benvolio deposited her shawl, and took a final look at herself in the glass. She again took the Yorkshireman's arm and entered the round ballroom, which, though low and out of all proportion, had an exceedingly gay appearance, from the judicious arrangement of the numerous lights, reflected in costly mirrors, and the simple elegance of the crimson drapery, festooned with flowers and evergreens against the gilded walls. Indeed, the hotel had been the residence of an ambassador before the first revolution, and this *entresol* had formed the private apartment of his Excellency. The door immediately opposite the one by which they entered, led into the Countess de Jackson's bedroom, which was also lighted up, with the best furniture exposed and her toilette-table set out with numberless scent bottles, vases, trinkets, and nick-nacks, while the *salle à manger* was converted into a card-room. Having been presented in due form to the hostess, the Yorkshireman and his new friend stood surveying the gay crowd of beautiful and well-dressed women, large frilled and well-whiskered men, all chatting, and bowing, and dancing, when a half-suppressed titter that ran through the room attracted their attention, and turning round, Mr. Jorrocks was seen poking his way through the crowd with a number of straws sticking to his feet, giving him the appearance of a feathered Mercury. The fact was, that Agamemnon had cleaned his shoes with the liquid varnish (french polish), and forgetting to dry it properly, the carrying away half the straw from the bottom of the *fiacre* was the consequence, and Mr. Jorrocks having paid the Jehu rather short, the latter had not cared to tell him about it.

The straws were, however, soon removed without interruption to the gaiety of the evening. Mr. Stubbs, of course, took an early opportunity of waltzing with the Countess Benvolio, who, as all French women are, was an admirable dancer, and Jorrocks stood by fingering and curling his mustachios, admiring her movements but apparently rather jealous of the Yorkshireman. "I wish," said he after the dance was over, "that you would sit down at *écarté* and let us try to win some of these mouncheers' tin, for I'm nearly cleaned out. Let us go into the cardroom, but first let us see if we can find anything in the way of nourishment, for I begin to be hungry. Garsoon," said he catching a servant with a trayful of *eau sucrée* glasses, "avez-vous kick-shaws to eat?" putting his finger in his mouth—"ge wouderay some refreshment." "Oh, oui," replied the garçon taking him to an open window overlooking the courtyard, and extending his hand in the air, "voilà, monsieur, de très bon rafraîchissement."

The ball proceeded with the utmost decorum, for though composed of shopkeepers and such like, there was nothing in their dress or manner to indicate anything but the best possible breeding. Jorrocks, indeed, fancied himself in the very élite of French society, and, but for a little incident, would have remained of that opinion. In an unlucky moment he took it into his head he could waltz, and surprised the Countess Benvolio by claiming her hand for the next dance. "It seems werry easy," said he to himself as he eyed the couples gliding round the room;—"at all ewents there's nothing like trying, 'for he who never makes an effort never risks a failure.'" The couples were soon formed and ranged for a fresh dance. Jorrocks took a conspicuous position in the centre of the room, buttoned his coat, and, as the music struck up, put his arm round the waist of his partner. The Countess, it seems, had some misgivings as to his prowess in the dancing line, and used all her strength to get him well off, but the majority of the dancers started before him. At length, however, he began to move, and went rolling away in something between a gallop and a waltz, effecting two turns, like a great cart-wheel, which brought him bang across the room, right into the track of another couple, who were swinging down at full speed, making a cannon with his head against both theirs, and ending by all four coming down upon the hard boards with a tremendous crash—the Countess Benvolio undermost, then the partner of the other Countess, then Jorrocks, and then the other Countess herself. Great was the commotion, and the music stopped; Jorrocks lost his wig, and split his Beelzebub breeches across the knees, while the other gentleman cracked his behind—and the Countess Benvolio and the other Countess were considerably damaged; particularly the other Countess, who lost four false teeth and broke an ear-ring. This, however, was not the worst, for as soon as they were all scraped together and set right again, the other Countess's partner attacked Jorrocks most furiously, calling him a *sacré-nom de-*

Dieu'd bête of an Englishman, a mauvais sujet, a cochon, etc., then spitting on the floor—the greatest insult a Frenchman can offer—he vapoured about being one of the "grand nation," "that he was brave—the world knew it," and concluded by thrusting his card—"Monsieur Charles Adolphe Eugene, Confiturier, No. 15 bis, Rue Poupée"—into Jorrocks's face. It was now Jorrocks's turn to speak, so doubling his fists, and getting close to him, he held one to his nose, exclaiming, "D—n ye, sir, je suis—JORROCKS!—Je suis an Englishman! je vous lick within an inch of your life! —Je vous kick!—je vous mill!—je vous flabbergaster!" and concluded by giving him his card, "Monsieur le Colonel Jorrocks, No 3, Rue des Mauvais-Garçons."

A friend of the confectioner's interposed and got him away, and Mr. Stubbs persuaded Mr. Jorrocks to return into the cardroom, where they were speedily waited upon by the friend of the former, who announced that the Colonel must make an apology or fight, for he said, although Jorrocks was a "Colonel Anglais," still Monsieur Eugene was of the Legion of Honour, and, consequently, very brave and not to be insulted with impunity. All this the Yorkshireman interpreted to Mr. Jorrocks, who was most anxious to fight, and wished it was light that they might go to work immediately. Mr. Stubbs therefore told the confectioner's friend (who was also his foreman), that the Colonel would fight him with pistols at six o'clock in the Bois de Boulogne, but no sooner was the word "pistols" mentioned than the friend exclaimed, with a grimace and shrug of his shoulders, "Oh horror, no! Monsieur Adolphe is brave, but he will not touch pistols—they're not weapons of his country." Jorrocks then proposed to fight him with broad swords, but this the confectioner's foreman declined on behalf of his principal, and at last the Colonel suggested that they could not do better than fight it out with fists. Now, the confectioner was ten years younger than Jorrocks, tall, long-armed, and not over-burthened with flesh, and had, moreover, taken lessons of Harry Harmer, when that worthy had his school in Paris, so he thought the offer was a good one, and immediately closed with it. Jorrocks, too, had been a patron of the prize-ring, having studied under Bill Richmond, the man of colour, and was reported to have exhibited in early life (incog.) with a pugilist of some pretensions at the Fives-court, so, all things considered, fists seemed a very proper mode of settling the matter, and that being agreed upon, each party quitted the Countess de Jackson's—the confectioner putting forth all manner of high-flown ejaculations and prayers for success, as he groped about the ante-room for his hat, and descended the stairs. "Oh! God of war!" said he, throwing up his hands, "who guided the victorious army of this grand nation in Egypt, when, from the pyramids, forty centuries beheld our actions—oh, brilliant sun, who shone upon our armies at Jaffa, at Naples, Montebello, Marengo, Austerlitz, Jena, and Algiers, who blessed our endeavours, who knowest that we are brave—brave as a hundred lions—look down on Charles Adolphe Eugene, and enable him to massacre and immolate on the altar of his wrath, this sacré-nom de-Dieu'd beastly hog of an Englishman"—and thereupon he spit upon the flags with all the venom of a viper.

Jorrocks, too, indulged in a few figures of speech, as he poked his way home, though of a different description. "Now blister my kidneys," said he, slapping his thigh, "but I'll sarve him out! I'll baste him as Randall did ugly Borrock. I'll knock him about as Belcher did the Big Ilkey Pigg. I'll damage his mug as Turner did Scroggins's. I'll fib him till he's as black as Agamemnon—for I do feel as though I could fight a few."

* * * * *

The massive folding doors of the Porte-Cocher at the Hôtel d'Hollande had not received their morning opening, when a tremendous loud, long, protracted rat-tat-tat-tat-tan, sounded like thunder throughout the extensive square, and brought numerous nightcapped heads to the windows, to see whether the hotel was on fire, or another revolution had broken out. The *maître d'hotel* screamed, the porter ran, the *chef de cuisine* looked out of his pigeon-hole window, and the *garçons* and male *femmes des chambres* rushed into the yard, with fear and astonishment depicted on their countenances, when on peeping through the grating of the little door, Mr. Jorrocks was descried, knocker in hand, about to sound a second edition. Now, nothing is more offensive to the nerves of a Frenchman than a riotous knock, and the impertinence was not at all migitated by its proceeding from a stranger who appeared to have arrived through the undignified medium of a co-cou.[23] Having scanned his dimensions and satisfied himself that, notwithstanding all the noise, Jorrocks was mere mortal man, the porter unbolted the door, and commenced a loud and energetic tirade of abuse against "Monsieur Anglais," for his audacious thumping, which he swore was enough to make every man of the National Guard rush "to arms." In the midst of the torrent, very little of which Mr. Jorrocks understood, the Yorkshireman appeared, whom he hurried into the *co-cou*, bundled in after him, cried "ally!" to the driver, and off they jolted at a miserably slow trot. A little before seven they reached the village of Passy, where it was arranged they should meet and proceed from thence to the Bois de Boulogne, to select a convenient place for the fight; but neither the confectioner nor his second, nor any one on his behalf, was visible and they walked the length and breadth of the village, making every possible inquiry without seeing or hearing anything of them. At length, having waited a couple of hours, Mr. Jorrocks's appetite overpowered his desire of revenge, and caused him to retire to the "Chapeau-Rouge" to indulge in a "fork breakfast." Nature being satisfied, he called for pen and ink, and with the aid of Mr. Stubbs drew up the following proclamation which to this day remains posted in the *salle à manger* a copy whereof was transmitted by post to the confectioner at Paris.

PROCLAMATION!

I, John Jorrocks, of Great Coram Street, in the County of Middlesex, Member of the Surrey Hunt, in England, and Colonel of the Army when I'm in France, having been grossly insulted by

---

[23] *Co-cous* are nondescript vehicles that ply in the environs of Paris. They are a sort of cross between a cab and a young Diligence.

Charles Adolphe Eugene of No. 15 bis, Rue Poupée, confectioner, this day repaired to Passy, with the intention of sarving him out with my fists; but, neither he nor any one for him having come to the scratch, I, John Jorrocks, do hereby proclaim the said Charles Adolphe Eugene to be a shabby fellow and no soldier, and totally unworthy the notice of a fox-hunter and a gentleman sportsman.

(Signed) JOHN JORROCKS.

(Countersigned) STUBBS.

This being completed, and the bill paid, they returned leisurely on foot to Paris, looking first at one object, then at another, so that the Countess Benvolio's dinner-hour was passed ere they reached the Tuileries Gardens, where after resting themselves until it began to get dusk, and their appetites returned, they repaired to the Café de Paris to destroy them again.—The lofty well-gilded salon was just lighted up, and the numberless lamps reflected in costly mirrors in almost every partition of the wall, aided by the graceful figures and elegant dresses of the ladies, interspersed among the sombre-coated gentry, with here and there the gay uniforms of the military, imparted a fairy air to the scene, which was not a little heightened by the contrast produced by Mr. Jorrocks's substantial figure, stumping through the centre with his hat on his head, his hands behind his back, and the dust of the day hanging about his Hessians.

"Garsoon," said he, hanging up his hat, and taking his place at a vacant table laid for two, "ge wouderai some wittles," and, accordingly, the spruce-jacketed, white-aproned *garçon* brought him the usual red-backed book with gilt edges, cut and lettered at the side, like the index to a ledger, and, as Mr. Jorrocks said, "containing reading enough for a month." "Quelle potage voulez vous, monsieur?" inquired the *garçon* at last, tired of waiting while he studied the *carte* and looked the words out in the dictionary. "*Avez-vous* any potted lobster?" "Non," said the *garçon*, "potage au vermicelle, au riz, a la Julienne, consommé, et potage aux choux." "Old shoe! who the devil do you think eats old shoes here? Have you any mock turtle or gravy soup?" "Non, monsieur," said the *garçon* with a shrug of the shoulders. "Then avez-vous any roast beef?" "Non, monsieur; nous avons boeuf au naturel—boeuf à la sauce piquante—boeuf aux cornichons—boeuf à la mode—boeuf aux choux—boeuf à la sauce tomate—bifteck aux pommes de terre." "Hold hard," said Jorrocks; "I've often heard that you can dress an egg a thousand ways, and I want to hear no more about it; bring me a beef-steak and pommes de terre for three." "Stop!" cried Mr. Stubbs, with dismay—"I see you don't understand ordering a dinner in France —let me teach you. Where's the *carte?*" "Here," said Mr. Jorrocks, "is 'the bill of lading,'" handing over the book.—"Garçon, apportez une douzaine des huîtres, un citron, et du beurre frais," said the Yorkshireman, and while they were discussing the propriety of eating them before or after the soup, a beautiful dish of little green oysters made their appearance, which were encored before the first supply was finished. "Now, Colonel," said the Yorkshireman, "take a bumper of Chablis," lifting a pint bottle out of the cooler. "It has had one plunge in the ice-pail and no more—see what a delicate rind it leaves on the glass!" eyeing it as he spoke. "Ay, but I'd rayther it should leave something in the mouth than on the side of the glass," replied Mr. Jorrocks; "I loves a good strong generous wine—military port, in fact—but here comes fish and soup— wot are they?" "Filet de sole au gratin, et potage au macaroni avec fromage de Parmesan. I'll take fish first, because the soup will keep hot longest." "So will I," said Mr. Jorrocks, "for I think you understand the thing—but they seem to give werry small penn'orths—it really looks like trifling with one's appetite—I likes the old joint—the cut-and-come-again system, such as we used to have at Sugden's in Cornhill—joint, wegitables, and cheese all for two shillings." "Don't talk of your joints here," rejoined the Yorkshireman—"I told you before, you don't understand the art of eating—the dexterity of the thing consists in titivating the appetite with delicate morsels so as to prolong the pleasure. A well-regulated French dinner lasts two hours, whereas you go off at score, and take the shine out of yourself before you turn the Tattenham Corner of your appetite. But come, take another glass of Chablis, for your voice is husky as though your throat was full of dust.—Will you eat some of this boulli-vert?" "No, not no bouleward for me thank ye." "Well, then, we will have the 'entrée de boeuf—beef with sauce tomate—and there is a côtelette de veau en papillotte;—which will you take?" "I'll trouble the beef, I think; I don't like that 'ere pantaloon cutlet much, the skin is so tough." "Oh, but you don't eat the paper, man; that is only put on to keep this nice layer of fat ham from melting; take some, if it is only that you may enjoy a glass of champagne after it. There is no meat like veal for paving the way for a glass of champagne." "Well, I don't care if I do, now you have explained how to eat it, for I've really been troubled with indigestion all day from eating one wholesale yesterday; but don't you stand potatoes—pommes de terre, as we say in France?" "Oh yes, fried, and à la maître d'hotel; here they come, smoking hot. Now, J—— for a glass of champagne—take it out of the pail—nay, man! not with both hands round the middle, unless you like it warm—by the neck, so," showing him how to do it and pouring him a glass of still champagne. "This won't do," said Jorrocks, holding it up to the candle; "garsoon! garsoon!—no good—no bon—no fizzay, no fizzay," giving the bottom of the bottle a slap with his hand to rouse it. "Oh, but this is still champagne," explained the Yorkshireman, "and far the best." "I don't think so," retorted Mr. Jorrocks, emptying the glass into his water-stand. "Well, then, have a bottle of the other," rejoined the Yorkshireman, ordering one. "And who's to pay for it?" inquired Mr. Jorrocks. "Oh, never mind that— care killed the cat—give a loose to pleasure for once, for it's a poor heart that never rejoices. Here it comes, and 'may you never know what it is to want,' as the beggar boys say.—Now, let's see you treat it like a philosopher—the wire is off, so you've nothing to do but cut the string, and press the cork on one side with your thumb.—Nay! you've cut both sides!" Fizz, pop, bang, and away went the cork close past the ear of an old deaf general, and bounded against the wall.—"Come, there's no mischief done, so pour out the wine.—Your good health, old boy, may you live for a thousand years, and I be there to count them!

—Now, that's what I call good," observed the Yorkshireman, holding up his glass, "see how it dulls the glass, even to the rim—champagne isn't worth a copper unless it's iced—is it, Colonel?" "Vy, I don't know—carn't say I like it so werry cold; it makes my teeth chatter, and cools my courage as it gets below— champagne certainly gives one werry gentlemanly ideas, but for a continuance, I don't know but I should prefer mild hale." "You're right, old boy, it does give one very gentlemanly ideas, so take another glass, and you'll fancy yourself an emperor.—Your good health again." "The same to you, sir. And now wot do you call this chap?" "That is a quail, the other a snipe—which will you take?" "Vy, a bit of both, I think; and do you eat these chaps with them?" "Yes, nothing nicer—artichokes á la sauce blanche; you get the real eating part, you see, by having them sent up this way, instead of like haystacks, as they come in England, diving and burning your fingers amid an infinity of leaves." "They are werry pretty eating, I must confess; and this upper Binjamin of ham the birds are cooked in is delicious. I'll trouble you for another plateful." "That's right, Colonel, you are yourself again. I always thought you would come back into the right course; and now you are good for a glass of claret of light Hermitage. Come, buck up, and give a loose to pleasure for once." "For once, ay, that's what you always say; but your once comes so werry often." "Say no more.— Garçon! un demi-bouteille de St. Julien; and here, J——, is a dish upon which I will stake my credit as an experienced caterer—a Charlotte de pommes—upon my reputation it is a fine one, the crust is browned to a turn, and the rich apricot sweet-meat lies ensconced in the middle, like a sleeping babe in its cradle. If ever man deserved a peerage and a pension it is this cook." "It's werry delicious— order another." "Oh, your eyes are bigger than your stomach, Mr. J——. According to all mathematical calculations, this will more than suffice. Ay, I thought so—you are regularly at a stand-still. Take a glass of whatever you like. Good—I'll drink Chablis to your champagne. And now, that there may be no mistake as to our country, we will have some cheese—fromage de Roquefort, Gruyère, Neufchatel, or whatever you like—and a beaker of Burgundy after, and then remove the cloth, for I hate dabbling in dowlas after dinner is done." "Rum beggars these French," said Mr. Jorrocks to himself, laying down the newspaper, and taking a sip of Churchman's chocolate, as on the Sunday morning he sat with the Countess Benvolio, discussing rolls and butter, with *Galignani's Messenger*, for breakfast.

"Rum beggars, indeed," said he, resuming the paper, and reading the programme of the amusements for the day, commencing with the hour of Protestant service at the Ambassador's Chapel, followed on by Palace and Gallery of Pictures of the Palais Royal—Review with Military Music in the Place du Carousel—Horse-races in the Champs de Mars—Fête in the Park of St. Cloud—Combat d'Animaux, that is to say, dog-fighting and bull-baiting, at the Barrière du Combat, Tivoli, etc., etc., "It's not werry right, but I suppose at Rome we must do as Romans do," with which comfortable reflection Mr. Jorrocks proposed that the Countess and he should go to the races. Madame was not partial to animals of any description, but having got a new hat and feathers she consented to show them, on condition that they adjoined to the fête at St. Cloud in the evening.

Accordingly, about noon, the ostler's man of a neighbouring English livery-stable drew up a dark-coloured job cab, with a red-and-white striped calico lining, drawn by a venerable long-backed white horse, at the Countess's gateway in the Rue des Mauvais-Garçons, into which Mr. Jorrocks having handed her ladyship, and Agamemnon, who was attired in his chasseur uniform, having climbed up behind, the old horse, after two or three flourishes of his dirty white tail, as a sort of acknowledgment of the whip on his sides, got himself into motion, and proceeded on his way to the races. The Countess being resolved to cut a dash, had persuaded our hero to add a smart second-hand cocked-hat, with a flowing red-and-white feather, to the rest of his military attire; and the end of a scarlet handkerchief, peeping out at the breast of his embroidered frock-coat, gave him the appearance of wearing a decoration, and procured him the usual salute from the soldiers and veterans of the Hospital of Invalids, who were lounging about the ramparts and walks of the edifice. The Countess's costume was simple and elegant; a sky-blue satin pelisse with boots to match, and a white satin bonnet with white feathers, tipped with blue, and delicate primrose-coloured gloves. Of course the head of the cab was well thrown back to exhibit the elegant inmates to the world.

Great respect is paid to the military in France, as Mr. Jorrocks found by all the hack, cab, and *fiacre* drivers pulling up and making way for him to pass, as the old crocodile-backed white horse slowly dragged its long length to the gateway of the Champ de Mars. Here the guard, both horse and foot, saluted him, which he politely acknowledged, under direction of the Countess, by raising his *chapeau bras*, and a subaltern was dispatched by the officer in command to conduct him to the place appointed for the carriages to stand. But for this piece of attention Mr. Jorrocks would certainly have drawn up at the splendid building of the École Militaire, standing as it does like a grand stand in the centre of the gravelly dusty plain of the Champ de Mars. The officer, having speared his way through the crowd with the usual courtesy of a Frenchman, at length drew up the cab in a long line of anonymous vehicles under the rows of stunted elms by the stone-lined ditch, on the southern side of the plain when, turning his charger round, he saluted Mr. Jorrocks, and bumped off at a trot. Mr. Jorrocks then stuck the pig-driving whip into the socket, and throwing forward the apron, handed out the Countess, and installed Agamemnon in the cab.

A fine day and a crowd make the French people thoroughly happy, and on this afternoon the sun shone brightly and warmly on the land;—still there was no apparently settled purpose for the assembling of the multitude, who formed themselves in groups upon the plain, or lined the grass-burnt mounds at the sides, in most independent parties. The Champ de Mars forms a regular parallelogram of 2700 feet by 1320, and the course, which is of an oblong form, comprises a circuit of the whole, and is marked out with strong posts and ropes. Within the course, equestrians—or more properly speaking, "men on horseback"—are admitted under the surveillance of a regiment of cavalry, while infantry and cavalry are placed in all directions with drawn swords and fixed bayonets to preserve order. Being a gravelly sandy soil, in almost daily requisition for the exercise and training of troops, no symptoms of vegetation can be expected, and the course is as hard as the ride in Rotten Row or up to Kensington Gardens.

About the centre of the south side, near where the carriages were drawn up, a few temporary stands were erected for the royal family and visitors, the stand for the former being in the centre, and hung with scarlet and gold cloth, while the others were tastefully arranged with tri-coloured drapery. These are entered by tickets only, but there are always plenty of platforms formed by tables and "chaises à louer" (chairs to let) for those who don't mind risking their necks for a sight. Some few itinerants tramped about the plain, offering alternately tooth-picks, play-bills, and race-lists for sale. Mr. Jorrocks, of course, purchased one of the latter, which was decorated at the top with a woodcut, representing three jockeys riding two horses, one with a whip as big as a broad sword. We append the list as a specimen of "Sporting in France," which, we are sorry to see, does not run into our pages quite so cleverly as our printer could wish.[24]

Foreigners accuse the English of claiming every good-looking horse, and every well-built carriage, met on the Continent, as their own, but we think that few would be ambitious of laying claim to the honour of supplying France with jockeys or racehorses. Mr. Jorrocks, indeed, indifferent as he is to the affairs of the turf, could not suppress his "conwiction" of the difference between the flibberty-gibberty appearance of the Frenchmen, and the quiet, easy, close-sitting jockeys of Newmarket. The former all legs and elbows, spurting and pushing to the front at starting, in tawdry, faded jackets, and nankeen shorts, just like the frowsy door-keepers of an Epsom gambling-booth; the latter in clean, neat-fitting leathers, well-cleaned boots, spick and span new jackets, feeling their horses' mouths, quietly in the rear, with their whip hands resting on their thighs. Then such riding! A hulking Norman with his knees up to his chin, and a long lean half-starved looking Frenchman sat astride like a pair of tongs, with a wet sponge applied to his knees before starting, followed by a runaway English stable lad, in white cords and drab gaiters, and half a dozen others equally singular, spurring and tearing round and round, throwing the gravel and sand into each other's faces, until the field was so separated as to render it difficult to say which was leading and which was tailing, for it is one of the rules of their races, that each heat must be run in a certain time, consequently, though all the horses may be distanced, the winner keeps working away. Then what an absence of interest and enthusiasm on the part of the spectators! Three-fourths of them did not know where the horses started, scarcely a man knew their names, and the few tenpenny bets that were made, were sported upon the colour of the jackets. A Frenchman has no notion of racing, and it is on record that after a heat in which the winning horse, after making a waiting race, ran in at the finish,

---

[24] Racing in France is, of course, now a very different business to the primitive sport it was when this sketch was written.—EDITOR.

a Parisian observed, that "although 'Annette' had won at the finish, he thought the greater honour was due to 'Hercule,' he having kept the lead the greater part of the distance." On someone explaining to him that the jockey on Annette had purposely made a waiting race, he was totally incredulous, asserting that he was sure the jockeys had too much *amour-propre* to remain in the rear at any part of the race, when they might be in front.

X
SPORTING IN FRANCE

PROGRAMME Des Courses De Chevaux

Qui Auront Lieu Au Champ-De-Mars Le Dimanche A Une Heure, En Presence De Ll. Mm. Le Roi Et La Reine, Et Des Princes De La Famille Royale

DEUX PRIX ROYAUX

NOMS Des Chevaux	SIGNALEMENS Et Ages	NOMS Des Proprietaires	POIDS à porter	NOMS Des Jockeys	COSTUMES Des Jockeys
Prix royal de 5000 fr. pour les chevaux et jumens de deuxième espèce.—En partie liée					
Moina	Bai-clair-4	Haras de Meudon	102 l.	Tom Hall	Veste rouge toque tricolore
Corisandre	Bai-brun-5	M. Bonvié fils	115	Tom Wilson	Veste orange, manches et toque noires.
Flore	Bai-cerise-4	M. de Laroque	102	Tony Montel	Veste noire, manches blanches toque noire.
Eleanor	Alezan-brulé-5	M. de Royère	112	Bernou	Veste verte, toque noire.
Diomède	Bai-4	M. le baron de la Bastide	105	Baptiste	Veste bleue, manches jaunes, toque bl. et j.
Cirus	Bai-brun-5	Lord Seymour	115	North	Veste orange, toque noire.
Aline	Bai-clair-4	M. Noel	102	Tom	Veste ponceau, manches blanches toque bleue.
Léonie	Alezan-doré-5	M. Belhomme	112	Pichon	Veste jaune, toque verte
Prix royal de 6000 fr. pour les chevaux de première espèce.—En partie liée					
Young-Milton	Bai-4	M. Fasquel	105 l	Tom Webb	Veste et toque noires.
Mouna	Bai-clair-4	M. de Laroque	102	Tony Montal	Veste noire, manches blanches toque noire
Paméla	Bai-4	Heras de Meudon	102	Tom Hall	Veste rouge, toque tricolore.
Eglé	Gris-sanguin-5	Lord Seymour	112	Mous	Veste orange, toque noire

Cédéric	Bai-5	M. le baron de	115	Baptiste	Veste bleue, manches jaunes, toque bl. et ja.
Young-Tandem	Bai-cerise-4	M. Schickler	105	Webb	Veste rouge, toque noire.
Oubiou	Alezan-6	MM. Salvador et Tassinari	121	Tom Johns	Veste bleue, manches blanches toque rouge.
Coradin	Bai-5	M. Moreil	115	René	Veste bleue, manches jaunes, toque bl.&jaune.

Nota. Les chevaux de première espèce sont ceux nés en France de pères et mères étrangers: ceux de la deuxième espèce sont ceux nés de pères et mères Français ou seulement de l'un des deux.—Chaque épreuve comprendra les deux tours du Champs de Mars.—Les courses commenceront par la première épreuve des chevaux de deuxième espèce.—La seconde course se fera pour la première épreuve des chevaux de première espèce: suivie de la deuxième épreuve des chevaux de deuxième espèce: et elles seront terminées par la deuxième épreuve des chevaux de première espèce.

Transcriber's note: The original document contains an additional column that could not be squeezed into the 80 characters allowed in this format. That column shows the pedigree of the horses, as follows:

Moina: Issu de Candide et de Miltonia.
Corisandre: Issu d'Holbein et de Lisbeth.
Flore: Issue de Tigris et Biche.
Eléanor: Issue de Moulay et de Cadette.
Diomède: Issu de Prémium et de Gabrielle.
Cirus: Issu de Toley et de Miss.
Aline: Issue de Snail et d'une jument Normande.
Léonie: Issue de Massoud et d'une fille de D-y-o.

Young-Milton: Issu de Milton et de Betzi.
Mouna: Issu de Rainbow et de Mouna.
Paméla: Issue de Candid et Géane
Eglé: Issue de Rainbow and Young-Urganda.
Cédéric: Issue de Candid et Prestesse.
Young-Tandem: Issu de Multum-in-Parvo et d'Oida.
Oubiou: Issu d'Oubiou et d'une fille de Stradlamlad.
Coradin: Issu de Candid et de Prestesse.

"Moderate sport," said Mr. Jorrocks to himself, curling his mustachios and jingling a handful of five-franc pieces in the pocket of his leathers—"moderate sport indeed," and therefore he turned his back to the course and walked the Countess off towards the cab.

From beneath a low tenth-rate-looking booth, called "The Cottage of Content," supported by poles placed on the stunted trees of the avenue, and exhibiting on a blue board, "John Jones, dealer in British beer," in gilt letters, there issued the sound of voices clamouring about odds, and weights and scales, and on looking in, a score of ragamuffin-looking grooms, imitation jockeys, and the usual hangers-on of the racehorses and livery-stables, were seen drinking beer, smoking, playing at cards, dice, and chuck-farthing. Before the well-patched canvas curtain that flapped before the entrance, a crowd had collected round one of the horses which was in the care of five or six fellows, one to hold him, another to whistle to him, a third to whisk the flies away with a horse's tail, a fourth to scrape him, a fifth to rinse his mouth out,—while the stud-groom, a tall, gaunt, hairy-looking fellow, in his shirt sleeves, with ear-rings, a blue apron and trousers (more like a gardener than a groom), walked round and round with mystified dignity, sacréing and muttering, "Ne parlez pas, ne parlez pas," as anyone approached who seemed likely to ask questions. Mr. Jorrocks, having well ascertained the importance of his hat and feather, pushed his way with the greatest coolness into the ring, just to cast his eye over the horse and see whether he was fit to go with the Surrey, and the stud-groom immediately took off his lavender-coloured foraging cap, and made two profound salaams, one to the Colonel, the other to the Countess. Mr. Jorrocks, all politeness, took off his *chapeau*, and no sooner was it in the air, than with a wild exclamation of surprise and delight, the groom screamed, "Oh, Monsieur Shorrock, mon ami, comment vous portez vous?" threw his arms round the Colonel's neck, and kissed him on each cheek.

"Hold!" roared the Colonel, half smothered in the embrace, and disengaging himself he drew back a few paces, putting his hand on the hilt of his sword, when in the training groom of Paris he recognised his friend the Baron of Newmarket. The abruptness of the incident disarmed Mr. Jorrocks of reflection, and being a man of impulse and warm affections, he at once forgave the novelty of the embrace, and most cordially joined hands with those of his friend. They then struck up a mixture of broken English and equally broken French, in mutual inquiries after each other's healths and movements, and presuming that Mr. Jorrocks was following up the sporting trade in Paris, the Baron most considerately gave him his best recommendations which horse to back, kindly betting with him himself, but, unfortunately, at each time assigning Mr. Jorrocks the losing horse. At length, being completely cleaned out, he declined any further transactions, and having got the Countess into the cab, was in the act of climbing in himself, when someone took him by the sword as he was hoisting himself up by the wooden apron, and drew him back to the ground. "Holloa, Stubbs, my boy!" cried he, "I'm werry 'appy to see ye," holding out his hand, and thereupon Mr. Stubbs took off his hat to the Countess. "Well now, the deuce be in these French," observed Mr. Jorrocks, confidentially, in an undertone as, resigning the reins to Agamemnon, he put his arm through the

Yorkshireman's and drew out of hearing of the Countess behind the cab—"the deuce be in them. I say. There's that beggarly Baron as we met at Newmarket has just diddled me out of four Naps and a half, by getting me to back 'osses that he said were certain to win, and I really don't know how we are to make 'tongue and buckle' meet, as the coachmen say. Somehow or other they are far too sharp for me. Cards, dominoes, dice, backgammon, and racing, all one—they inwariably beat me, and I declare I haven't as much pewter as will coach me to Calais." The Yorkshireman, as may be supposed, was not in a condition of any great pecuniary assistance, but after a turn or two along the mound, he felt it would be a reproach on his country if he suffered his friend to be done by a Frenchman, and on consideration he thought of a trick that Monsieur would not be up to. Accordingly, desiring Mr. Jorrocks to take him to the Baron, and behave with great cordiality, and agree to the proposal he should make, they set off in search of that worthy, who, after some trouble, they discovered in the "Cottage of Content," entertaining John Jones and his comrades with an account of the manner in which he had fleeced Monsieur Shorrock. The Yorkshireman met him with the greatest delight, shook hands with him over and over again, and then began talking about racing, pigeon-shooting, and Newmarket, pretended to be full of money, and very anxious for the Baron's advice in laying it out. On hearing this, the Baron beckoned him to retire, and joining him in the avenue, walked him up and down, while he recommended his backing a horse that was notoriously amiss. The Yorkshireman consented, lost a Nap with great good humour, and banteringly told the Baron he thought he could beat the horse on foot. This led them to talk of foot-racing and at last the Yorkshireman offered to bet that Mr. Jorrocks would run fifty yards with him on his back, before the Baron would run a hundred. Upon this the Baron scratched his head and looked very knowing, pretended to make a calculation, when the Yorkshireman affected fear, and professed his readiness to withdraw the offer. The Baron then plucked up his courage, and after some haggling, the match was made for six Naps, the Yorkshireman reckoning the Baron might have ten francs in addition to what he had won of Mr. Jorrocks and himself. The money was then deposited in the hands of the Countess Benvolio, and away went the trio to the "Cottage of Content," to get men and ropes to measure and keep the ground. The English jockeys and lads, though ready enough to pigeon a countryman themselves, have no notion of assisting a foreigner to do so, unless they share in the spoil, and the Baron being a notorious screw, they all seemed heartily glad to find him in a trap. Out then they all sallied, amid cheers and shouts, while John Jones, with a yard-wand in his hand, proceeded to measure a hundred yards along the low side of the mound. This species of amusement being far more in accordance with the taste of the French than anything in which horses are concerned, an immense mob flocked to the scene, and the Baron having explained how it was, and being considered a safe man to follow, numerous offers were made to bet against the performance of the match. The Yorkshireman being a youth of discretion and accustomed to bet among strangers, got on five Naps more with different parties, who to "prevent accidents" submitted to deposit the money with the Countess, and all things being adjusted, and the course cleared by a picket of infantry, Mr. Jorrocks ungirded his sword, and depositing it with his frock-coat in the cab, walked up to the fifty yards he was to have for start. "Now, Colonel," said the Yorkshireman, backing him to the mound, so that he might leap on without shaking him, "put your best leg first, and it's a hollow thing; if you don't fall, you must win,"—and thereupon taking Mr. Jorrocks's cocked hat and feather from his head, he put it sideways on his own, so that he might not be recognised, and mounted his man. Mr. Jorrocks then took his place as directed by John Jones, and at a signal from him—the dropping of a blue cotton handkerchief—away they started amid the shouts, the clapping of hands, and applause of the spectators, who covered the mound and lined the course on either side. Mr. Jorrocks's action was not very capital, his jack-boots and leathers rather impeding his limbs, while the Baron had as little on him as decency would allow. The Yorkshireman feeling his man rather roll at the start, again cautioned him to take it easy, and after a dozen yards he got into a capital run, and though the lanky Baron came tearing along like an ill-fed greyhound, Mr. Jorrocks had full two yards to spare, and ran past the soldier, who stood with his cap on his bayonet as a winning-post, amid the applause of his backers, the yells of his opponents, and the general acclamation of the spectators.

The Countess, anticipating the victory of her hero, had dispatched Agamemnon early in the day for a chaplet of red-and-yellow immortelles, and having switched the old cab horse up to the winning-post, she gracefully descended, without showing more of her foot and ankle than was strictly correct, and decorated his brow with the wreath, as the Yorkshireman dismounted. Enthusiasm being always the order of the day in France, this act was greeted with the loudest acclamations, and, without giving him time to recover his wind, the populace bundled Mr. Jorrocks neck and shoulders into the cab, and seizing the old horse by the head, paraded him down the entire length of the Champ de Mars, Mr. Jorrocks bowing and kissing his hands to the assembled multitude, in return for the vivas! the clapping of hands, and the waving of ribbons and handkerchiefs that greeted him as he went.

Popularity is but a fickle goddess, and in no country more fickle than in France. Ere the procession reached the end of the dusty plain, the mob had tailed off very considerably, and as the leader of the old white horse pulled him round to return, a fresh commotion in the distance, caused by the apprehension of a couple of pickpockets, drew away the few followers that remained, and the recently applauded and belauded Mr. Jorrocks was left alone in his glory. He then pulled up, and taking the chaplet of immortelles from his brow, thrust it under the driving cushion of the cab, and proceeded to reinstate himself in his tight military frock, re-gird himself with his sword, and resume the cocked hat and feather.

Nothing was too good for Mr. Stubbs at that moment, and, had a pen and ink been ready, Mr. Jorrocks would have endorsed him a bill for any amount. Having completed his toilette he gave the Yorkshireman the vacant seat in the cab, flopped the old horse well about the ears with the pig-driving whip, and trotted briskly up the line he had recently passed in triumphal procession, and wormed his way among the crowd in search of the Countess. There was nothing, however, to be seen of her, and after driving about, and poking his way on foot into all the crowds he could find, bolting up to every lady in blue, he looked at his great double-cased gold repeater, and finding it was near three o'clock and recollecting the fête of St. Cloud, concluded her ladyship must have gone on, and Agamemnon being anxious to see it, of course was of the same opinion; so, again flopping the old horse about the ears, he cut away down the Champ de Mars, and by the direction of Agamemnon crossed the Seine by the Pont des Invalides, and gained the route to Versailles.

Here the genius of the people was apparent, for the road swarmed with voitures of every description, diligences, gondoles, co-cous, cabs, fiacres, omnibuses, dame-blanches, all rolling and rumbling along, occasionally interrupted by the lilting and tilting of a light English cab or tilbury, drawn by a thoroughbred, and driven by a dandy. The spirit of the old white horse even seemed roused as he got among the carriages and heard the tramping of hoofs and the jingling of bells round the necks of other horses, and he applied himself to the shafts with a vigour his enfeebled-looking frame appeared incapable of supplying. So they trotted on, and after a mile travelling at a foot's pace after they got into close line, they reached the porte Maillot, and resigning the cab to the discretion of Agamemnon, Mr. Jorrocks got himself brushed over by one of the gentry who ply in that profession at all public places, and tucking his sword under one arm, he thrust the other through Mr. Stubbs's, and, John-Bull-like, strutted up the long broad grass avenue, through the low part of the wood of St. Cloud, as if all he saw belonged to himself. The scene was splendid, and nature, art, and the weather appeared confederated for effect. On the lofty heights arose the stately place, looking down with placid grandeur on the full foliage of the venerable trees, over the beautiful gardens, the spouting fountains, the rushing cascades, and the gay and countless myriads that swarmed the avenues, while the circling river flowed calmly on, without a ripple on its surface, as if in ridicule of the sound of trumpets, the clang of cymbals, and the beat of drums, that rent the air around.

Along the broad avenue were ranged shows of every description—wild beasts, giants, jugglers, tumblers, mountebanks, and monsters, while in spots sheltered from the sun by lofty trees were dancing-places, swings, roundabouts, archery-butts, pistol-ranges, ball-kicking and head-thumping places, montagnes-Suisses, all the concomitants of fairs and fêtes—beating "Bartlemy Fair," as Mr. Jorrocks candidly confessed, "all to nothing."

The chance of meeting the Countess Benvolio in such a multitude was very remote indeed, but, to tell the truth, Mr. Jorrocks never once thought of her, until having eat a couple of cold fowls and drank a bottle of porter, at an English booth, he felt in his pocket for his purse, and remembered it was in her keeping. Mr. Stubbs, however, settled the account, and in high glee Mr. Jorrocks resumed his peregrinations, visiting first one show, then another, shooting with pea-guns, then dancing a quadrille, until he was brought up short before a splendid green-and-gold roundabout, whose magic circle contained two lions, two swans, two black horses, a tiger, and a giraffe. "Let's have a ride," said he, jumping on to one of the black horses and adjusting the stirrups to his length. The party was soon made up, and as the last comer crossed his tiger, the engine was propelled by the boys in the centre, and away they went at Derby pace. In six rounds Mr. Jorrocks lost his head, turned completely giddy, and bellowed out to them to stop. They took no heed—all the rest were used to it—and after divers yells and ineffectual efforts to dismount, he fell to the ground like a sack. The machine was in full work at the time, and swept round three or four times before they could stop it. At last Mr. Stubbs got to him, and a pitiable plight he was in. He had fallen on his head, broken his feather, crushed his chapeau bras, lost off his mustachios, was as pale as death, and very sick. Fortunately the accident happened near the gate leading to the town of St. Cloud, and thither, with the aid of two gendarmes, Mr. Stubbs conveyed the fallen hero, and having put him to bed at the Hôtel d'Angleterre, he sent for a "médecin," who of course shook his head, looked very wise, ordered him to drink warm water—a never-failing specific in France—and keep quiet. Finding he had an Englishman for a patient, the "médecin" dropped in every two hours, always concluding with the order "encore l'eau chaud." A good sleep did more for Mr. Jorrocks than the doctor, and when the "médecin" called in the morning, and repeated the injunction "encore l'eau chaud," he bellowed out, "Cuss your *l'eau chaud*, my stomach ain't a reservoir! Give me some wittles!" The return of his appetite being a most favourable symptom, Mr. Stubbs discharged the doctor, and forthwith ordered a *déjeuner à la fourchette*, to which Mr. Jorrocks did pretty fair justice, though trifling in comparison with his usual performances. They then got into a Versailles diligence that stopped at the door, and rattling along at a merry pace, very soon reached Paris and the Rue des Mauvais-Garçons.

"Come up and see the Countess," said Mr. Jorrocks as they arrived at the bottom of the flight of dirty stairs, and, with his hands behind his back and his sword dragging at his heels, he poked upstairs, and opening the outer door entered the apartment. He passed through the small ante-room without observing his portmanteau and carpet-bag on the table, and there being no symptoms of the Countess in the next one, he walked forward into the bedroom beyond.

Before an English fire-place that Mr. Jorrocks himself had been at the expense of providing, snugly ensconced in the luxurious depths of a well-cushioned easy chair, sat a monstrous man with a green patch on his right eye, in slippers, loose hose, a dirty grey woollen dressing-gown, and black silk nightcap, puffing away at a long meerschaum pipe, with a figure of Bacchus on the bowl. At a sight so unexpected Mr. Jorrocks started back, but the smoker seemed quite unconcerned, and casting an unmeaning grey eye at the intruder, puffed a long-drawn respiration from his mouth.

"How now!" roared Mr. Jorrocks, boiling into a rage, which caused the monster to start upon his legs as though he were galvanised. "Vot brings you here?"

"Sprechen sie Deutsch?" responded the smoker, opening his eye a little wider, and taking the pipe from his mouth. "Speak English, you fool," bawled Mr. Jorrocks. "Sie sind sehr unverschämt" (you are very impudent), replied the Dutchman with a thump on the table. "I'll run you through the gizzard!" rejoined Mr. Jorrocks, half drawing his sword,—"skin you alive, in fact!" when in rushed the Countess and threw herself between them.

Now, Mynheer Van Rosembom, a burgomaster of Flushing, was an old friend of the Countess's, and an exceedingly good paying one, and having cast up that morning quite unexpectedly by the early diligence from Dunkirk, and the Countess being enraged at Mr. Jorrocks for not sharing the honours of his procession in the cab on the previous day, and believing, moreover, that his treasury was pretty well exhausted, thought she could not do better than instal Rosembom in his place, and retain the stakes she held for the Colonel's board and lodging.

This arrangement she kept to herself, simply giving Rosembom, who was not a much better Frenchman than Col. Jorrocks, to understand that the room would be ready for him shortly, and Agamemnon was ordered to bundle Mr. Jorrocks's clothes into his portmanteau and bag, and place them in readiness in the ante-room. Rosembom, fatigued with his journey, then retired to enjoy his pipe at his ease, while the Countess went to the Marche St. Honoré to buy some sour crout, roast beef, and prunes for his dinner.

"Turn this great slush-bucket out of my room!" cried Mr. Jorrocks, as the Countess rushed into his apartment. "Vot's he doing here?"

"Doucement, mon cher Colonel," said she, clapping him on the back, "he sall be my brodder." "Never such a thing!" roared Mr. Jorrocks, eyeing him as he spoke. "Never such a thing! no more than myself—out with him, I say, or I'll cut my stick—*toute suite*—directly!"

"Avec tout mon coeur!" replied the Countess, her choler rising as she spoke. "You're another," rejoined Mr. Jorrocks, judging by her manner that she called him something offensive—"Vous ête one mauvaise woman!" "Monsieur," said the Countess, her eyes flashing as she spoke, "vous êtes un polisson!—von rascal!—von dem villain!—un charlatan!—von nasty—bastely—ross bif!—dem dog!" and thereupon she curled her fingers and set her teeth on edge as though she would tear his very eyes out. Rosembom, though he didn't exactly see the merits of the matter, exchanged his pipe for the poker, so what with this, the sword, and the nails, things wore a very belligerent aspect.

Mr. Stubbs, as usual, interposed, and the Countess, still keeping up the semblance of her rage, ordered them to quit her apartment directly, or she would have recourse to her old friends the police. Mr. Stubbs was quite agreeable to go, but he hinted that she might as well hand over the stakes that had been entrusted to her keeping on the previous day, upon which she again indulged in a torrent of abuse, swore they were a couple of thieves, and that Mr. Jorrocks owed her far more than the amount for board and lodging. This made the Colonel stare, for on the supposition that he was a visitor, he had been firing away his money in all directions, playing at everything she proposed, buying her bonnets, Perigord pies, hiring remises, and committing every species of extravagance, and now to be charged for what he thought was pure friendship, disgusted him beyond expression.

The Countess speedily summoned the porter, the man of letters of the establishment, and with his aid drew Mr. Jorrocks out a bill, which he described as "reaching down each side of his body and round his waist," commencing with 2 francs for savon, and then proceeding in the daily routine of café, 1 franc; déjeuner à la fourchette, 5 francs; diner avec vin, 10 francs; tea, 1 franc; souper, 3 francs; bougies, 2 francs; appartement, 3 francs; running him up a bill of 700 francs; and when Mr. Stubbs remonstrated on the exorbitance of the charges, she replied, "It sall be, sare, as small monnaie as sail be consistent avec my dignified respectability, you to charge."

There seemed no help for the matter, so Mr. Stubbs paid the balance, while Mr. Jorrocks, shocked at the duplicity of the Countess, the impudence of Rosembom, and the emptiness of his own pockets, bolted away without saying a word.

That very night the Malle-Poste bore them from the capital, with two cold fowls, three-quarters of a yard of bread, and a bottle of porter, for Mr. Jorrocks on the journey, and ere another sun went down, the sandy suburbs of Calais saw them toiling towards her ramparts, and rumbling over the drawbridges and under the portcullis, that guard the entrance to her gloomy town. Calais! cold, cheerless, lifeless Calais! Whose soul has ever warmed as it approached thy town? but how many hearts have turned with sickening sorrow from the mirthless tinkling of thy bells!

"We'll not stay here long I guess," said Mr. Jorrocks as the diligence pulled up at the post-office, and the conducteur requested the passengers to descend. "That's optional," said a bystander, who was waiting for his letters, looking at Mr. Jorrocks with an air as much as to say, what a rum-looking fellow you are, and not without reason, for the Colonel was attired in a blue sailor's jacket, white leathers, and jack-boots, with the cocked hat and feather. The speaker was a middle-aged, middle-statured man, with a quick intelligent eye, dressed in a single-breasted green riding-coat, striped toilinette waistcoat, and drab trousers, with a whip in his hand. "Thank you for nothing!" replied Mr. Jorrocks, eyeing him in return, upon which the speaker turned to the clerk and asked if there were any letters for Monsieur Apperley or Nimrod. "NIMROD!" exclaimed Mr. Jorrocks, dropping on his knees as though he were shot. "Oh my vig what have I done? Oh dear! oh dear! what a dumbfounderer—flummoxed I declare!"

"Hold up! old 'un," said Nimrod in astonishment; "why, what's the matter now? You don't owe me anything I dare say!"

"Owe you anything! yes, I does," said Mr. Jorrocks, rising from the ground, "I owes you a debt of gratitude that I can never wipe off—you'll be in the day-book and ledger of my memory for ever and a year."

"Who are you?" inquired Nimrod, becoming more and more puzzled, as he contrasted his dialect with his dress.

"Who am I? Why, I'm Mister Jorrocks."

"Jorrocks, by Jove! Who'd have thought it! I declare I took you for a horse-marine. Give us your hand, old boy. I'm proud to make your acquaintance."

"Ditto to you, sir, twice repeated. I considers you the werry first man of the age!"—and thereupon they shook hands with uncommon warmth.

"You've been in Paris, I suppose," resumed Nimrod, after their respective digits were released; "were you much gratified with what you saw? What pleased you most—the Tuileries, Louvre, Garden of Plants, Père la Chaise, Notre Dame, or what?"

"Why now, to tell you the truth, singular as it may seem, I saw nothing but the Tuileries and Naughty Dame.—I may say a werry naughty dame, for she fleeced me uncommonly, scarcely leaving me a dump to carry me home."

"What, you've been among the ladies, have you? That's gay for a man at your time of life."

"Yes, I certainlie have been among the ladies,—countesses I may say—but, dash my vig, they are a rum set, and made me pay for their acquaintance. The Countess Benwolio certainlie is a bad 'un."

"Oh, the deuce!—did that old devil catch you?" inquired Nimrod.

"Vot, do you know her?"

"Know her! ay—everybody here knows her with her black boy. She's always on the road, and lives now by the flats she catches between Paris and the coast. She was an agent for Morison's Pills—but having a fractious Scotch lodger that she couldn't get out, she physicked him so dreadfully that he nearly died, and the police took her licence away. But you are hungry, Mr. Jorrocks, come to my house and spend the evening, and tell me all about your travels."

Mr. Stubbs objected to this proposition, having just learned that the London packet sailed in an hour, so the trio adjourned to Mr. Roberts's, Royal Hotel, where over some strong eau-de-vie they cemented their acquaintance, and Mr. Jorrocks, finding that Nimrod was to be in England the following week, insisted upon his naming a day for dining in Great Coram Street.

"Permits" to embark having been considerately granted "gratis" by the Government for a franc apiece, at the hour of ten our travellers stepped on board, and Mr. Jorrocks, having wrapped himself up in his martial cloak, laid down in the cabin and, like Ulysses in Ithaca, as Nimrod would say, "arrived in London Asleep."

XI
A RIDE TO BRIGHTON ON "THE AGE"

(IN a very "Familiar Letter" to Nimrod)

DEAR NIMROD,

You have favoured myself, and the sporting world at large, with a werry rich high-flavoured account of the great Captain Barclay, and his extonishing coach, the "Defiance"; and being werry grateful to you for that and all other favours, past, present, and to come, I take up my grey goose quill to make it "obedient to my will," as Mr. Pope, the poet, says, in relating a werry gratifying ride I had on the celebrated "Brighton Age," along with Sir Wincent Cotton, Bart., and a few other swells. Being, as you knows, of rather an emigrating disposition, and objecting to make a nick-stick of my life by marking down each Christmas Day over roast-beef and plum pudding, cheek-by-jowl with Mrs. J—— at home, I said unto my lad Binjimin—and there's not a bigger rogue unhung—"Binjimin, be after looking out my Sunday clothes, and run down to the Regent Circus, and book me the box-seat of the 'Age,' for I'm blow'd if I'm not going to see the King at Brighton (or 'London-sur-Mary,' as James Green calls it), and tell the pig-eyed book-keeper it's for Mr. Jorrocks, and you'll be sure to get it."

Accordingly, next day, I put in my appearance at the Circus, dressed in my best blue Saxony coat, with metal buttons, yellow waistcoat, tights, and best Hessians, with a fine new castor on my head, and a carnation in my button-hole. Lots of chaps came dropping in to go, and every one wanted the box-seat. "Can I have the box-seat?" said one.—"No, sir; Mr. Jorrocks has it." "Is the box-seat engaged?" asked another.—"Yes, sir; Mr. Jorrocks has taken it." "Book me the box," said a third with great dignity.—"It's engaged already." "Who by?"—"Mr. Jorrocks"; and so they went on to the tune of near a dozen. Presently a rattling of pole chains was heard, and a cry was raised of "Here's Sir Wincent!" I looks out, and saw a werry neat, dark, chocolate-coloured coach, with narrow red-striped wheels, and a crest, either a heagle or a unicorn (I forgets which), on the door, and just the proprietors' names below the winder, and "The Age," in large gilt letters, below the gammon board, drawn by four blood-like, switch-tailed nags, in beautiful highly polished harness with brass furniture, without bearing reins—driven by a swellish-looking young chap, in a long-backed, rough, claret-coloured benjamin, with fancy-coloured tyes, and a bunch of flowers in his button-hole—no coachman or man of fashion, as you knows, being complete without the flower. There was nothing gammonacious about the turn-out; all werry neat and 'andsome, but as plain as plain could be; and there was not even a bit of Christmas at the 'orses' ears, which I observed all the other coaches had. Well, down came Sir Wincent, off went his hat, out came the way-bill, and off he ran into the office to see what they had for him. "Here, coachman," says a linen-draper's "elegant extract," waiting outside, "you've to deliver this (giving him a parcel) in the Marine Parade the instant you get to Brighton. It's Miss—— 's bustle, and she'll be waiting for it to put on to go out to dinner, so you musn't lose a moment, and you may charge what you like for your trouble." "Werry well," says Sir Wincent, laughing, "I'll take care of her bustle. Now, book-keeper, be awake. Three insides here, and six out. Pray, sir," touching his hat to me, "are you booked here? Oh! Mr. Jorrocks, I see. I begs your pardon. Jump up, then; be lively! what luggage have you?" "Two carpet-bags, with J. J., Great Coram Street, upon them." "There, then we'll put them in the front boot, and you'll have them under you. All right behind? Sit tight!" Hist! off we go by St. Mertain's Church into the Strand, to the booking-office there.

The streets were werry full, but Sir Wincent wormed his way among the coal-wagons, wans, busses, coaches, bottom-over-tops,—in wulgar French, "cow sur tate," as they calls the new patent busses—trucks, cabs, &c., in a marvellous workmanlike manner, which seemed the more masterly, inasmuch as the leaders, having their heads at liberty, poked them about in all directions, all a mode Francey, just as they do in Paris. At the Marsh gate we were stopped. A black job was going through on one side, and a haw-buck had drawn a great yellow one 'oss Gravesend cruelty wan into the other, and was fumbling for his coin.

"Now, Young Omnibus!" cried Sir Wincent, "don't be standing there all day." The man cut into his nag, but the brute was about beat. "There, don't 'it him so 'ard (hard)," said Sir Wincent, "or you may hurt him!"

When we got near the Helephant and Castle, Timothy Odgkinson, of Brixton Hill, a low, underselling grocer, got his measly errand cart, with his name and address in great staring white letters, just in advance of the leaders, and kept dodging across the road to get the sound ground, for the whole line was werry "woolley" as you calls it. "Come, Mister independent grocer! go faster if you can," cries Sir Wincent, "though I think you have bought your horse where you buy your tea, for he's werry sloe." A little bit farther on a chap was shoving away at a truck full of market-baskets. "Now, Slavey," said he, "keep out of my way!" At the Helephant and Castle, and, indeed, wherever he stopped, there were lots of gapers assembled to see the Baronet coachman, but Sir Wincent never minded them, but bustled about with his way-bill, and shoved in his parcels, fish-baskets, and oyster-barrels like a good 'un. We pulled up to grub at the Feathers at Merstham, and 'artily glad I was, for I was far on to famish, having ridden whole twenty-five miles in a cold, frosty air without morsel of wittles of any sort. When the Bart. pulled up, he said, "Now, ladies and gentlemen— twenty minutes allowed here, and let me advise you to make the most of it." I took the 'int, and heat away like a regular bagman, who can always dispatch his ducks and green peas in ten minutes.

We started again, and about one hundred yards below the pike stood a lad with a pair of leaders to clap on, for the road, as I said before, was werry woolley. "Now, you see, Mr. Jorrocks," said Sir Wincent, "I do old Pikey by having my 'osses on this side. The old screw drew me for four shillings one day for my leaders, two each way, so, says I, 'My covey, if you don't draw it a little milder, I'll send my 'osses from the stable through my friend Sir William Jolliffe's fields to the other side of your shop,' and as he wouldn't, you see here they are, and he gets nothing."

The best of company, they say, must part, and Baronets "form no exception to the rule," as I once heard Dr. Birkbeck say. About a mile below the halfway 'ouse another coach hove in sight, and each pulling up, they proved to be as like each other as two beans, and beneath a mackintosh, like a tent cover, I twigged my friend Brackenbury's jolly phiz. "How are you, Jorrocks?" and "How are you, Brack?" flew across like billiard-balls, while Sir Wincent, handing me the ribbons, said, "Ladies and gentlemen, I wish you all a good morning and a pleasant ride," and Brack having done the same by his coach and passengers, the two heroes met on terry firmey, as we say in France, to exchange way-bills and directions about parcels. "Now," said Sir Wincent, "you'll find Miss——'s bustle under the front seat—send it off to the Marine Parade the instant you get in, for she wants it to make herself up to-night for a party." "By Jove, that's lucky," said Brackenbury, "for I'll be hanged if I haven't got old Lady——'s false dinner-set of ivories in my waistcoat pocket, which I should have forgot if you hadn't mentioned t'other things, and then the old lady would have lost her blow-out this Christmas. Here they are," handing out a small box, "and mind you leave them yourself, for they tell me they are costly, being all fixed in coral, with gold springs, and I don't know what—warranted to eat of themselves, they say." "She has lost her modesty with her teeth, it seems," said Sir Wincent. "Old women ought to be ashamed to be seen out of their graves after their grinders are gone. I'll pound it the old tabby carn't be under one hundred. But quick! who does that d——d parrot and the cock-a-too belong to that you've got stuck up there? and look, there's a canary and all! I'll be d——d if you don't bring me a coach loaded like Wombwell's menagerie every day! Well, be lively! 'Twill be all the same one hundred years hence.—All right? Sit tight! Good night!"

"Well, Mr. Jorrocks, it's long since we met," said Brackenbury, looking me over—"never, I think, since I showed you way over the Weald of Sussex from Torrington Wood, on the gallant wite with the Colonel's 'ounds! Ah, those were rare days, Mr. Jorrocks! we shall never see their like again! But you're looking fresh. Time lays a light hand on your bearing-reins! I hope it will be long ere you are booked by the Gravesend Buss. You don't lush much, I fancy?" added he, putting a lighted cigar in his mouth. "Yes, I does," said I—"a good deal; but I tells you what, Brackenbury, I doesn't fumigate none—it's the fumigation that does the mischief," and thereupon we commenced a hargument on the comparitive mischief of smoking and drinking, which ended without either being able to convince the other. "Well, at all events, you gets beefey, Brackenbury," said I; "you must be a couple of stone heavier than when we used to talliho the 'ounds together. I think I could lead you over the Weald now, at all ewents if the fences were out of the way," for I must confess that Brack was always a terrible chap at the jumps, and could go where few would follow.

We did the journey within the six hours—werry good work, considering the load and the state of the roads. No coach like the "Age"—in my opinion. I was so werry much pleased with Brack's driving, that I presented him with a four-in-hand whip.

I put up at Jonathan Boxall's, the Star and Garter, one of the pleasantest and best-conducted houses in all Brighton. It is close to the sea, and just by Mahomed, the sham-poor's shop. I likes Jonathan, for he is a sportsman, and we spin a yarn together about 'unting, and how he used to ride over the moon when he whipped in to St. John, in Berkshire. But it's all talk with Jonathan now, for he's more like a stranded grampus now than a fox-hunter. In course I brought down a pair of kickseys and pipe-cases, intending to have a round with the old muggers, but the snow put a stop to all that. I heard, however, that both the Telscombe Tye and the Devil's Dike dogs had been running their half-crown rounds after hares, some of which ended in "captures," others in "escapes," as the newspapers terms them. I dined at the Albion on Christmas Day, and most misfortunately, my appetite was ready before the joints, so I had to make my dinner off Mary Ann cutlets, I think they call them, that is to say, chops screwed up in large curl papers, and such-like trifles. I saw some chaps drinking small glasses of stuff, so I asked the waiter what it was, and, thinking he said "Elixir of Girls," I banged the table, and said, "Elixir of Girls! that's the stuff for my money—give me a glass." The chap laughed, and said, "Not Girls, sir, but Garus"; and thereupon he gave another great guffaw.

It is a capital coffee-room, full of winders, and finely-polished tables, waiters in silk stockings, and they give spermaceti cheese, and burn Parmesan candles. The chaps in it, however, were werry unsociable, and there wasn't a man there that I would borrow half a crown to get drunk with. Stickey is the landlord, but he does not stick it in so deep as might be expected from the looks of the house, and the cheese and candles considered. It was a most tempestersome night, and, having eaten and drank to completion, I determined to go and see if my aunt, in Cavendish Street, was alive; and after having been nearly blown out to France several times, I succeeded in making my point and running to ground. The storm grew worser and worser, and when I came to open the door to go away, I found it blocked with snow, and the drifts whirling about in all directions. My aunt, who is a werry feeling woman, insisted on my staying all night, which only made the matter worse, for when I came to look out in the morning I found the drift as high as the first floor winder, and the street completely buried in snow. Having breakfasted, and seeing no hopes of emancipation, I hangs out a flag of distress—a red wipe—which, after flapping about for some time, drew three or four sailors and a fly-man or two. I explained from the winder how dreadfully I was situated, prayed of them to release me, but the wretches did nothing but laugh, and ax wot I would give to be out. At last one of them, who acted as spokesman, proposed that I should put an armchair out of the winder, and pay them five shillings each for carrying me home on their shoulders. It seemed a vast of money, but the storm continuing, the crowd increasing, and I not wishing to kick up a row at my aunt's, after offering four and sixpence, agreed to their terms, and throwing out a chair, plumped up to the middle in a drift. Three cheers followed the feat, which drew all the neighbours to the winders, when about half a dozen fellows, some drunk, some sober, and some half-and-half, pulled me into the chair, hoisted me on to their shoulders, and proceeded into St. James's Street, bellowing out, "Here's the new member for Brighton! Here's the boy wot sleeps in Cavendish Street! Huzzah, the old 'un for ever! There's an elegant man for a small tea-party! Who wants a fat chap to send to their friends this Christmas?" The noise they made was quite tremendious, and the snow in many places being up to their middles, we made werry slow progress, but still they would keep me in the chair, and before we got to the end of the street the crowd had increased to some hundreds. Here they began snow-balling, and my hat and wig soon went flying, and then there was a fresh holloa. "Here's Mr. Wigney, the member for Brighton," they cried out; "I say, old boy, are you for the ballot? You must call on the King this morning; he wants to give you a Christmas-box." Just then one of the front bearers tumbled, and down we all rolled into a drift, just opposite Daly's backey shop. There were about twenty of us in together, but being pretty near the top, I was soon on my legs, and seeing an opening, I bolted right forward—sent three or four fellows flying—dashed down the passage behind Saxby's wine vaults, across the Steyne, floundering into the drifts, followed by the mob, shouting and pelting me all the way. This double made some of the beggars over-shoot the mark, and run past the statute of George the Fourth, but, seeing their mistake, or hearing the other portion of the pack running in the contrary direction, they speedily joined heads and tails, and gave me a devil of a burst up the narrow lane by the Wite 'Orse 'Otel. Fortunately Jonathan Boxall's door was open, and Jonathan himself in the passage bar, washing some decanters. "Look sharp, Jonathan!" said I, dashing past him as wite as a miller, "look sharp! come out of that, and be after clapping your great carcase against the door to keep the Philistines out, or they'll be the death of us both." Quick as thought the door was closed and bolted before ever the leaders had got up, but, finding this the case, the mob halted and proceeded to make a deuce of a kick-up before the house, bellowing and shouting like mad fellows, and threatening to pull it down if I did not show. Jonathan got narvous, and begged and intreated me to address them. I recommended him to do it himself, but he said he was quite unaccustomed to public speaking, and he would stand two glasses of "cold without" if I would. "Hot with," said I, "and I'll do it." "Done," said he, and he knocked the snow off my coat, pulled my wig straight, and made me look decent, and took me to a bow-winder'd room on the first floor, threw up; the sash, and exhibited me to the company outside. I bowed and kissed my hand like a candidate. They cheered and shouted, and then called for silence whilst; I addressed them. "Gentlemen," said I, "Who are you?" "Why, we be the men wot carried your honour's glory from Cavendish Street, and wants to be paid for it."; "Gentlemen," said I, "I'm no orator, but I'm a honest man; I pays everybody twenty shillings in the pound. and no mistake (cheers). If you had done your part of the bargain, I would have done mine, but 'ow can you expect to be paid after spilling me? This is a most inclement day, and, whatever you may say to the contrary, I'm not Mr. Clement Wigney."— "No, nor Mr. Faithful neither," bellowed one of the bearers.—said I, "you'll get the complaints of the season, chilblains and influhensa, if you stand dribbling there in the snow. Let me advise you to mizzle, for, if you don't, I'm blowed if I don't divide a whole jug of cold water equally amongst you. Go home to your wives and children, and don't be after annoying an honest, independent, amiable publican, like Jonathan Boxall. That's all I've got to say, and if I was to talk till I'm black in the face, I couldn't say nothing more to the purpose; so, I wishes you all 'A Merry Christmas and an 'Appy New Year.'"

But I'm fatiguing you, Mr. Nimrod, with all this, which is only hinteresting to the parties concerned, so will pass on to other topics. I saw the King riding in his coach with his Sunday coat on. He looked werry well, but his nose was rather blueish at the end, a sure sign that he is but a mortal, and feels the cold just like any other man. The Queen did not show, but I saw some of her maids of honour, who made me think of the Richmond cheesecakes. There were a host of pretty ladies, and the cold gave a little colour to their noses, too, which, I think, improved their appearance wastly, for I've always remarked that your ladies of quality are rather pasty, and do not generally show their high blood in their cheeks and noses. I'm werry fond of looking at pretty girls, whether maids of 'onour or maids of all work.

The storm stopped all wisiting, and even the Countess of Winterton's ball was obliged to be put off. Howsomever, that did not interfere at all with Jonathan Boxall and me, except that it, perhaps, made us take a bottom of brandy more than usual, particularly after Jonathan had run over again one of his best runs.

Now, dear Nimrod, adieu. Whenever you comes over to England, I shall be werry 'appy to see you in Great Coram Street, where dinner is on the table punctually at five on week days, and four on Sundays; and with best regards to Mrs. Nimrod, and all the little Nimrods,

I remain, for Self and Co., yours to serve,

JOHN JORROCKS.

XII
MR. JORROCKS'S DINNER PARTY

THE general postman had given the final flourish to his bell, and the muffin-girl had just begun to tinkle hers, when a capacious yellow hackney-coach, with a faded scarlet hammer-cloth, was seen jolting down Great Coram Street, and pulling up at Mr. Jorrocks's door.

Before Jarvey had time to apply his hand to the area bell, after giving the usual three knocks and a half to the brass lion's head on the door, it was opened by the boy Benjamin in a new drab coat, with a blue collar, and white sugar-loaf buttons, drab waistcoat, and black velveteen breeches, with well-darned white cotton stockings.

The knock drew Mr. Jorrocks from his dining-room, where he had been acting the part of butler, for which purpose he had put off his coat and appeared in his shirtsleeves, dressed in nankeen shorts, white gauze silk stockings, white neckcloth, and white waistcoat, with a frill as large as a hand-saw. Handing the bottle and corkscrew to Betsey, he shuffled himself into a smart new blue saxony coat with velvet collar and metal buttons, and advanced into the passage to greet the arrivers.

"Oh! gentlemen, gentlemen," exclaimed he, "I'm so 'appy to see you—so werry 'appy you carn't think," holding out both hands to the foremost, who happened to be Nimrod; "this is werry kind of you, for I declare it's six to a minute. 'Ow are you, Mr. Nimrod? Most proud to see you at my humble crib. Well, Stubbs, my boy, 'ow do you do? Never knew you late in my life," giving him a hearty slap on the back. "Mr. Spiers, I'm werry 'appy to see you. You are just what a sporting publisher ought to be—punctuality itself. Now, gentlemen, dispose of your tiles, and come upstairs to Mrs. J——, and let's get you introduced." "I fear we are late, Mr. Jorrocks," observed Nimrod, advancing past the staircase end to hang up his hat on a line of pegs against the wall.

"Not a bit of it," replied Mr. Jorrocks—"not a bit of it—quite the contrary—you are the first, in fact!"

"Indeed!" replied Nimrod, eyeing a table full of hats by where he stood—"why here are as many hats as would set up a shop. I really thought I'd got into Beaver (Belvoir) Castle by mistake!"

"Haw! haw! haw! werry good, Mr. Happerley, werry good indeed—I owes you one."

"I thought it was a castor-oil mill," rejoined Mr. Spiers.

"Haw! haw! haw! werry good, Mr. Spiers, werry good indeed—owes you one also—but I see what you're driving at. You think these hats have a coconut apiece belonging to them upstairs. No such thing I assure you; no such thing. The fact is, they are what I've won at warious times of the members of our hunt, and as I've got you great sporting coves dining with me, I'm a-going to set them out on my sideboard, just as racing gents exhibit their gold and silver cups, you know. Binjimin! I say, Binjimin! you blackguard," holloaing down the kitchen stairs, "why don't you set out the castors as I told you? and see you brush them well!" "Coming, sir, coming, sir!" replied Benjamin, from below, who at that moment was busily engaged, taking advantage of Betsey's absence, in scooping marmalade out of a pot with his thumb. "There's a good lot of them," said Mr. Jorrocks, resuming the conversation, "four, six, eight, ten, twelve, thirteen—all trophies of sporting prowess. Real good hats. None o' your nasty gossamers, or dog-hair ones. There's a tile!" said he, balancing a nice new white one with green rims on the tip of his finger. "I won that in a most miraculous manner. A most wonderful way, in fact. I was driving to Croydon one morning in my four-wheeled one-'oss chay, and just as I got to Lilleywhite, the blacksmith's, below Brixton Hill, they had thrown up a drain—a 'gulph' I may call it—across the road for the purpose of repairing the gas-pipe—I was rayther late as it was, for our 'ounds are werry punctual, and there was nothing for me but either to go a mile and a half about, or drive slap over the gulph. Well, I looked at it, and the more I looked at it the less I liked it; but just as I was thinking I had seen enough of it, and was going to turn away, up tools Timothy Truman in his buggy, and he, too, began to crane and look into the abyss—and a terrible place it was, I assure you—quite frightful, and he liked it no better than myself. Seeing this, I takes courage, and said, 'Why, Tim, your 'oss will do it!' 'Thank'e, Mr. J——,' said he, 'I'll follow you.' 'Then,' said I, 'if you'll change wehicles'—for, mind ye, I had no notion of damaging my own—'I'll bet you a hat I gets over.' 'Done,' said he, and out he got; so I takes his 'oss by the head, looses the bearing-rein, and leading him quietly up to the place and letting him have a look at it, gave him a whack over the back, and over he went, gig and all, as clever as could be!"

Stubbs. Well done, Mr. J——, you are really a most wonderful man! You have the most extraordinary adventures of any man breathing—but what did you do with your own machine?

Jorrocks. Oh! you see, I just turned round to Binjimin, who was with me, and said, You may go home, and, getting into Timothy's buggy, I had my ride for nothing, and the hat into the bargain. A nice hat it is too—regular beaver—a guinea's worth at least. All true what I've told you, isn't it, Binjimin?

"Quite!" replied Benjamin, putting his thumb to his nose, and spreading his fingers like a fan as he slunk behind his master.

"But come, gentlemen," resumed Mr. Jorrocks, "let's be after going upstairs.—Binjimin, announce the gentlemen as your missis taught you. Open the door with your left hand, and stretch the right towards her, to let the company see the point to make up to."

The party ascend the stairs one at a time, for the flight is narrow and rather abrupt, and Benjamin, obeying his worthy master's injunctions, threw open the front drawing-room door, and discovered Mrs. Jorrocks sitting in state at a round table, with annuals and albums spread at orthodox distances around. The possession of this room had long been a bone of contention between Mr. Jorrocks and his spouse, but at length they had accommodated matters by Mr. Jorrocks gaining undivided possession of the back drawing-room (communicating by folding-doors), with the run of the front one equally with Mrs. Jorrocks on non-company days. A glance, however, showed which was the master's and which the mistress's room. The front one was papered with weeping willows, bending under the weight of ripe cherries on a white ground, and the chair cushions were covered with pea-green cotton velvet with yellow worsted bindings.

The round table was made of rosewood, and there was a "whatnot" on the right of the fire-place of similar material, containing a handsomely-bound collection of Sir Walter Scott's Works, in wood. The carpet-pattern consisted of most dashing bouquets of many-coloured flowers, in winding French horns on a very light drab ground, so light, indeed, that Mr. Jorrocks was never allowed to tread upon it except in pumps or slippers. The bell-pulls were made of foxes' brushes, and in the frame of the looking-glass, above the white marble mantelpiece, were stuck visiting-cards, notes of invitation, thanks for "obliging inquiries," etc. The hearth-rug exhibited a bright yellow tiger, with pink eyes, on a blue ground, with a flossy green border; and the fender and fire-irons were of shining brass. On the wall, immediately opposite the fire-place, was a portrait of Mrs. Jorrocks before she was married, so unlike her present self that no one would have taken it for her. The back drawing-room, which looked out upon the gravel walk and house-backs beyond, was papered with broad scarlet and green stripes in honour of the Surrey Hunt uniform, and was set out with a green-covered library table in the centre, with a red morocco hunting-chair between it and the window, and several good strong hair-bottomed mahogany chairs around the walls. The table had a very literary air, being strewed with sporting magazines, odd numbers of *Bell's Life*, pamphlets, and papers of various descriptions, while on a sheet of foolscap on the portfolio were ten lines of an elegy on a giblet pie which had been broken in coming from the baker's, at which Mr. Jorrocks had been hammering for some time. On the side opposite the fire-place, on a hanging range of mahogany shelves, were ten volumes of *Bell's Life in London*, the *New Sporting Magazine*, bound gilt and lettered, the *Memoirs of Harriette Wilson*, *Boxiana*, Taplin's *Farriery*, Nimrod's *Life of Mytton*, and a backgammon board that Mr. Jorrocks had bought by mistake for a history of England.

Mrs. Jorrocks, as we said before, was sitting in state at the far side of the round table, on a worsted-worked ottoman exhibiting a cock pheasant on a white ground, and was fanning herself with a red-and-white paper fan, and turning over the leaves of an annual. How Mr. Jorrocks happened to marry her, no one could ever divine, for she never was pretty, had very little money, and not even a decent figure to recommend her. It was generally supposed at the time, that his brother Joe and he having had a deadly feud about a bottom piece of muffin, the lady's friends had talked him into the match, in the hopes of his having a family to leave his money to, instead of bequeathing it to Joe or his children. Certain it is, they never were meant for each other; Mr. Jorrocks, as our readers have seen, being all nature and impulse, while Mrs. Jorrocks was all vanity and affectation. To describe her accurately is more than we can pretend to, for she looked so different in different dresses, that Mr. Jorrocks himself sometimes did not recognise her. Her face was round, with a good strong brick-dust sort of complexion, a turn-up nose, eyes that were grey in one light and green in another, and a middling-sized mouth, with a double chin below. Mr. Jorrocks used to say that she was "warranted" to him as twelve years younger than himself, but many people supposed the difference of age between them was not so great. Her stature was of the middle height, and she was of one breadth from the shoulders to the heels. She was dressed in a flaming scarlet satin gown, with swan's-down round the top, as also at the arms, and two flounces of the same material round the bottom. Her turban was of green velvet, with a gold fringe, terminating in a bunch over the left side, while a bird-of-paradise inclined towards the right. Across her forehead she wore a gold band, with a many-coloured glass butterfly (a present from James Green), and her neck, arms, waist (at least what ought to have been her waist) were hung round and studded with mosaic-gold chains, brooches, rings, buttons, bracelets, etc., looking for all the world like a portable pawnbroker's shop, or the lump of beef that Sinbad the sailor threw into the Valley of Diamonds. In the right of a gold band round her middle, was an immense gold watch, with a bunch of mosaic seals appended to a massive chain of the same material; and a large miniature of Mr. Jorrocks when he was a young man, with his hair stiffly curled, occupied a place on her left side. On her right arm dangled a green velvet bag with a gold cord, out of which one of Mr. Jorrocks's silk handkerchiefs protruded, while a crumpled, yellowish-white cambric one, with a lace fringe, lay at her side.

On an hour-glass stool, a little behind Mrs. Jorrocks, sat her niece Belinda (Joe Jorrocks's eldest daughter), a nice laughing pretty girl of sixteen, with languishing blue eyes, brown hair, a nose of the "turn-up" order, beautiful mouth and teeth, a very fair complexion, and a gracefully moulded figure. She had just left one of the finishing and polishing seminaries in the neighbourhood of Bromley, where, for two hundred a year and upwards, all the teasing accomplishments of life are taught, and Mrs. Jorrocks, in her own mind, had already appropriated her to James Green, while Mr. Jorrocks, on the other hand, had assigned her to Stubbs. Belinda's dress was simplicity itself; her silken hair hung in shining tresses down her smiling face, confined by a plain tortoiseshell comb behind, and a narrow pink velvet band before. Round her swan-like neck was a plain white cornelian necklace; and her well-washed white muslin frock, confined by a pink sash, flowing behind in a bow, met in simple folds across her swelling bosom. Black sandal shoes confined her fairy feet, and with French cotton stockings, completed her toilette. Belinda, though young, was a celebrated eastern beauty, and there was not a butcher's boy in Whitechapel, from Michael Scales downwards, but what eyed her with delight as she passed along from Shoreditch on her daily walk.

The presentations having been effected, and the heat of the day, the excellence of the house, the cleanliness of Great Coram Street—the usual topics, in short, when people know nothing of each other—having been discussed, our party scattered themselves about the room to await the pleasing announcement of dinner. Mr. Jorrocks, of course, was in attendance upon Nimrod, while Mr. Stubbs made love to Belinda behind Mrs. Jorrocks.

Presently a loud long-protracted "rat-tat-tat-tat-tan, rat-tat-tat-tat-tan," at the street door sounded through the house, and Jorrocks, with a slap on his thigh, exclaimed, "By Jingo! there's Green. No man knocks with such wigorous wiolence as he does. All Great Coram Street and parts adjacent know when he comes. Julius Caesar himself couldn't kick up a greater row." "What Green is it, Green of Rollestone?" inquired Nimrod, thinking of his Leicestershire friend. "No," said Mr. Jorrocks, "Green of Tooley Street. You'll have heard of the Greens in the borough, 'emp, 'op, and 'ide (hemp, hop, and hide) merchants— numerous family, numerous as the 'airs in my vig. This is James Green, jun., whose father, old James Green, jun., *verd antique*, as I calls him, is the son of James Green, sen., who is in the 'emp line, and James is own cousin to young old James Green, sen., whose father is in the 'ide line." The remainder of the pedigree was lost by Benjamin throwing open the door and announcing Mr. Green; and Jemmy, who had been exchanging his cloth boots for patent-leather pumps, came bounding upstairs like a racket-ball. "My dear Mrs. Jorrocks," cried he, swinging through the company to her, "I'm delighted to see you looking so well. I declare you are fifty per cent younger than you were. Belinda, my love, 'ow are you? Jorrocks, my friend, 'ow do ye do?"

"Thank ye, James," said Jorrocks, shaking hands with him most cordially, "I'm werry well, indeed, and delighted to see you. Now let me present you to Nimrod."

"Ay, Nimrod!" said Green, in his usual flippant style, with a nod of his head, "'ow are ye, Nimrod? I've heard of you, I think—Nimrod Brothers and Co., bottle merchants, Crutched Friars, ain't it?"

"No," said Jorrocks, in an undertone with a frown—Happerley Nimrod, the great sporting hauthor."

"True," replied Green, not at all disconcerted, "I've heard of him— Nimrod—the mighty 'unter before the lord. Glad to see ye, Nimrod. Stubbs, 'ow are ye?" nodding to the Yorkshireman, as he jerked himself on to a chair on the other side of Belinda.

As usual, Green was as gay as a peacock. His curly flaxen wig projected over his forehead like the roof of a Swiss cottage, and his pointed gills were supported by a stiff black mohair stock, with a broad front and black frill confined with jet studs down the centre. His coat was light green, with archery buttons, made very wide at the hips, with which he sported a white waistcoat, bright yellow ochre leather trousers, pink silk stockings, and patent-leather pumps. In his hand he carried a white silk handkerchief, which smelt most powerfully of musk; and a pair of dirty wristbands drew the eye to sundry dashing rings upon his fingers.

Jonathan Crane, a little long-nosed old city wine-merchant, a member of the Surrey Hunt, being announced and presented, Mrs. Jorrocks declared herself faint from the heat of the room, and begged to be excused for a few minutes. Nimrod, all politeness, was about to offer her his arm, but Mr. Jorrocks pulled him back, whispering, "Let her go, let her go." "The fact is," said he in an undertone after she was out of hearing, "it's a way Mrs. J—— has when she wants to see that dinner's all right. You see she's a terrible high-bred woman, being a cross between a gentleman-usher and a lady's-maid, and doesn't like to be supposed to look after these things, so when she goes, she always pretend to faint. You'll see her back presently," and, just as he spoke, in she came with a half-pint smelling-bottle at her nose. Benjamin followed immediately after, and throwing open the door proclaimed, in a half-fledged voice, that "dinner was sarved," upon which the party all started on their legs.

"Now, Mr. Happerley Nimrod," cried Jorrocks, "you'll trot Mrs. J—— down—according to the book of etiquette, you know, giving her the wall side.[25] Sorry, gentlemen, I havn't ladies apiece for you, but my sally-manger, as we say in France, is rayther small, besides which I never like to dine more than eight. Stubbs, my boy, Green and you must toss up for Belinda—here's a halfpenny, and let be 'Newmarket'[26] if you please. Wot say you? a voman! Stubbs wins!" cried Mr. Jorrocks, as the halfpenny fell head downwards. "Now, Spiers, couple up with Crane, and James and I will whip in to you. But stop, gentlemen!" cried Mr. Jorrocks, as he reached the top of the stairs, "let me make one request—that you von't eat the windmill you'll see on the centre of the table. Mrs. Jorrocks has hired it for the evening, of Mr. Farrell, the confectioner, in Lamb's Conduit Street, and it's engaged to two or three evening parties after it leaves this." "Lauk, John! how wulgar you are. What matter can it make to your friends where the windmill comes from!" exclaimed Mrs. Jorrocks in an audible voice from below, Nimrod, with admirable skill, having piloted her down the straights and turns of the staircase. Having squeezed herself between the backs of the chairs and the wall, Mrs. Jorrocks at length reached the head of the table, and with a bump of her body and wave of her hand motioned Nimrod to take the seat on her right. Green then pushed past Belinda and Stubbs, and took the place on Mrs. Jorrocks's left, so Stubbs, with a dexterous manoeuvre, placed himself in the centre of the table, with Belinda between himself and her uncle. Crane and Spiers then filled the vacant places on Nimrod's side, Mr. Spiers facing Mr. Stubbs.

The dining-room was the breadth of the passage narrower than the front drawing-room, and, as Mr. Jorrocks truly said, was rayther small—but the table being excessively broad, made the room appear less than it was. It was lighted up with spermaceti candles in silver holders, one at each corner of the table, and there was a lamp in the wall between the red-curtained windows, immediately below a brass nail, on which Mr. Jorrocks's great hunting-whip and a bunch of boot garters were hung. Two more candles in the hands of bronze Dianas on the marble mantelpiece, lighted up a coloured copy of Barraud's picture of John Warde on Blue Ruin; while Mr. Ralph Lambton, on his horse Undertaker, with his hounds and men, occupied a frame on the opposite wall. The old-fashioned cellaret sideboard, against the wall at the end, supported a large bright-burning

---

[25] "In your passage from one room to another, offer the lady the wall in going downstairs," etc,—*Spirit of Etiquette.*

[26] "We have repeatedly decided that Newmarket is *one* toss."—*Bell's Life.*

brass lamp, with raised foxes round the rim, whose effulgent rays shed a brilliant halo over eight black hats and two white ones, whereof the four middle ones were decorated with evergreens and foxes' brushes. The dinner table was crowded, not covered. There was scarcely a square inch of cloth to be seen on any part. In the centre stood a magnificent finely spun barley-sugar windmill, two feet and a half high, with a spacious sugar foundation, with a cart and horses and two or three millers at the door, and a she-miller working a ball-dress flounce at a lower window.

The whole dinner, first, second, third, fourth course —everything, in fact, except dessert—was on the table, as we sometimes see it at ordinaries and public dinners. Before both Mr. and Mrs. Jorrocks were two great tureens of mock-turtle soup, each capable of holding a gallon, and both full up to the brim. Then there were two sorts of fish; turbot and lobster sauce, and a great salmon. A round of boiled beef and an immense piece of roast occupied the rear of these, ready to march on the disappearance of the fish and soup—and behind the walls, formed by the beef of old England, came two dishes of grouse, each dish holding three brace. The side dishes consisted of a calf's head hashed, a leg of mutton, chickens, ducks, and mountains of vegetables; and round the windmill were plum-puddings, tarts, jellies, pies, and puffs.

Behind Mrs. Jorrocks's chair stood "Batsay" with a fine brass-headed comb in her hair, and stiff ringlets down her ruddy cheeks. She was dressed in a green silk gown, with a coral necklace, and one of Mr. Jorrocks's lavender and white coloured silk pocket-handkerchiefs made into an apron. "Binjimin" stood with the door in his hand, as the saying is, with a towel twisted round his thumb, as though he had cut it.

"Now, gentlemen," said Mr. Jorrocks, casting his eye up the table, as soon as they had all got squeezed and wedged round it, and the dishes were uncovered, "you see your dinner, eat whatever you like except the windmill—hope you'll be able to satisfy nature with what's on—would have had more but Mrs. J—— is so werry fine, she won't stand two joints of the same sort on the table."

Mrs. J. Lauk, John, how can you be so wulgar! Who ever saw two rounds of beef, as you wanted to have? Besides, I'm sure the gentlemen will excuse any little defishency, considering the short notice we have had, and that this is not an elaborate dinner.

Mr. Spiers. I'm sure, ma'm, there's no de*fish*ency at all. Indeed, I think there's as much fish as would serve double the number—and I'm sure you look as if you had your soup "on sale or return," as we say in the magazine line.

Mr. J. Haw! haw! haw! werry good, Mr. Spiers. I owe you one. Not bad soup though—had it from Birch's. Let me send you some; and pray lay into it, or I shall think you don't like it. Mr. Happerley, let me send you some—and, gentlemen, let me observe, once for all, that there's every species of malt liquor under the side table. Prime stout, from the Marquess Cornwallis, hard by. Also ale, table, and what my friend Crane there calls lamen*table*—he says, because it's so werry small—but, in truth, because I don't buy it of him. There's all sorts of drench, in fact, except water—thing I never touch—rots one's shoes, don't know what it would do with one's stomach if it was to get there. Mr. Crane, you're eating nothing. I'm quite shocked to see you; you don't surely live upon hair? Do help yourself, or you'll faint from werry famine. Belinda, my love, does the Yorkshireman take care of you? Who's for some salmon?—bought at Luckey's, and there's both Tallyho and Tantivy sarce to eat with it. Somehow or other I always fancies I rides harder after eating these sarces with fish. Mr. Happerley Nimrod, you are the greatest man at table, consequently I axes you to drink wine first, according to the book of etiquette—help yourself, sir. Some of Crane's particklar, hot and strong, real stuff, none of your wan de bones (vin de beaume) or rot-gut French stuff—hope you like it—if you don't, pray speak your mind freely, now that we have Crane among us. Binjimin, get me some of that duck before Mr. Spiers, a leg and a wing, if you please, sir, and a bit of the breast.

Mr. Spiers. Certainly, sir, certainly. Do you prefer a right or left wing, sir?

Mr. Jorrocks. Oh, either. I suppose it's all the same.

Mr. Spiers. Why no, sir, it's not exactly all the same; for it happens there is only one remaining, therefore it must be the *left* one.

Mr. J. (chuckling). Haw! haw! haw! Mr. S——, werry good that—werry good indeed. I owes you two.

"I'll trouble you for a little, Mr. Spiers, if you please," says Crane, handing his plate round the windmill.

"I'm sorry, sir, it is all gone," replies Mr. Spiers, who had just filled Mr. Jorrocks's plate; "there's nothing left but the neck," holding it up on the fork.

"Well, send it," rejoins Mr. Crane; "neck or nothing, you know, Mr. Jorrocks, as we say with the Surrey."

"Haw! haw! haw!" grunts Mr. Jorrocks, who is busy sucking a bone; "haw! hawl haw! werry good, Crane, werry good—owes you one. Now, gentlemen," added he, casting his eye up the table as he spoke, "let me adwise ye, before you attack the grouse, to take the hedge (edge) off your appetites, or else there won't be enough, and, you know, it does not do to eat the farmer after the gentlemen. Let's see, now—three and three are six, six brace among eight—oh dear, that's nothing like enough. I wish, Mrs. J——, you had followed my adwice, and roasted them all. And now, Binjimin, you're going to break the windmill with your clumsiness, you little dirty rascal! Why von't you let Batsay arrange the table? Thank you, Mr. Crane, for your assistance—your politeness, sir, exceeds your beauty." [A barrel organ strikes up before the window, and Jorrocks throws down his knife and fork in an agony.] "Oh dear, oh dear, there's that cursed horgan again. It's a regular annihilator. Binjimin, run and kick the fellow's werry soul out of him. There's no man suffers so much from music as I do. I wish I had a pocketful of sudden deaths, that I might throw one at every thief of a musicianer that comes up the street. I declare the scoundrel has set all my teeth on edge. Mr. Nimrod, pray take another glass of wine after your roast beef.— Well, with Mrs. J—— if you choose, but I'll join you—always says that you are the werry cleverest man of the day—read all your writings—anny-tommy (anatomy) of gaming, and all. Am a hauthor myself, you know—once set to, to write a werry long and elaborate harticle on scent, but after cudgelling my brains, and turning the thing over and over again in my mind, all that I could brew on the subject was, that scent was a werry rum thing; nothing rummer than scent, except a woman."

"Pray," cried Mrs. Jorrocks, her eyes starting as she spoke, "don't let us have any of your low-lifed stable conversation here—you think to show off before the ladies," added she, "and flatter yourself you talk about what we don't understand. Now, I'll be bound to say, with all your fine sporting hinformation, you carn't tell me whether a mule brays or neighs!"

"Vether a mule brays or neighs?" repeated Mr. Jorrocks, considering. "I'll lay I can!"

"Which, then?" inquired Mrs. Jorrocks.

"Vy, I should say it brayed."

"Mule bray!" cried Mrs. Jorrocks, clapping her hands with delight, "there's a cockney blockhead for you! It brays, does it?"

Mr. Jorrocks. I meant to say, neighed.

"Ho! ho! ho!" grinned Mrs. J——, "neighs, does it? You are a nice man for a fox-'unter—a mule neighs—thought I'd catch you some of these odd days with your wain conceit."

"Vy, what does it do then?" inquired Mr. Jorrocks, his choler rising as he spoke. "I hopes, at all ewents, he don't make the 'orrible noise you do."

"Why, it screams, you great hass!" rejoined his loving spouse.

A single, but very resolute knock at the street door, sounding quite through the house, stopped all further ebullition, and Benjamin, slipping out, held a short conversation with someone in the street, and returned.

"What's happened now, Binjimin?" inquired Mr. Jorrocks, with anxiety on his countenance, as the boy re-entered the room; "the 'osses arn't amiss, I 'ope?"

"Please, sir, Mr. Farrell's young man has come for the windmill—he says you've had it two hours," replied Benjamin.

"The deuce be with Mr. Farrell's young man! he does not suppose we can part with the mill before the cloth's drawn—tell him to mizzle, or I'll mill him. 'Now's the day and now's the hour'; who's for some grouse? Gentlemen, make your game, in fact. But first of all let's have a round robin. Pass the wine, gentlemen. What wine do you take, Stubbs."

"Why, champagne is good enough for me."

Mr. Jorrocks, I dare say; but if you wait till you get any here, you will have a long time to stop. Shampain, indeed! had enough of that nonsense abroad—declare you young chaps drink shampain like hale. There's red and wite port, and sherry, in fact, and them as carn't drink, they must go without.

    X. was expensive and soon became poor,

    Y. was the wise man and kept want from the door.

"Now for the grouse!" added he, as the two beefs disappeared, and they took their stations at the top and bottom of the table. "Fine birds, to be sure! Hope you havn't burked your appetites, gentlemen, so as not to be able to do justice to them—smell high—werry good—gamey, in fact. Binjimin. take an 'ot plate to Mr. Nimrod—sarve us all round with them."

The grouse being excellent, and cooked to a turn, little execution was done upon the pastry, and the jellies had all melted long before it came to their turn to be eat. At length everyone, Mr. Jorrocks and all, appeared satisfied, and the noise of knives and forks was succeeded by the din of tongues and the ringing of glasses, as the eaters refreshed themselves with wine or malt liquors. Cheese and biscuit being handed about on plates, according to the *Spirit of Etiquette*. Binjimin and Batsay at length cleared the table, lifted off the windmill, and removed the cloth. Mr. Jorrocks then delivered himself of a most emphatic grace.

The wine and dessert being placed on the table, the ceremony of drinking healths all round was performed. "Your good health, Mrs. J——.—Belinda, my loove, your good health—wish you a good 'usband.—Nimrod, your good health.—James Green, your good health.—Old *verd antique's* good health.—Your uncle's good health.—All the Green family.—Stubbs, your good health.— Spiers, Crane, etc." The bottles then pass round three times, on each of which occasions Mrs. Jorrocks makes them pay toll. The fourth time she let them pass; and Jorrocks began to grunt, hem, and haw, and kick the leg of the table, by way of giving her a hint to depart. This caused a dead silence, which at length was broken by the Yorkshireman's exclaiming "horrid pause!"

"Horrid paws!" vociferated Mrs. J——, in a towering rage, "so would yours, let me tell you, sir, if you had helped to cook all that dinner": and gathering herself up and repeating the words "horrid paws, indeed, I like your imperence," she sailed out of the room like an exasperated turkey-cock; her face, from heat, anger, and the quantity she had drank, being as red as her gown. Indeed, she looked for all the world as if she had been put into a furnace and blown red hot. Jorrocks having got rid of his "worser half," as he calls her, let out a reef or two of his acre of white waistcoat, and each man made himself comfortable according to his acceptation of the term. "Gentlemen," says Jorrocks, "I'll trouble you to charge your glasses, 'eel-taps off—a bumper toast—no skylights, if you please. Crane, pass the wine—you are a regular old stop-bottle—a turnpike gate, in fact. I think you take back hands—gentlemen, are you all charged?—then I'll give you THE NOBLE SPORT OF FOX-'UNTING! gentlemen, with three times three, and Crane will give the 'ips—all ready—now, ip, 'ip, 'ip, 'uzza, 'uzza, 'uzza—'ip, 'ip, 'ip, 'uzza, 'uzza, 'uzza—'ip, 'ip, 'ip, 'uzza, 'uzza, 'uzza.—one cheer more, 'UZZA!" After this followed "The Merry Harriers," then came "The Staggers," after that "The Trigger, and bad luck to Cheatum," all bumpers; when Jorrocks, having screwed his courage up to the sticking-place, called for another, which being complied with, he rose and delivered himself as follows:

"Gentlemen, in rising to propose the toast which I am now about to propose—I feel—I feel—(Yorkshireman—'very queer?') J—— No, not verry queer, and I'll trouble you to hold your jaw (laughter). Gentlemen, I say, in rising to propose the toast which I am about to give, I feel—I feel—(Crane—'werry nervous?') J—— No, not werry nervous, so none of your nonsense; let me alone, I say. I say, in rising to propose the toast which I am about to give, I feel—(Mr. Spiers—'very foolish?' Nimrod—'very funny?' Crane—'werry rum?') J—— No, werry proud of the distinguished honour that has been conferred upon me—conferred upon me—conferred upon me—distinguished honour that has been conferred upon me by the presence, this day, of one of the most distinguished men—distinguished men—by the presence, this day, of one of the most distinguished men and sportsmen—of modern times (cheers.) Gentlemen—this is the proudest moment of my life! the eyes of England are upon us! I give you the health of Mr. Happerley Nimrod." (Drunk with three times three.)

When the cheering, and dancing of the glasses had somewhat subsided, Nimrod rose and spoke as follows:

"Mr. Jorrocks, and gentlemen",

"The handsome manner in which my health has been proposed by our worthy and estimable host, and the flattering reception it has met with from you, merit my warmest acknowledgments. I should, indeed, be unworthy of the land which gave me birth, were I insensible of the honour which has just been done me by so enlightened and distinguished an assembly as the present. My friend, Mr. Jorrocks, has been pleased to designate me as one of the most distinguished sportsmen of the day, a title, however, to which I feel I have little claim: but this I may say, that I have portrayed our great national sports in their brightest and most glowing colours, and that on sporting subjects my pen shall yield to none (cheers). I have ever been the decided advocate of many sports and exercises, not only on account of the health and vigour they inspire, but because I feel that they are the best safeguards on a nation's energies, and the best protection against luxury, idleness, debauchery, and effeminacy (cheers). The authority of all history informs us, that the energies of countries flourished whilst manly sports have flourished, and decayed as they died away (cheers). What says Juvenal, when speaking of the entry of luxury into Rome?"

Saevior armis
Luxuria incubuit, victumque ulciscitur orbem.

"And we need only refer to ancient history, and to the writings of Xenophon, Cicero, Horace, or Virgil, for evidence of the value they have all attached to the encouragement of manly, active, and hardy pursuits, and the evils produced by a degenerate and effeminate life on the manners and characters of a people (cheers). Many of the most eminent literary characters of this and of other countries have been ardently attached to field sports; and who, that has experienced their beneficial results, can doubt that they are the best promoters of the *mens sana in corpore sano*—the body sound and the understanding clear (cheers)? Gentlemen, it is with feelings of no ordinary gratification that I find myself at the social and truly hospitable board of one of the most distinguished ornaments of one of the most celebrated Hunts in this great country, one whose name and fame have reached the four corners of the globe—to find myself after so long an absence from my native land—an estrangement from all that has ever been nearest and dearest to my heart—once again surrounded by these cheerful countenances which so well express the honest, healthful pursuits of their owners. Let us then," added Nimrod, seizing a decanter and pouring himself out a bumper, "drink, in true Kentish fire, the health and prosperity of that brightest sample of civic sportsmen, the great and renowned JOHN JORROCKS!"

Immense applause followed the conclusion of this speech, during which time the decanters buzzed round the table, and the glasses being emptied, the company rose, and a full charge of Kentish fire followed; Mr. Jorrocks, sitting all the while, looking as uncomfortable as men in his situation generally do.

The cheering having subsided, and the parties having resumed their seats, it was his turn to rise, so getting on his legs, he essayed to speak, but finding, as many men do, that his ideas deserted him the moment the "eyes of England" were turned upon him, after two or three hitches of his nankeens, and as many hems and haws, he very coolly resumed his seat, and spoke as follows:

"Gentlemen, unaccustomed as I am to public speaking, I am taken quite aback by this werry unexpected compliment (cheers); never since I filled the hancient and honerable hoffice of churchwarden in the populous parish of St. Botolph Without, have I experienced a gratification equal to the present. I thank you from the werry bottom of my breeches-pocket (applause). Gentlemen, I'm no horator, but I'm a honest man (cheers). I should indeed be undeserving the name of a sportsman—undeserving of being a member of that great and justly celebrated 'unt, of which Mr. Happerley Nimrod has spun so handsome and flattering a yarn, if I did not feel deeply proud of the compliment you have paid it. It is unpossible for me to follow that great sporting scholar fairly over the ridge and furrow of his werry intricate and elegant horation, for there are many of those fine gentlemen's names—French, I presume—that he mentioned, that I never heard of before, and cannot recollect; but if you will allow me to run 'eel a little, I would make a few hobservations on a few of his hobservations.—Mr. Happerley Nimrod, gentlemen, was pleased to pay a compliment to what he was pleased to call my something 'ospitality. I am extremely obliged to him for it. To be surrounded by one's friends is in my mind the 'Al' of 'uman 'appiness (cheers). Gentlemen, I am most proud of the honour of seeing you all here to-day, and I hope the grub has been to your likin' (cheers), if not, I'll discharge my butcher. On the score of quantity there might be a little deficiency, but I hope the quality was prime. Another time this shall be all remedied (cheers). Gentlemen, I understand those cheers, and I'm flattered by them—I likes 'ospitality!—I'm not the man to keep my butter in a 'pike-ticket, or my coals in a quart pot (immense cheering). Gentlemen, these are my sentiments, I leaves the flowers of speech to them as is better acquainted with botany (laughter)—I likes plain English, both in eating and talking, and I'm happy to see Mr. Happerley Nimrod has not forgot his, and can put up with our homely fare, and do without pantaloon cutlets, blankets of woe,[27] and such-like miseries."

---

[27] "Blanquette de veau."

"I hates their 'orse douvers (hors-d'oeuvres), their rots, and their poisons (poissons); 'ord rot 'em, they near killed me, and right glad am I to get a glass of old British black strap. And talking of black strap, gentlemen, I call on old Crane, the man what supplies it, to tip us a song. So now I'm finished—and you, Crane, lap up your liquor and begin!" (applause).

Crane was shy—unused to sing in company—nevertheless, if it was the wish of the party, and if it would oblige his good customer, Mr. Jorrocks, he would try his hand at a stave or two made in honour of the immortal Surrey. Having emptied his glass and cleared his windpipe, Crane commenced:

"Here's a health to them that can ride!
Here's a health to them that can ride!
And those that don't wish good luck to the cause.
May they roast by their own fireside!
It's good to drown care in the chase,
It's good to drown care in the bowl.
It's good to support Daniel Haigh and his hounds,
Here's his health from the depth of my soul."

CHORUS
"Hurrah for the loud tally-ho!
Hurrah for the loud tally-ho!
It's good to support Daniel Haigh and his hounds.
And echo the shrill tally-ho!"

"Here's a health to them that can ride!
Here's a health to them that ride bold!
May the leaps and the dangers that each has defied,
In columns of sporting be told!
Here's freedom to him that would walk!
Here's freedom to him that would ride!
There's none ever feared that the horn should be heard
Who the joys of the chase ever tried."

"Hurrah for the loud tally-ho!
Hurrah for the loud tally-ho!
It's good to support Daniel Haigh and his hounds,
And halloo the loud tally-ho!"

"Beautiful! beautiful!" exclaimed Jorrocks, clapping his hands and stamping as Crane had ceased.

"A werry good song, and it's werry well sung.
Jolly companions every one!"

"Gentlemen, pray charge your glasses—there's one toast we must drink in a bumper if we ne'er take a bumper again. Mr. Spiers, pray charge your glass—Mr. Stubbs, vy don't you fill up?—Mr. Nimrod, off with your 'eel taps, pray—I'll give ye the 'Surrey 'Unt,' with all my 'art and soul. Crane, my boy, here's your werry good health, and thanks for your song!" (All drink the Surrey Hunt and Crane's good health, with applause, which brings him on his legs with the following speech):

"Gentlemen, unaccustomed as I am to public speaking (laughter), I beg leave on behalf of myself and the absent members of the Surrey 'Unt, to return you our own most 'artfelt thanks for the flattering compliment you have just paid us, and to assure you that the esteem and approbation of our fellow-sportsmen is to us the magnum bonum of all earthly 'appiness (cheers and laughter). Gentlemen, I will not trespass longer upon your valuable time, but as you seem to enjoy this wine of my friend Mr. Jorrocks's, I may just say that I have got some more of the same quality left, at from forty-two to forty-eight shillings a dozen, also some good stout draught port, at ten and sixpence a gallon—some ditto werry superior at fifteen; also foreign and British spirits, and Dutch liqueurs, rich and rare." The conclusion of the vintner's address was drowned in shouts of laughter. Mr. Jorrocks then called upon the company in succession for a toast, a song, or a sentiment. Nimrod gave, "The Royal Staghounds"; Crane gave, "Champagne to our real friends, and real pain to our sham friends"; Green sung, "I'd be a butterfly"; Mr. Stubbs gave, "Honest men and bonnie lasses"; and Mr. Spiers, like a patriotic printer, gave, "The liberty of the Press," which he said was like fox-hunting—"if we have it not we die"—all of which Mr. Jorrocks applauded as if he had never heard them before, and drank in bumpers. It was evident that unless tea was speedily announced he would soon become;

O'er the ills of life victorious,

for he had pocketed his wig, and had been clipping the Queen's English for some time. After a pause, during which his cheeks twice changed colour, from red to green and back to red, he again called for a bumper toast, which he prefaced with the following speech, or parts of a speech:

"Gentlemen—in rising—propose toast about to give—feel werry—feel werry—(Yorkshireman, 'werry muzzy?') J—— feel werry—(Mr. Spiers, 'werry sick?') J—— werry—(Crane, 'werry thirsty?') J—— feel werry —(Nimrod, 'werry wise?') J—— no; but werry sensible —great compliment—eyes of England upon us—give you the health—Mr. Happerley Nimrod—three times three!"

He then attempted to rise for the purpose of marking the time, but his legs deserted his body, and after two or three lurches down he went with a tremendous thump under the table. He called first for "Batsay," then for "Binjimin," and, game to the last, blurted out, "Lift me up!—tie me in my chair!—fill my glass!"

XIII. THE DAY AFTER THE FEAST
AN EPISODE BY THE YORKSHIREMAN

ON the morning after Mr. Jorrocks's "dinner party" I had occasion to go into the city, and took Great Coram Street in my way. My heart misgave me when I recollected Mrs. J—— and her horrid paws, but still I thought it my duty to see how the grocer was after his fall. Arrived at the house I rang the area bell, and Benjamin, who was cleaning knives below, popped his head up, and seeing who it was, ran upstairs and opened the door. His master was up, he said, but "werry bad," and his misses was out. Leaving him to resume his knife-cleaning occupation, I slipped quietly upstairs, and hearing a noise in the bedroom, opened the door, and found Jorrocks sitting in his dressing-gown in an easy chair, with Betsey patting his bald head with a damp towel.

"Do that again, Batsay! Do that again!" was the first sound I heard, being an invitation to Betsey to continue her occupation. "Here's the Yorkshireman, sir," said Betsey, looking around.

"Ah, Mr. York, how are you this morning?" said he, turning a pair of eyes upon me that looked like boiled gooseberries—his countenance indicating severe indisposition. "Set down, sir; set down—I'm werry bad—werry bad indeed—bad go last night. Doesn't do to go to the lush-crib this weather. How are you, eh? tell me all about it. Is Mr. Nimrod gone?"

"Don't know," said I; "I have just come from Lancaster Street, where I have been seeing an aunt, and thought I would take Great Coram Street in my way to the city, to ask how you do—but where's Mrs. Jorrocks?"

Jorrocks. Oh, cuss Mrs. J——; I knows nothing about her—been reading the Riot Act, and giving her red rag a holiday all the morning—wish to God I'd never see'd her—took her for better and worser, it's werry true; but she's a d——d deal worser than I took her for. Hope your hat may long cover your family. Mrs. J——'s gone to the Commons to Jenner—swears she'll have a diworce, a *mensa et thorax*, I think she calls it—wish she may get it—sick of hearing her talk about it—Jenner's the only man wot puts up with her, and that's because he gets his fees. Batsay, my dear! you may damp another towel, and then get me something to cool my coppers—all in a glow, I declare—complete fever. You whiles go to the lush-crib, Mr. Yorkshireman; what now do you reckon best after a regular drench?

Yorkshireman. Oh, nothing like a glass of soda-water with a bottom of brandy—some people prefer a sermon, but that won't suit you or I. After your soda and brandy take a good chivy in the open air, and you'll be all right by dinner-time.

Jorrocks. Right I Bliss ye, I shall niver be right again. I can scarce move out of my chair, I'm so bad—my head's just fit to split in two—I'm in no state to be seen.

Yorkshireman. Oh, pooh!—get your soda-water and brandy, then have some strong coffee and a red herring, and you'll be all right, and if you'll find cash, I'll find company, and we'll go and have a lark together.

Jorrocks. Couldn't really be seen out—besides, cash is werry scarce. By the way, now that I come to think on it, I had a five-pounder in my breeches last night. Just feel in the pocket of them 'ere nankeens, and see that Mrs. J—— has not grabbed it to pay Jenner's fee with.

Yorkshireman (feels). No—all right—here it is—No. 10,497—I promise to pay Mr. Thos. Rippon, or bearer, on demand, five pounds! Let's demand it, and go and spend the cash.

Jorrocks. No, no—put it back—or into the table-drawer, see—fives are werry scarce with me—can't afford it—must be just before I'm generous.

Yorkshireman. Well, then, J——, you must just stay at home and get bullied by Mrs. J——, who will be back just now, I dare say, perhaps followed by Jenner and half Doctors' Commons.

Jorrocks. The deuce! I forgot all that—curse Mrs. J—— and the Commons too. Well, Mr. Yorkshireman, I don't care if I do go with you—but where shall it be to? Some place where we can be quiet, for I really am werry bad, and not up to nothing like a lark.

Yorkshireman. Suppose we take a sniff of the briny—Margate—Ramsgate—Broadstairs?

Jorrocks. No, none of them places—over-well-known at 'em all—can't be quiet—get to the lush-crib again, perhaps catch the cholera and go to Gravesend by mistake. Let's go to the Eel Pye at Twickenham and live upon fish.

Yorkshireman. Fish! you old flat. Why, you know, you'd be the first to cry out if you had to do so. No, no—let's have no humbug—here, drink your coffee like a man, and then hustle your purse and see what it will produce. Why, even Betsey's laughing at the idea of your living upon fish.

Jorrocks. Don't shout so, pray—your woice shoots through every nerve of my head and distracts me (drinks). This is grand Mocho—quite the cordial balm of Gilead—werry fine indeed. Now I feel rewived and can listen to you.

Yorkshireman. Well, then, pull on your boots—gird up your loins, and let's go and spend this five pounds—stay away as long as it lasts, in fact.

Jorrocks. Well, but give me the coin—it's mine you know—and let me be paymaster, or I know you'll soon be into dock again. That's right; and now I have got three half-crowns besides, which I will add.

Yorkshireman. And I've got three pence, which, not to be behind-hand in point of liberality, I'll do the same with, so that we have got five pounds seven shillings and ninepence between us, according to Cocker.

Jorrocks. Between us, indeed! I likes that. You're a generous churchwarden.

Yorkshireman. Well—we won't stand upon trifles the principle is the thing I look to—and not the amount. So now where to, your honour?

After a long parley, we fixed upon Herne Bay. Our reasons for doing so were numerous, though it would be superfluous to mention them, save that the circumstance of neither of us ever having been there, and the prospect of finding a quiet retreat for Jorrocks to recover in, were the principal ones. Our arrangements were soon made. "Batsay," said J—— to his principessa of a cook, slut, and butler, "the Yorkshireman and I are going out of town to stay five pounds seven and ninepence, so put up my traps." Two shirts (one to wash the other as he said), three pairs of stockings, with other etceteras, were stamped into a carpet-bag, and taking a cab, we called at the "Piazza," where I took a few things, and away we drove to Temple Bar. "Stop here with the bags," said Jorrocks, "while I go to the Temple Stairs and make a bargain with a Jacob Faithful to put us on board, for if they see the bags they'll think it's a case of necessity, and ask double; whereas I'll pretend I'm just going a-pleasuring, and when I've made a bargain, I'll whistle, and you can come." Away he rolled, and after the lapse of a few minutes I heard a sort of shilling-gallery cat-call, and obeying the summons, found he had concluded a bargain for one and sixpence. We reached St. Catherine's Docks just as the Herne Bay boat—the *Hero*—moored alongside, consequently were nearly the first on board.

Herne Bay being then quite in its infancy, and this being what the cits call a "weekday," they had rather a shy cargo, nor had they any of that cockney tomfoolery that generally characterises a Ramsgate or Margate crew, more particularly a Margate one. Indeed, it was a very slow cargo, Jorrocks being the only character on board, and he was as sulky as a bear with a sore head when anyone approached. The day was beautifully fine, and a thin grey mist gradually disappeared from the Kentish hills as we passed down the Thames. The river was gay enough. Adelaide, Queen of Great Britain and Ireland, was expected on her return from Germany, and all the vessels hung out their best and gayest flags and colours to do her honour. The towns of Greenwich and Woolwich were in commotion. Charity schools were marching, and soldiers were doing the like, while steamboats went puffing down the river with cargoes to meet and escort Her Majesty. When we got near Tilbury Fort, a man at the head of the steamer announced that we should meet the Queen in ten minutes, and all the passengers crowded on to the paddle-box of the side on which she was to pass, to view and greet her. Jorrocks even roused himself up and joined the throng. Presently a crowd of steamers were seen in the distance, proceeding up the river at a rapid pace, with a couple of lofty-masted vessels in tow, the first of which contained the royal cargo. The leading steamboat was the celebrated *Magnet*—considered the fastest boat on the river, and the one in which Jorrocks and myself steamed from Margate, racing against and beating the *Royal William*. This had the Lord Mayor and Aldermen on board, who had gone down to the extent of the city jurisdiction to meet the Queen, and have an excuse for a good dinner. The deck presented a gay scene, being covered with a military band, and the gaudy-liveried lackeys belonging to the Mansion House, and sheriffs whose clothes were one continuous mass of gold lace and frippery, shining beautifully brilliant in the midday sun. The royal yacht, with its crimson and gold pennant floating on the breeze, came towering up at a rapid pace, with the Queen sitting under a canopy on deck. As we neared, all hats were off, and three cheers—or at least as many as we could wedge in during the time the cortège took to sweep past us—were given, our band consisting of three brandy-faced musicians, striking up *God save the King*—a compliment which Her Majesty acknowledged by a little mandarining; and before the majority of the passengers had recovered from the astonishment produced by meeting a live Queen on the Thames, the whole fleet had shot out of sight. By the time the ripple on the water, raised by their progress, had subsided, we had all relapsed into our former state of apathy and sullenness. A duller or staider set I never saw outside a Quakers' meeting. Still the beggars eat, as when does a cockney not in the open air? The stewards of these steamboats must make a rare thing of their places, for they have plenty of custom at their own prices. In fact, being in a steamboat is a species of personal incarceration, and you have only the option between bringing your own prog, or taking theirs at whatever they choose to charge—unless, indeed, a person prefers going without any. Jorrocks took nothing. He laid down again after the Queen had passed, and never looked up until we were a mile or two off Herne Bay.

With the reader's permission, we will suppose that we have just landed, and, bags in hand, ascended the flight of steps that conduct passengers, as it were, from the briny ocean on to the stage of life.

"My eyes!" said Jorrocks, as he reached the top, "wot a pier, and wot a bit of a place! Why, there don't seem to be fifty houses altogether, reckoning the windmill in the centre as one. What's this thing?" said he to a ticket-porter, pointing to a sort of French diligence-looking concern which had just been pushed up to the landing end. "To carry the lumber, sir—live and dead— gentlemen and their bags, as don't like to walk." "Do you charge anything for the ride?" inquired Jorrocks, with his customary caution. "Nothing," was the answer. "Then, let's get on the roof," said J——, "and take it easy, and survey the place as we go along." So, accordingly, we clambered on to the top of the diligence, "summâ diligentiâ," and seated ourselves on a pile of luggage; being all stowed away, and as many passengers as it would hold put inside, two or three porters proceeded to propel the machine along the railroad on which it runs. "Now, Mr. Yorkshireman," said Jorrocks, "we are in a strange land, and it behoves us to proceed with caution, or we may spend our five pounds seven and sixpence before we know where we are."

Yorkshireman. Seven and ninepence it is, sir.

Jorrocks. Well, be it so—five pounds seven and ninepence between two, is by no means an impossible sum to spend, and the trick is to make it go as far as we can. Now some men can make one guinea go as far as others can make two, and we will try what we can do. In the first place, you know I makes it a rule never to darken the door of a place wot calls itself an 'otel, for 'otel prices and inn prices are werry different. You young chaps don't consider these things, and as long as you have got a rap in the world you go swaggering about, ordering claret and waxlights, and everything wot's expensive, as though you must spend money because you are in an inn. Now, that's all gammon. If a man haven't got money he can't spend it; and we all know that many poor folks are obliged at times to go to houses of public entertainment, and you don't suppose that they pay for fire and waxlights, private sitting-rooms, and all them 'ere sort of things. Now, said he, adjusting his hunting telescope and raking the town of Herne Bay, towards which we were gently approaching on our dignified eminence, but as yet had not got near enough to descry "what was what" with the naked eye, I should say yon great staring-looking shop directly opposite us is the cock inn of the place (looks through his glass). I'm right P-i-e-r, Pier 'Otel I reads upon the top, and that's no shop for my money. Let's see what else we have. There's nothing on the right, I think, but here on the left is something like our cut—D-o-l dol, p-h-i-n phin, Dolphin Inn. It's long since I went the circuit, as the commercial gentlemen (or what were called bagmen in my days) term it, but I haven't forgot the experience I gained in my travels, and I whiles turn it to werry good account now.

"Coach to Canterbury, Deal, Margate, sir, going directly," interrupted him, and reminded us that we had got to the end of the pier, and ought to be descending. Two or three coaches were drawn up, waiting to carry passengers on, but we had got to our journey's end. "Now," said J——, "let's take our bags in hand and draw up wind, trying the 'Dolphin' first."

Rejecting the noble portals of the Pier Hotel, we advanced towards Jorrocks's chosen house, a plain unpretending-looking place facing the sea, which is half the battle, and being but just finished had every chance of cleanliness. "Jonathan Acres" appeared above the door as the name of the landlord, and a little square-built, hatless, short-haired chap, in a shooting-jacket, was leaning against the door. "Mr. Hacres within?" said Jorrocks. "My name's Acres," said he of the shooting-jacket. "Humph," said J——, looking him over, "not Long Acre, I think." Having selected a couple of good airy bedrooms, we proceeded to see about dinner. "Mr. Hacres," said Jorrocks, "I makes it a rule never to pay more than two and sixpence for a feed, so now just give us as good a one as you possibly can for that money": and about seven o'clock we sat down to lamb-chops, ducks, French beans, pudding, etc.; shortly after which Jorrocks retired to rest, to sleep off the remainder of his headache. He was up long before me the next morning, and had a dip in the sea before I came down. "Upon my word," said he, as I entered the room, and found him looking as lively and fresh as a four-year-old, "it's worth while going to the lush-crib occasionally, if it's only for the pleasure of feeling so hearty and fresh as one does on the second day. I feel just as if I could jump out of my skin, but I will defer the performance until after breakfast. I have ordered a fork one, do you know, cold 'am and boiled bacon, with no end of eggs, and bread of every possible description. By the way, I've scraped acquaintance with Thorp, the baker hard by, who's a right good fellow, and says he will give me some shooting, and has some werry nice beagles wot he shoots to. But here's the grub. Cold 'am in abundance. But, waiter, you should put a little green garnishing to the dishes, I likes to see it, green is so werry refreshing to the eye; and tell Mr. Hacres to send up some more bacon and the bill, when I rings the bell. Nothing like having your bill the first morning, and then you know what you've got to pay, and can cut your coat according to your cloth." The bacon soon disappeared, and the bell being sounded, produced the order.

"Humph," said J——, casting his eyes over the bill as it lay by the side of his plate, while he kept pegging away at the contents of the neighbouring dish—

"pretty reasonable, I think—dinners, five shillings, that's half a crown each; beds, two shillings each; breakfasts, one and ninepence each, that's cheap for a fork breakfast; but, I say, you had a pint of sherry after I left you last night, and PALE sherry too! How could you be such an egreggorus (egregious) ass! That's so like you young chaps, not to know that the only difference between pale and brown sherry is, that one has more of the pumpaganus aqua in it than the other. You should have made it pale yourself, man. But look there. Wot a go!"

Our attention was attracted to a youth in spectacles, dressed in a rich plum-coloured coat, on the outside of a dingy-looking, big-headed, brown nag, which he was flogging and cramming along the public walk in front of the "Dolphin," in the most original and ludicrous manner. We presently recognised him as one of our fellow-passengers of the previous day, respecting whom Jorrocks and I had had a dispute as to whether he was a Frenchman or a German. His equestrian performances decided the point. I never in all my life witnessed such an exhibition, nor one in which the performer evinced such self-complacency. Whether he had ever been on horseback before or not I can't tell, but the way in which he went to work, using the bridle as a sort of rattle to frighten the horse forward, the way in which he shook the reins, threw his arms about, and belaboured the poor devil of an animal in order to get him into a canter (the horse of course turning away every time he saw the blow coming), and the free, unrestrained liberty he gave to his head, surpassed everything of the sort I ever saw, and considerably endangered the lives of several of His Majesty's lieges that happened to be passing. Instead of getting out of their way, Frenchmanlike, he seemed to think everything should give way to an equestrian; and I saw him scatter a party of ladies like a covey of partridges, by riding slap amongst them, and not even making the slightest apology or obeisance for the rudeness. There he kept, cantering (or cantering as much as he could induce the poor rip to do) from one end of the town to the other, conceiving, I make not the slightest doubt, that he was looked upon with eyes of admiration by the beholders. He soon created no little sensation, and before he was done a crowd had collected near the Pier Hotel, to see him get his horse past (it being a Pier Hotel nag) each time; and I heard a primitive sort of postman, who was delivering the few letters that arrive in the place, out of a fish-basket, declare "that he would sooner kill a horse than lend it to such a chap." Having fretted his hour away, the owner claimed the horse, and Monsieur was dismounted.

After surveying the back of the town, we found ourselves rambling in some beautiful picturesque fields in the rear. Kent is a beautiful county, and the trimly kept gardens, and the clustering vines twining around the neatly thatched cottages, remind one of the rich, luxuriant soil and climate of the South. Forgetting that we were in search of sea breezes, we continued to saunter on, across one field, over one stile and then over another, until after passing by the side of a snug-looking old-fashioned house, with a beautifully kept garden, the road took a sudden turn and brought us to some parkish-looking well-timbered ground in front, at one side of which Jorrocks saw something that he swore was a kennel.

"I knows a hawk from a hand-saw," said he, "let me alone for that. I'll swear there are hounds in it. Bless your heart, don't I see a gilt fox on one end, and a gilt hare on the other?"

Just then came up a man in a round fustian jacket, to whom Jorrocks addressed himself, and, as good luck would have it, he turned out to be the huntsman (for Jorrocks was right about the kennel), and away we went to look at the hounds. They proved to be Mr. Collard's, the owner of the house that we had just passed, and were really a very nice pack of harriers, consisting of seventeen or eighteen couple, kept in better style (as far as kennel appearance goes) than three-fourths of the harriers in England. Bird, the huntsman, our cicerone, seemed a regular keen one in hunting matters, and Jorrocks and he had a long confab about the "noble art of hunting," though the former was rather mortified to find on announcing himself as the "celebrated Mr. Jorrocks" that Bird had never heard of him before.

After leaving the kennel we struck across a few fields, and soon found ourselves on the sea banks, along which we proceeded at the rate of about two miles an hour, until we came to the old church of Reculvers. Hard by is a public-house, the sign of the "Two Sisters," where, having each taken a couple of glasses of ale, we proceeded to enjoy one of the (to me at least) greatest luxuries in life—viz. that of lying on the shingle of the beach with my heels just at the water's edge.

The day was intensely hot, and after occupying this position for about half an hour, and finding the "perpendicular rays of the sun" rather fiercer than agreeable, we followed the example of a flock of sheep, and availed ourselves of the shade afforded by the Reculvers. Here for a short distance along the beach, on both sides, are small breakwaters, and immediately below the Reculvers is one formed of stake and matting, capable of holding two persons sofa fashion. Into this Jorrocks and I crept, the tide being at that particular point that enabled us to repose, with the water lashing our cradle on both sides, without dashing high enough to wet us.

"Oh, but this is fine!" said J——, dangling his arm over the side, and letting the sea wash against his hand. "I declare it comes fizzing up just like soda-water out of a bottle—reminds me of the lush-crib. By the way, Mr. Yorkshireman, I heard some chaps in our inn this morning talking about this werry place, and one of them said that there used to be a Roman station, or something of that sort, at it. Did you know anything of them 'ere ancient Romans? Luxterous dogs, I understand. If Mr. Nimrod was here now he could tell us all about them, for, if I mistake not, he was werry intimate with some of them—either he or his father, at least."

A boat that had been gradually advancing towards us now run on shore, close by where we were lying, and one of the crew landed with a jug to get some beer. A large basket at the end attracted Jorrocks's attention, and, doglike, he got up and began to hover about and inquire about their destination of the remaining crew, four in number. They were a cockney party of pleasure, it seemed, going to fish, for which purpose they had hired the boat, and laid in no end of bait for the fish, and prog for themselves. Jorrocks, though no great fisherman (not having, as he says, patience enough), is never at a loss if there is plenty of eating; and finding that they had got a great chicken pie, two tongues, and a tart, agreed to pay for the boat if they would let us in upon equal terms with themselves as to the provender, which was agreed to without a debate. The messenger having returned with a gallon of ale, we embarked, and away we slid through the "glad waters of the dark blue sea." It was beautifully calm, scarcely a breeze appearing on the surface. After rowing for about an hour, one of the boatmen began to adjust the lines and bait the hooks; and having got into what he esteemed a favourite spot, he cast anchor and prepared for the sport. Each man was prepared with a long strong cord line, with a couple of hooks fastened to the ends of about a foot of whalebone, with a small leaden plummet in the centre. The hooks were baited with sandworms, and the instructions given were, after sounding the depth, to raise the hooks a little from the bottom, so as to let them hang conveniently for the fish to swallow. Great was the excitement as we dropped the lines overboard, as to who should catch the first whale. Jorrocks and myself having taken the fishermen's lines from them, we all met upon pretty equal terms, much like gentlemen jockeys in a race. A dead silence ensued. "I have one!" cried the youngest of our new friends. "Then pull him up," responded one of the boatmen, "gently, or you'll lose him." "And so I have, by God! he's gone." "Well, never mind," said the boatmen, "let's see your bait— aye, he's got that, too. We'll put some fresh on—there you are again—all right. Now drop it gently, and when you find you've hooked him, wind the line quickly, but quietly, and be sure you don't jerk the hook out of his mouth at starting." "I've got one!" cries Jorrocks—"I've got one—now, my wig, if I can but land him. I have him, certainly—by Jove! he's a wopper, too, judging by the way he kicks. Oh, but it's no use, sir—come along—come along—here he is— doublets, by crikey—two, huzza! huzza! What fine ones!—young haddocks or codlings, I should call them—werry nice eating, I dare say—I'm blow'd if this arn't sport." "I have one," cries our young friend again. "So have I," shouts another; and just at the same moment I felt the magic touch of my bait, and in an instant I felt the thrilling stroke. The fish were absolutely voracious, and we had nothing short of a miraculous draught. As fast as we could bait they swallowed, and we frequently pulled them up two at a time. Jorrocks was in ecstasies. "It was the finest sport he had ever encountered," and he kept halloaing and shouting every time he pulled them up, as though he were out with the Surrey. Having just hooked a second couple, he baited again and dropped his line. Two of our new friends had hooked fish at the same instant, and, in their eagerness to take them, overbalanced the boat, and Jorrocks, who was leaning over, went head foremost down into the deeps!

* * * * *

A terrible surprise came over us, and for a second or two we were so perfectly thunderstruck as to be incapable of rendering any assistance. A great splash, followed by a slight gurgling sound, as the water bubbled and subsided o'er the place where he went down, was all that denoted the exit of our friend.

After a considerable dive he rose to the surface, minus his hat and wig, but speedily disappeared. The anchor was weighed, oars put out, and the boat rowed to the spot where he last appeared. He rose a third time, but out of arms' reach, apparently lifeless, and just as he was sinking, most probably for ever, one of the men contrived to slip the end of an oar under his arm, and support him on the water until he got within reach from the boat.

The consternation when we got him on board was tremendous! Consisting, as we did, of two parties, neither knowing where the other had come from, we remained in a state of stupefied horror, indecision, and amazement for some minutes. The poor old man lay extended in the bottom of the boat, apparently lifeless, and even if the vital spark had not fled, there seemed no chance of reaching Herne Bay, whose pier, just then gilded by the rich golden rays of the setting sun, appeared in the far distance of the horizon. Where to row to was the question. No habitation where effective succour could be procured appeared on the shore, and to proceed without a certain destination was fruitless. How helpless such a period as this makes a man feel! "Let's make for Grace's," at length exclaimed one of the boatmen, and the other catching at the proposition, the head of the boat was whipped round in an instant, and away we sped through the glassy-surfaced water. Not a word broke upon the sound of the splashing oars until, nearing the shore, one of the men, looking round, directed us to steer a little to the right, in the direction of a sort of dell or land-break, peculiar to the Isle of Thanet; and presently we ran the head of the boat upon the shingle, just where a small rivulet that, descending from the higher grounds, waters the thickly wooded ravine, and discharges itself into the sea. The entrance of this dell is formed by a lofty precipitous rock, with a few stunted overhanging trees on one side, while the other is more open and softened in its aspect, and though steep and narrow at the mouth, gently slopes away into a brushwood-covered bank, which, stretching up the little valley, becomes lost in a forest of lofty oaks that close the inland prospect of the place. Here, to the left (just after one gets clear of the steeper part), commanding a view of the sea, and yet almost concealed from the eye of a careless traveller, was a lonely hut (the back wall formed by an excavation of the sandy rock) and the rest of clay, supporting a wooden roof, made of the hull of a castaway wreck, the abode of an old woman, called Grace Ganderne, well known throughout the whole Isle of Thanet as a poor harmless secluded widow, who subsisted partly on the charity of her neighbours, and partly on what she could glean from the smugglers, for the assistance she affords them in running their goods on that coast; and though she had been at work for forty years, she had never had the misfortune to be detected in the act, notwithstanding the many puncheons of spirits and many bales of goods fished out of the dark woods near her domicile.

To this spot it was, just as the "setting sun's pathetic light" had been succeeded by the grey twilight of the evening, that we bore the body of our unfortunate companion. The door was closed, but Grace being accustomed to nocturnal visitors, speedily answered the first summons and presented herself. She was evidently of immense age, being nearly bowed double, and her figure, with her silvery hair, confined by a blue checked cotton handkerchief, and palsied hand, as tremblingly she rested upon her staff and eyed the group, would have made a subject worthy of the pencil of a Landseer. She was wrapped in an old red cloak, with a large hood, and in her ears she wore a pair of long gold-dropped earrings, similar to what one sees among the Norman peasantry—the gift, as I afterwards learned, of a drowned lover. After scrutinising us for a second or two, during which time a large black cat kept walking to and fro, purring and rubbing itself against her, she held back the door and beckoned us to enter. The little place was cleanly swept up, and a faggot and some dry brushwood, which she had just lighted for the purpose of boiling her kettle, threw a gleam of light over the apartment, alike her bedchamber, parlour, and kitchen. Her curtainless bed at the side, covered with a coarse brown counterpane, was speedily prepared for our friend, into which being laid, our new acquaintances were dispatched in search of doctors, while the boatman and myself, under the direction of old Grace, applied ourselves to procuring such restoratives as her humble dwelling afforded.

"Let Grace alone," said the younger of the boatmen, seeing my affliction at the lamentable catastrophe, "if there be but a spark of life in the gentleman, she'll bring him round—many's the drowning man—aye, and wounded one, too—that's been brought in here during the stormy nights, and after fights with the coast-guard—that she's recovered."

Hot bottles, and hot flannels, and hot bricks were all applied, but in vain; and when I saw hot brandy, too, fail of having the desired effect, I gave my friend up as lost, and left the hut to vent my grief in the open air. Grace was more sanguine and persevering, and when I, after a half-hour's absence, I could distinctly feel a returning pulse. Still, he gave no symptoms of animation, and it might only be the effect produced by the applications—as he remained in the same state for several hours. Fresh wood was added to the fire, and the boatmen having returned to their vessel, Grace and I proceeded to keep watch during the night, or until the arrival of a doctor. The poor old body, to whom scenes such as this were matter of frequent occurrence, seemed to think nothing of it, and proceeded to relate some of the wonderful escapes and recoveries she had witnessed, in the course of which she dropped many a sigh to the memory of some of her friends—the bold smugglers. There were no such "braw lads" now as formerly, she said, and were it not that "she was past eighty, and might as weel die in one place as anither, she wad gang back to the bonny blue hulls (hills) of her ain canny Scotland."

In the middle of one of her long stories I thought I perceived a movement of the bedclothes, and, going to look, I found a considerable increase in the quickness of pulsation, and also a generous sort of glow upon the skin. "An' ded I no tell ye I wad recover him?" said she, with a triumphant look. "Afore twa mair hours are o'er he'll spak to ye." "I hope so, I'm sure," said I, still almost doubting her. "Oh, trust to me," said she, "he'll come about—I've seen mony a chiel in a mickle worse state nor him recovered. Pray, is the ould gintleman your father or your grandfather?"

Yorkshireman. Why, I can't say that he's either exactly—but he's always been as good as a grandmother to me, I know.

Grace was right. About three o'clock in the morning a sort of revulsion of nature took place, and after having lain insensible, and to all appearance lifeless, all that time, he suddenly began to move. Casting his eye wildly around, he seemed lost in amazement. He muttered something, but what it was I could not catch.

"Lush-crib again, by Jove!" were the first words he articulated, and then, appearing to recollect himself, he added, "Oh, I forgot, I'm drowned—well drowned, too—can't be help'd, however—wasn't born to be hanged—and that seems clear." Thus he kept muttering and mumbling for an hour, until old Grace thinking him so far recovered as to remove all danger from sudden surprise, allowed me to take her seat at the bedside. He looked at me long and intensely, but the light was not sufficiently strong to enable him to make out who I was.

"Jorrocks!" at length said I, taking him by the hand, "how are you, my old boy?" He started at the sound of his name. "Jorrocks," said he, "who's that?" "Why, the Yorkshireman; you surely have not forgotten your old friend and companion in a hundred fights!"

Jorrocks. Oh, Mr. York, it's you, is it? Much obliged by your inquiries, but I'm drowned.

Yorkshireman. Aye, but you are coming round, you'll be better before long.

Jorrocks. Never! Don't try to gammon me. You know as well as I do that I'm drowned, and a drowned man never recovers. No, no, it's all up with me, I feel. Set down, however, while I say a few words to you. You're a good fellow, and I've remembered you in my will, which you'll find in the strong port-wine-bin, along with nine pounds secret service money. I hopes you'll think the legacy a fat one. I meant it as such. If you marry Belinda, I have left you a third of my fourth in the tea trade. Always said you were cut out for a grocer. Let Tat sell my stud. An excellent man, Tat—proudish perhaps—at least, he never inwites me to none of his dinners—but still a werry good man. Let him sell them, I say, and mind give Snapdragon a charge or two of shot before he goes to the 'ammer, to prevent his roaring. Put up a plain monument to my memory—black or white marble, whichever's cheapest—but mind, no Cupids or seraphums, or none of those sort of things—quite plain—with just this upon it—*Hic jacet Jorrocks.* And now I'll give you a bit of news. Neptune has appointed me huntsman to his pack of haddocks. Have two dolphins for my own riding, and a young lobster to look after them. Lord Farebrother whips in to me—he rides a turtle. "And now, my good friend," said he, grasping my hands with redoubled energy, "do you think you could accomplish me a rump-steak and oyster sauce?—also a pot of stout?—but, mind, blow the froth off the top, for it's bad for the kidneys!"

THE END

Printed in the United States
153147LV00001B/71/A